The Dimensions of Love

7 Steps to Divine Love

The Dimensions of Love

7 Steps to Divine Love

Padma Aon Prakasha

BOOKS

Winchester, UK
Washington, USA

First published by O-Books, 2013
O-Books is an imprint of John Hunt Publishing Ltd., Laurel House, Station Approach,
Alresford, Hants, SO24 9JH, UK
office1@jhpbooks.net
www.johnhuntpublishing.com

For distributor details and how to order please visit the 'Ordering' section on our website.

Text copyright: Padma Aon Prakasha 2012

ISBN: 978 1 78099 513 7

A CIP catalogue record for this book is available from the British Library.

Design: Stuart Davies

Printed and bound by CPI Group (UK) Ltd, Croydon, CR0 4YY

We operate a distinctive and ethical publishing philosophy in all
areas of our business, from our global network of authors to
production and worldwide distribution.

CONTENTS

THE DIMENSIONS OF LOVE:
THE 7 STEPS TO DIVINE LOVE

What is love ... and what is it not? Why is love the most misused word on this planet? Is love meant to hurt? Is the love between me, my partner and family the greatest love I can ever experience? Or is there more? Is there a map to love that I can follow?

The soul's journey to God, as described by the greatest mystics in history, takes Seven Steps. This Path that Christ, Magdalene, Rumi, St Francis, Kabir, Teresa of Avila and Hafiz walked on was of Seven Spheres or Dimensions of Love.

Each ascending Sphere holds ever increasing, vaster amounts of love, with this love gradually becoming part of the very fabric of your soul. As we drink in this Love, It inexorably transforms our human soul into a Divine Soul. This is the Grace Filled Path where by following divine laws so simple a child could understand them, and through deep desire for God, one reaches Union with the Beloved.

This involves deep humility and a steadfast anchoring into the center of your own, pure soul, along the way feeling all the emotions you have never dared to feel. The soul is made of your emotions and your deeper feelings. To come closer to this Divine Love, we need to realize what love is, what it is not, and our beliefs and pains around love. We come to recognize and feel the five forms of love, and the ones we can grow into more.

The Pathway to God's Divine Love, the simplest pathway on Earth, has been obscured by our own forgetting of who God Is: a

Great Soul who created your soul and deeply desires to give you Divine Love. *The Dimensions of Love: 7 Steps to God* contains new, interesting and sometimes radical truths for the soul in the 21st century, and shares it as direct experience.

The Dimensions of Love: 7 Steps to God is a beautiful, simple, poignant and profound book. Soulful and insightful, it contains a message that cannot be missed.

'If you find anything good in this book which helps you to learn to know God better, you can be quite sure that it is His Majesty Who has said it, and if you find anything bad, then it has been said by me.'

St Teresa of Avila

The FIVE FORMS of LOVE

There are five main forms of love we can engage in:

- Love for God, and receiving God's Divine Love

- Love for our soul mate, and receiving our soul mate's love

- Self Love: loving our own soul as God Loves it

- Natural Love: loving others, and receiving other humans' love for us in our natural Love for all souls, creatures and the Earth, and receiving their love

- Love for our Friends of the Heart, and receiving their love

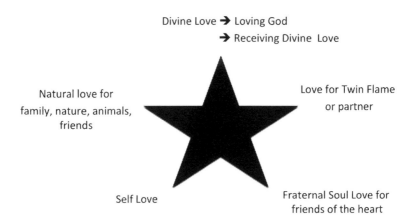

DIVINE LOVE

'God, help me to receive more of your Divine Love.'

Divine Love nurtures the growth of all other forms of human or natural love into their ultimate potential, based on universal laws of Divine Truth and harmony – the Divine Design. This Divine Design leads to the greatest love and enjoyment for us in all aspects of life if we follow Divine laws and consistently ask for and receive Divine Love. God's Divine Love is the foundation for our truest happiness in all ways, and indeed is our ultimate happiness.

Divine Love is the most powerful, transformative and alchemical Power in all universes. God is waiting and desiring to give this Greatest of All Loves to you through your desire and sincere yearning for It. This desire comes from imploring and asking from the depths of your heart, sincerely, passionately and whole-heartedly, for Divine Love, humbly bowing to God to receive It.

This desire is like an arrow of love piercing your heart, pointing straight and true towards its target, praying as though you were 'interrogating your own soul about its deepest, most hidden longings.'

This desire searches every single last part of you, known and unknown, discovering the inner gnawing and boiling, burning desire within you. Your desires are powerful, and desire for God is the most powerful; angels look on in awe, appreciation and wonder when a human truly desires God from the depths of their soul. True desire is as if you were driving a tent stake home deep into the depths and recesses of your soul, striking a clear musical note.

A Lover of God is a soul of fire.[1]

Pure, deep yearning desire for God is like a flame that attracts the moths of benevolent spirit guides, Divine Love spirits, angels and ultimately God. Pure desire is a beacon shining in the darkness that God and His helpers cannot ignore. Inexorably drawn to this flame like a magnet by the very nature and substance of their souls, they cannot help but come to, serve, and answer a soul's desire if it is in alignment with Truth and Love. This is the truth.

'Ask and it shall be given to you; seek and you will find; Knock and it shall be opened to you.'[2]

And if a desire is not in alignment, circumstances are provided to enable a humble soul to see the error of their desire, OR the desire may manifest and they will see in the manifestation of the desire the error in it; then they will have to clean up the error and the unfelt pain within them that created such a creation.

Pure desire is a shining lantern, a lighthouse in the darkness, a searchlight of aspiration and yearning for Love and Truth that helps you both in seeing Divine Truths and your own personal truths that shield one from following Divine Truth, and receiving Divine Love. It is the fuel of desire allied with humility that brings wisdom, which sorts out the wheat from the chaff, separating out truth from untruth,[3] like oil and water.

With pure flaming desire sustained, you will Realize everything eventually.

Longing itself brings the cure.[4]

Receiving Divine Love transforms your soul forever. It makes anew all things by helping you to see and feel everything in your soul that stands in Its Way. It is the center, the fulcrum, around which all other forms of love merely travel. Divine Love is the only quality and substance which can ever fulfill you completely, eventually changing the very substance and nature of your soul from what you know and identify now as your human soul, to the greater Perfection and transformation into a Divine soul, distinct from your human soul, human laws and human love as you know it today.

Divine Laws are how Divine Love operates in the universe. They are the Laws of Love, codes of Living Light that maintain the harmony of the cosmos, and once followed FULLY lead to God. The Laws surrounding Divine Love are the most powerful Laws in existence, and the fastest way to learn these Divine Laws is to connect to God via His Love, for we only truly understand Laws of Divine Love in our soul. All of God's Laws are loving in their operation, and have loving consequences upon the soul.[5]

Your soul, before Divine Love FULLY enters and changes it, is finite. It does not have within it the essence of Divine Love. Before Divine Love enters your soul fully and stabilizes within it to a large degree, your soul is a creation made in the image of God, a mere reflection. God is not in you *as yet*. What is within you is natural love, that which your soul was automatically created with. It is not Divine as yet.

Divine Love was never given to us as a perfect and complete gift, but as a gift that is waiting for your own efforts, it is meant to be received by you. Without continual asking, It can never become part of you, although God is always waiting to answer your Calls. This Love forms no part of you *unless* your yearnings and prayers have opened up your soul, so that It may flow in and fill you with its Presence.

We are naturally good. God created us this way. The love we were originally created in enables us to love God and love others the way we love our own self. This is a part of natural love, and yet is still not Divine Love.

When we arrive at the Original state of goodness that was ours in the beginning of our creation, we will simply have embraced, healed and let go of all our false needs, substitutes, ancestral, parental and childhood wounds, appetites, thoughts and desires that are not in harmony with Love, that make us unhappy now, and are actually alien to our true nature. In this process, we become humble, for we realize we cannot do this journey by ourselves.

This Work is largely a work of feeling, for healing. We have to clear enough space within us to allow this Divine Love to flow in. When enough space is revealed within your soul, Love can flow in to fill this space, further releasing all the negative emotions held in your soul. Then the stage is set for Divine Love to enter us more fully in our humility and desire for It.

It is important to understand that all the objects of God's creation, like all humans, by reason of being objects, are made in the image of the Divine. *But this is not the Divine.* Humans are a creation of God, and our souls are but images of our Creator, but this creation was not made of God. Our souls existed before we had physical bodies and *'resembled the Great Soul of God, although the soul that was given to humans was not a part of the Great Soul, merely a likeness of it.'*

The Divine is the essence and nature of God, and not that which is merely the object of his creation. You are not Divine until you have completely cleared your soul. In truth, there is nothing in you that is Divine until this occurs. *You can never have in you any part of the Divine unless you receive and have developed Divine Love.*

You, with the help of God, make your own destiny. The desire to know your Creator, That which has created you, instills a deeper longing within you to ask for and receive more and more Divine Love, for what greater thing is there? Over time, you will cease to be *just* a created being, but become a new, Celestial Soul born of the Divine, not born of the human.

Many (including myself until I had actually received Divine Love and felt the vast difference between it and natural love, realizing how I had not had it until this time, and indeed until I had received Divine Love many, many times) believe that everyone possesses 'a Divine spark,,' that there is some divinity within us which only needs development to make us Divine.

This is wrong, and reminds us that a huge part of Christ's Message was ignored, avoided and minimized. His deepest and simplest Message, given to him by God, is that we do not have within us the Divine or the divine spark, and never can or will have, until we receive and develop Divine Love through the simplest ways of deep desire, educated choice, constant humility, deep prayer and vulnerable, transparent and total, honest release of the soul's wounds.

'In all God's universe and creation of things material and spiritual, the only one of His creatures who can possibly have within them anything of a Divine nature is one who possesses Divine Love.'
Christ Yeshua

What we do have within us, that many mistake for God, or the Divine spark, or the God Self, is the pristine and perfect human soul in natural love that we were created as *by God*. This is what we may mistake as being God, because it is so pure, loving and has no error or blemish to it. This is also because we have not actually experienced Divine Love, and so mistake it for something else. Once you do fully experience Divine Love, there is no mistaking it for anything else!

It is a false belief that we return home to God. We return first back to feeling our soul, and then into feeling the pure soul we were created as, which is still not Divine or part of God's Essence. *We have never been At-One with God ever*, and the thing we recognize as pure is our created soul, free of error and wounding, which we mistakenly call God and Home.

But when Divine Love does enter into your soul, piece-by-piece, day-by-day, the soul begins to transform; it begins to become Divine. The very substance of the soul changes, and it is deeply felt. And again, the transformation occurs through your openness, your yearning for Divine Love, your willingness to search for, embrace and heal any and all soul wounds that stand in its way, with continual dedication, self inquiry and prayer.
The most important thing is to do this, because once a soul *walks through this door*, once Divine Love is tasted and allowed in fully, once enough wounding is removed by Divine Love, then Divine Love can *always be asked for and received*.

Whenever you ask for it, in one second it will come and fill you. Ask and you shall receive, knock on the door and the door will open. This is a massive key and is worth giving EVERYTHING for. For this is what you have always secretly wanted, so secretly you have forgotten what it is. Unconditional love from God.

Walk through this door of Divine Love, opened through your sacred wounds, for once the door is opened, once you start to receive Divine Love, then you will never, ever wish to close this door again; and once you keep going, it is sure that you will become closer to God.

God always loves us in our weakness. We may only feel Divine Love in glimpses and flashes because we only allow ourselves to feel this Love briefly. Only you yourself can block God's Love. This Love is always waiting to enter you through your deep desire for it. It is the negative emotions and veils, your sacred wounds, which block It. Feel these fully, and breathe deeply and powerfully through your belly whilst praying to feel them completely.

There may be times of stagnation and apparent separation or loss of this Divine Love as you go through your healing process. Rest assured that the transformation is always taking place once the door has been opened and you continue to walk through it.

The more your soul receives this Love, the more it journeys into becoming At-One with God, ceasing to be a mere image, becoming transformed into Her substance. Then the possession of this Divine Love will *dissolve* the soul you were created with, the soul you think is you at this moment. This soul, your human soul, will disappear, and leave only Divine qualities of Divine Love. A new soul, a new birth, a new you is born.

'*Divine Love is the primary Quality of God. Divine Love is an emotion of God, and as such is a substance that God can transmit to humans. Divine Love can be received by the human soul if the human soul exercises its Free Will to receive Divine Love, and desires to eradicate all those emotions within itself that prevents the flow and demonstration of Love.*

Divine Love, when received continuously, transforms the Human Soul into a Divine Angel through the process of the New Birth, or being Born Again. Divine Love flows into the soul through the operation of the Holy Spirit, which is the conduit God establishes between Himself and the soul longing for His Love.'[6]

Divine Love is given to us in:

- Prayer to receive Divine Love
- Prayer to feel your soul wounds as gateways to Divine Love
- Spontaneous moments of Grace as desired by God
- Soul Mate Love in harmony with desire for God
- Receiving and praying for Divine Love in making love
- Following Divine Laws and Truths at all costs
- Being chosen as a vessel, conduit or Teacher of Divinity. Being surrendered and dependent on God enables Divine Love to flow through a dedicated human soul, to others, through humility and giving of all glory to God by the soul.

Each human being has a unique place in God's Creation. Each and every one of us is designed to be God's delegate on Earth. Ask yourself: how often do you behave like God's delegate?

The feelings of Divine Love

Divine Love is a definite and profound feeling of the soul. Tangible, always available once one is in the Third Sphere[7] and above, it is unlimited and Here for all souls all the time if we but ask sincerely. We feel Divine Love entering us firstly through gentle, soft, humbling, kind and loving feelings, independent of any other person. This can be experienced as gently overwhelming as it increases, dependent on the depth of our desire for It.

As we heal further, and more of our negative, repressed emotions and causal soul wounds are removed, the entering of Divine Love into our souls becomes stronger and stronger, bringing deep tears, powerful sensations and expansions in the heart and soul in immense gratitude, humility and feelings of great love and even more yearning for God.

There may also be whole body tingling and sensations, crown chakra and heart explosions, feelings of being fully bathed in love and light, great feelings of humility, awe and wonder at the indescribable nature of God's Love, and at how much He loves you.

Receiving Divine Love can feel like being immersed in a bath of love all over, in every part of you, every cell. Deep peace, joy and waves of ecstasy, rapture and bliss arise and flow all over, and great humility washes over the soul. Immense love for God as the most wondrous, awe inspiring Soul that He Is is felt. A deepening into the essence of your pure soul occurs, along with the deep desire to give more of your soul to God.

You feel deeply nurtured and embraced in God's Arms. There is nothing better than resting and dropping into This. You feel the purity of His Love that is the most pleasurable feeling your soul will ever experience. Heat, pressure, inner and outer movements, pulsing, physical shifts and alignments can occur as you open and embody more Divine Love and the feeling of Blessedness this brings. This Blessedness also arises in felt feelings of forgiveness and mercy.

Divine Love is Perfect in its trust and tenderness. We become more and more like a child; innocent, joyful, playful and beautiful as we were created to Be. This play is a pure and glorious sensation, wishing to share itself freely and touching all others.

Receiving Divine Love can also become so powerful that we are brought to our knees in immense gratitude, rapture, pain and bliss, sometimes all at once. Receiving Divine Love in its fullness is overwhelming, and can even be physically painful in the heart as it inflows to such a degree that the heart actually stretches to accommodate It all. It is both rapturous and ecstatic, as the body may rock, sway and stretch as it receives more and more Divine Love.[8]

There is no better feeling in all universes than to receive this Greatest Love of all loves, the most pleasurable feelings a soul can experience as it has actually been designed this way, yet our physical bodies cannot take too much of it at one time!

When I receive Divine Love in a rapturous way, it is blissful to the soul yet sometimes painful to the physical. Sometimes I have to stop praying as the body becomes too tired. Yet I trust in my Father's love, and know that He is opening my body and soul more and more to Him. And receiving this power of Divine Love also brings healing afterwards, as it reaches into deeper recesses, nooks and crannies of the soul to reveal more emotions to feel and release.

As we receive Divine Love, parts of us may arise that resist this. We may feel a sense of separation, of distance, of missing God as we receive His Love, realizing the distance between Him and us that we have created, and realizing how beautiful a feeling we have left out of our lives. We may feel unworthy and small; we may feel pain and disconnection to God rapidly followed by connection and peace as we oscillate between our wounds and the truth of our pure soul that loves God. Pure honesty and total vulnerability arises.

If you sincerely, earnestly, deeply ask and pray to God that you want God, that you desire God above all else, then God will orchestrate circumstances in your life in such a way that you will see what you have to do to enact your desire. All the events and relationships in your life will provide you with the means to show yourself how much you want Him or Her, *and what you have to do to be At-One with God.*

Once this Call is sincerely put out from your heart, many times, every day, your Law of Attraction will provide all the means necessary for you to achieve this, through your actions in all you do, and with everyone you know. This is guaranteed. This can be a beautiful unfolding of God's Love for you in your life, which can be totally unexpected, mind blowing and delightful, as well as challenging.

The thirst for human affection and love is a need usually masking a wound or a lack of some kind, but underneath this lies a primordial urge within us to be with our Creator, an urge and hidden desire that *can only ever be satisfied by Divine Love.* This satisfaction, this quenching of the thirst within you for love, happens as you follow Divine laws, the way Divine Love operates. As long as we seek any form of satisfaction or solace from human beings, this urge will always be disappointed.

When we turn our faces away from getting this love from other mortals, and turn our face fully towards God as our sustenance, the only true permanent love, we realize love has no demand, no expectation, no need and has no desire to compromise or sacrifice itself. Love is not sacrifice or martyrdom, and those who do this out of a sense of duty, religious belief, low self-esteem or family/societal obligation often end up repressed, bitter, resentful and angry, tying up their soul into more knots.

In not compromising how you are being, at any time to any person for any reason, your pure soul voice becomes stronger, clearer. Loving your own soul will always benefit everyone around you, even if it does not seem to be at the time because of your own fears.

To receive the fullness of Divine Love, which is to become At-One with God, all other loves are de-prioritized so Divine Love becomes the center of your being, the center of your desires, the center of your life and your very existence, the central pillar in your soul around which all else revolves.

Then, all other things, all other loves, can be added on for your relative happiness, and will in fact be given to you with little effort or strategizing on your behalf because they will now be in their rightful place and context in your life: behind your desire for Divine Love, led by Divine Love, and therefore free of need, demand, pain, sacrifice and expectation. Love is freely received, given and transmitted, all at the same time. God comes first, everything else second.

Living without expectation in love is a process that becomes applied to every single aspect of your life, your soul and your relationships. This is sobering, humbling, an internal reference and feeling, smoothing out the kinks and edges in the equanimity, presence and roundedness of your loving soul. The pure soul you are, and its feelings and voice, becomes stronger, clearer and the center of yourself. *This center is what God communes with directly.*

When one receives more and more Divine Love, the value of human love diminishes – its importance becomes less and less. Paradoxically, this enables one to become more and more humanly loving with others. A gentle, soft and loving 'detaching' occurs because no more is human love needed. *You get given all these things when you no longer 'need' them to fill yourself up.* And it matters not when you are given them, because your very center is no longer focused on or needing this AT ALL.

Human love is a gift freely given and received without charge – in peace, presence and equanimity, with no disturbance, without going towards it or being repelled by it, without hope or expectation, only with the best interests of your soul and another's soul progressing towards God, with whatever that entails. There is no more personal interest, as there is nothing personal about it; there is nothing to gain or lose from it.

Why we do not receive Divine Love

The reason we may not feel Divine Love coming into us, even though we pray for It, is because we ourselves are blocking it. We refuse to let it in because we are unwilling to feel our own wounds, and are not truly willing to feel these pains, even if we say we do. This is where we have to be honest with ourselves and investigate our own inner resistances, asking God to help us feel the fear and pain within us, to Be with us, to take our hand as we dive down into the depths of our own suffering.

It may not be easy at first to feel the inflow of God's Love due to there not being a sensitivity to It, and due to the breaking up and releasing of the armor of the soul which can feel more like pain than love. Yet this too is the action of Divine Love!

You may be receiving Divine Love, but not be conscious of it because of the strong emotions that are being released at the same time. If we are clearing things emotionally, we may find that we do not feel the more overt feelings of Divine Love until after the emotions have cleared. As we clear more, more Divine Love can come to us.

If Divine Love is not coming to us when we ask, we have to look deeply at our own selves, inquire within, to see where we are blocking it, *and what emotions we are most scared of, for it is these emotions that we have to feel in order to allow God in.*

People can believe Truth, Divine Laws and God, and still not receive Divine Love. This is because Divine Love is not an intellectual undertaking or belief system, but rather a direct, soulful experience, the deepest feelings a soul can ever have, and is received through your soul's earnest yearnings. It cannot be received any other way except through the soul's desires, beyond mental understanding, thought and undertaking.

We do not feel God's Love because we have chosen to become self-reliant. It is hard for Divine Love to come in when you say 'Ah, there is no God,' or 'I can do this without God.' We think we can do it all ourselves. Deep in your soul you know there is a God, but it is surrounded with many layers of betrayal, denial and abandonment.

You do not feel Divine Love because you do not *yet* feel or put into action your burning desire for God, you do not *yet* feel the passion for Truth. You are still identified with the wound. It is by choice and desires that you separated from God, and it is by choice and desire that you come to Union with God also.

If you are not receiving Divine Love, and yet you 'feel' you are longing for it, then the cause for your not receiving It is that your own longings and desires are not pure, truthful or sincerely motivated, and that you are maybe using these longings to escape feeling your own emotions. This means YOU are lying to yourself, refusing to see your own wounds and be humble to them, being in victim mode or giving your power away to God, hoping He will make it all better.

If you lie to yourself, others or God, even if you do not think you are lying, even if you do not think you are covering over something, even if you ignore your mirrors and reflections in this world thinking it is not you, you are covering over the truth, and then your connection with Divine Love is broken. It can no longer flow into your soul. Without honest self-examination of the truth about yourself, truth about how you are relating with others, and knowing and following Divine Truths in every aspect of your life, Divine Love will not flow fully.

God waits for US to become conscious of the mistakes within OURSELVES before He can give us more Divine Love. It is our responsibility to find the errors within ourselves, to do this work. If you do not do this work, then Divine Love will not come! This is the barometer.

Your desire for God is shown in your willingness to find all the hurts, veils and masks you have created to stop Him from entering. Your refusal to see these things within you creates a wall where Divine Love cannot enter. Trust God here – He knows what is best for you. If you are not receiving Divine Love, it is because your longing is not strong enough.

Ask and you shall receive. You can have the support of God, guides, those in a better spiritual condition than yourself, and 'mirroring' events with other people or situations which can demonstrate your own errors to you, IF YOU ARE HONEST AND TRUTHFUL ABOUT YOURSELF.

If you are not receiving Divine Love every day in your prayers, something is not clicking, and you are blocking it. Shame, feeling bad and guilt may arise from realizing how easy it is to slip into victim mode with God or in fact any other perceived authority figure.

We may think we are trying hard, but nothing is happening. We may pray to let go, to fall apart, to stop the defenses, but the opposite is happening. This too is a sign. Honesty is the Key. Sit with God and ask yourself: Am I longing enough? Am I not pure, truthful or sincere?

Then say, No, I am not ... and then you may go into blame and self-punishment around this: 'it's my fault, it's his fault,' or 'I am not worthy to receive such a great Love' which again is showing you part of your own wound which needs to be fully felt.

Search in yourself and feel the times of your burning desire for God. Pray: how do I block myself from Your Divine Love? What unfelt emotions block me from feeling Your Love more?

The answer could also be that *you are not loving yourself*, that you are judging yourself, that you are living in a false hope, that you have abandoned your love for yourself in your life, that you give it away cheaply to others, that you compromise it because you think it is the right thing to do, that to be a martyr is right, that to ignore your own feelings is the spiritual way.

This is not what God desires for you at all! Yet we give away this, our closest link to God, found right in our very own self, in our relationships, with our families, our sexual partners, to placate and keep them close to you in fear of what might happen; and this shows even in our unwillingness to have intimate relationships.

As long as you cannot accept yourself (self love) and how you are really feeling about anything and everything, God cannot help you – no matter how much you think you are praying. Self love and deep desire go hand in hand.

God Loves us Perfectly, and if we are not receiving Divine Love it is because He is showing us something about our self that is actually the best thing for us, even if we do not like or understand it. In our desire for God, we can understand this and then inquire into why we are not receiving Divine Love, despite our 'efforts.'

Often there are two parts within us. The one with some type of desire to go to God, and a separated, heavy, pain-filled part that does not wish to go *at all* to God. This other part is the pain of our errors and wounds; we have dipped our toes into the pain and quickly backed off, subsequently making conclusions from this, and building a whole reality and belief system around this.

This then becomes the false wisdom of our wounds. The belief is that following the deep desire for God is too hurtful, too painful, that you will have to give up too much (which is true) and therefore this involves a belief that the desire is not safe and not good because it hurts. So you are aware of the desire, but do not follow it all the way through. You compromise it and are not complete in it, not whole and total in it. One has to be total in it. Give all to receive all.

So, substitutes and addictions come in so you can control these feelings, so you do not have to go there. Deep desire in true humility leads to the pain of feeling your deepest wounds, and the *loss of control*, security and to dependence solely on your own self, which is one of the greatest fears one can have.

This is where courage comes in, the action of desire for God in all aspects of your life. Pray for courage to be soft and vulnerable to feelings. Submit to being weak, humble and vulnerable, which is true strength. Submit to the real feelings – surrender to them. This is part of your deep desire for God put into action. Then help will come in abundance.

Happiness and Divine Love are received by accepting, feeling into and then living in these truths, because Love and Truth are in harmony. We do not receive Divine Love because we do not exercise our own gift of free will (out of fear) to *emotionally accept* the truth about our own self and about God. Once these truths are accepted, the deep desires and longings of the soul can be felt and freed, as if from a walled-up dam, as the veils to them are removed, and Divine Love will flow in.

On the Divine Love path, life becomes simpler and simpler. You do not bother with 95 percent of what most people are fascinated with and following on the 'spiritual' path because it is totally irrelevant to your soul. It is really fascinating to the mind, but once you know your soul, this does not matter, because it is not helping your soul to evolve. And that is the desire. So you live that all the time, and it stays with you every day. It is your foundation.

And every day I pray many, many times – 40, 50, 60 times a day. I pray without words in pure feelings, which is the language of the soul communicating directly with God, and this sharing and communion happens in two seconds. This is what you will start to experience and know. A whole prayer can be felt and received, and Divine Love can be shared with you in just two seconds. 'God, help me to receive more of your Divine Love,' or words/feelings to that effect; it is as simple as that.

One can pray and receive Divine Love walking into dinner, in the bathroom, in the shower, lying on the ground, making love, hugging a friend, in the supermarket … wherever and whatever. All the time. And the prayer is received and the heart physically swells and bursts. If you start to have this relationship with God, borne from humility and yearning for Him and Him alone, and it is clear and deep, then prayer will happen in seconds.

And you get the feelings in your heart of wonder, humility, love and reverence for God. It is more powerful to spontaneously pray like this, and be touched by the Divine in one moment, than spend hours mumbling religious incantations.

Focus on your desire for Divine Love. Feel and release the wounds of your soul and their deepest causes. And then, you will be given something far more amazing than you could think of when you had all your wounds, because many of the intentions you had when you were living in your wounds will largely be error based because they are coming from the false information generated by your wounds.

So forget about them. Do not intend anything. Just desire God and everything will be given, everything will be added unto you, and it will be far more amazing, glorious and loving than whatever you can think about right now. This is True abundance.

A soul receiving Divine Love will see the results of this Love in their own life, as it will spill over into all they do, and all they feel within. They will see with the eyes of the soul more and more how God loves us, and then they will treat others more and more like this. This will especially be seen in intimate relationships, where confirmation of your own changes become more mirrored.

In receiving more and more Divine Love, all needs become fulfilled by God, freeing you to then expansively and truly love self and others as God loves them. There is no more grasping for others or what they can give to you; none of this matters anymore.

You are fulfilled and can simply share love with whoever crosses your path, without the need to give or not to give, without the need to receive or not to receive. In receiving Divine Love more and more, we walk sublimely, humbly and as ordinary folk on the Earth, able to connect with all souls wherever they are in their own understanding.

NATURAL LOVE

God created the human soul of natural love, which when it is Realized within us returns us to this pure love or Original Innocence. This is just one journey, however. The most profound journey that brings us into the Greatest of All Loves is the Love from God that transforms us and dissolves this natural or human love soul into a Divine or Celestial Soul.

Natural love does not give us the highest degree of happiness. It changes with our own changes and growth in life, with our changes in ideas, desires, affections and understanding. It is temporary. Natural love has no stability or constancy in its affections. This love is for the present only, and when you think this love can never change or leave you, that you will always have it, it is but a hope and wish. This love is temporary, subject to change and death; it is not absolute or unending, neither is it full or complete in itself.[9]

However, without natural love we would be in an unhappy condition. Natural love is the love *within us* that comes from within our own heart-soul, is felt and then shared outwards to other people, creatures, nature, the Earth, and to all within our environment; it is the love we feel when others love us, appreciate us and are kind to us. Of course, it is the love we give in our desire and love for God.

Natural love brings us a sense of unity, enabling us to live happy lives. Without it, there would be no harmony, for only our love for each other can make the Earth, and our lives, a happy and desirable place to be. This human love is felt and expressed primarily for our parents, brothers and sisters, sexual partners, friends, soul companions, children, pets and nature. It includes our self love, love for our own soul, and loving, intimate sexual exchanges and the magnetic attraction of opposites.

Natural love seeks to fulfill itself by giving and receiving these loves, in all its expressions. Here there is value, goodness, safety, security, joy, peace and fulfillment. This love is necessary to help us to progress through human life in ways that will produce ever-greater harmony and happiness as we deal with the ups and downs, the difficulties, cares and disappointments of our lives.

Natural love is designed by God to be enjoyed as a secondary aspect of Love. With Divine Love firmly installed as the priority in your heart and soul, natural love can then be enjoyed for what it is, and actually more of it can then be given and shared with others in a totally non-attached and open-hearted way. The more Divine Love you have, the more natural love naturally overflows from you, but in a different manner than before *when you still needed something from this love and from others because there were wounds there.*

And one always remembers and holds dear in one's heart, that this natural love is not Divine Love; it is not our potential for the greatest love, joy, happiness and fulfillment. *It is a love that dies.* It is a mortal love, for mortals.

The greatest mistake and illusion in today's culture and society, fueled by Hollywood movies, modern music, advertising, art, society and literature is that human or natural love is the love worth dying for, that it is the love to yearn for, desire and value above all else, that it is the answer to all our problems, and that once possessed our life will change and we will live happily ever after.

This belief is so pernicious that our whole lives become centered on this quest to GET love from others in various ways, thereby breaking the law of free will in numerous manners. This all stems from our need to fill the hole and yearning for Divine Love with the substitute of natural love from others, not just romantically or sexually, but with our parents, children, friends, pets, drugs and more.[10]

Most of us simply do not know any better than this, as we are told on a daily basis by almost everything and everyone around us that this is 'right.' This indoctrination ensures we will always be looking to imperfect others for this imperfect love, based on our own wounds and beliefs.

And the truth is they can never give us that which we desire. Ever. They can temporarily cover and veil a hole, but once they are gone, the hole is revealed again. We think this is heartbreak, that we are missing our partner, family or children. This heartbreak is showing us our own wounds, which if investigated would lead us to much healing.

If we took this heartbreak to its root cause, we would see that it was revealing our deep missing and pining for Divine Love, our keenly felt loss of It, and the pain of substituting It with something and someone else, almost like a false god that we have erected in God's place. Feeling all of this can lead to feeling the deep desire, yearning and longing we have for God, which then leads to experiencing Divine Love, which then leads to natural love being recognized for what it is, put into its right place, and enjoyed without need, expectation, demand or injury.

Our parents are often our first substitute for Divine Love. To us, as a child, they approximated God in some dim way. Next are our children, who see us as such in some ways, but it is the way we use children to fill our own holes and yearning for love that is the saddest. We condition them through our own wounds, and refuse to feel the mirrors they bring up to us of our own unfelt and unexpressed feelings. We use our sexual partners as a substitute for Love, and then our pets and animals, as they do not talk back, are simple in their expressions and are a safe bet to not hurt us.

And of course, there are genuine expressions of these loves, free of need, worry, demand, expectation and truly unconditional. This unconditional love is truly possible once you are receiving Divine Love consistently into your soul and have healed your soul's wounds, for then there is no need for any human love, and thus it can be enjoyed truly as it was designed to be.
Doing your familial and moral duty, good works for society and others, works of charity and faith, karmic contracts and obligations, things which society deems to be righteous, while these will help you in developing a pleasant and culturally desirable moral and intellectual character, they will never bring your soul to God.

Without Divine Love, the longed for utopia of a unity of humanity, a brotherhood of humanity, will never have a solid and permanent foundation to it, and it will always collapse back into individual agendas, selfishness and the wounded self. There may be occasions of great disaster and catastrophe where the unity of humanity comes to the fore, where we all selflessly help each other for a day, make a donation, give a bag of food and a tent, but then this coming together and selfless giving dissipates back into the cavern of the heart from whence it came.

For this form of selfless giving, unity and charity to all beings, the height of natural love, to be sustained, it needs something greater than itself to aspire to: Divine Love, that which is permanent, absolute and not relative, which can transform everything.

By going to the next octave beyond natural love, natural love reaches its true expression. It is only at the next octave beyond where the issue lies that the issue can be solved. Yet, it is easy to love a perfect God, unblemished and infallible as He is. He always loves us, yet humans rarely will for our highest good. It is far more difficult to love fellow human beings with all their imperfections and defects. One can only know what one is capable of loving. There is no wisdom without love. Unless we learn to love God's Creation, we can neither truly love nor truly know God. Yet to love God first and foremost, receiving Her Love, allows us to love all of God's Creation unconditionally, and in its right place.

SOUL MATE LOVE

There is a Celestial Book called The Book of Lives which contains the names of those marked by God to be One throughout all eternity. When the Guardian of the Book is consulted, the soul mate coupling is found. If the soul mate is married, then the name cannot be told.[11]

Before coming into physical form, the human soul had a consciousness of its existence, of its relationship to God, and of its twin character. Our souls were made male and female, having only One Soul – two in One – and with this was given them a love – not two loves, but only One – which was possessed equally by each part of the soul, and which will always remain One.

When the time comes for a soul to come into form, these two parts separate. This separation is necessary for the individualization of each part of this One complete Soul, yet the two parts never lose their inter-relationship, or the binding qualities that existed before their separation. Their love is never cut, separated or split, for throughout all eternity these two parts are bound as One.[12]

Each soul mate can meet again on Earth; this is a possibility for each and every one of us. If both soul mates do not meet again on earth, they will meet again in the spirit world to reunite in a complete One, *unless* in their individual soul development barriers have arisen that prevent their reuniting.

Soul mate love was a part of our soul's very creation. So we cannot ever be deprived of it. For many, it is simply known about as an indefinable knowing from an early age, and an equally desired fulfillment. Soul mate love is the greatest human companionship and love a human can ever experience, yet also the most challenging.

In *The Symposium*, Plato shares a myth that in early times, the human beings who inhabited the Earth were simultaneously male and female. They were spherical in shape, with four arms, four legs, two faces, two sets of genital organs, and so on. These extraordinarily vigorous and masterful creatures were so keenly aware of their power that they dared to attack the gods themselves.

Faced with this threat, the gods sought a way to disarm them, and it was Zeus who found that the solution was to split them in two. This is why, from that day, these separate halves of single beings, yearning to unite and recover their original wholeness, roam the world in search of their missing half.[13]

This idea of a primitive, androgynous being, a perfect being who possessed the characteristics of both sexes, is found in one form or another in most of the major religious and philosophical traditions. Even in Genesis, God makes Eve from one of Adam's ribs, a separation of the sexes.

All these traditions express the idea that creation is the result of the polarization of unity. Each human being is one half of a whole, and as men and women sense this, they have a constant sense of being incomplete and cannot rest until they find their other half. Men and women throughout the world pursue this goal. They have an instinct, an inner voice, that tells them that in this way they will recover their original wholeness.[14]

This fundamental part of the human soul desires to be met, received and commune with its other half, its twin. This desire is actually how we have been created by God, and is an innate and implanted part of us. It is what drives us into romantic relationships, and why 'Finding the One' is such a natural and basic need, especially amongst women and more sensitive men.

It is this soul desire that needs to be fulfilled in some way, shape or form as part of the human experience, as part of the completion of the human soul, before it moves on from its human station to start becoming a Divine Soul in the Seventh Sphere.

One's human soul purpose also needs to be fulfilled totally before one can move forwards into this next great step in evolution, where there is nothing left of the human being as it is known, as all human desires, needs and experiences have been recognized, dived into, met, fulfilled, let go of and therefore transcended.

Suffering is caused by unfulfilled desire *and* mis-directed use of desire. Desire is the most powerful force in the universe, along with love and ecstatic orgasm linked to the divine. Desire makes the world go around, but what really is the essence of this desire? It is the desire of the incomplete soul to become whole, by reuniting with its Soul Mate, and with the Source of their One Soul. Desire cannot be extinguished and fulfilled *in the soul* until it joyfully joins male and female halves into an essential unity in one body.

'We are trying to find the one we love – our other. To do this we must find ourselves. To find our true love we must find who and what we are.'[15]

Many people today are interested in finding their twin flame or soul mate. But this full meeting of souls cannot take place until one has integrated enough of the male and female halves within oneself. When two soul halves who have integrated both qualities within themselves meet, *soul union* takes place. As each person is whole enough in him or herself, they are full circles, and when these two full circles meet, their union takes the form of the infinity symbol.

Greatness practice

We may not like some things or people, but really what we do not like is ourselves. There is no evil – just wounded souls and mistakes committed from out of this pain. Feel and speak to this place within. Speak to the glorious place within that hides greatness, compassion, mercy and the innate love we have been created from. We all possess this place for we have been created like this. The more we tune into this space, the more healing occurs. It is from this space that we receive the most Divine Love too, when we ask for it.

One of the greatest goods we can do for others is not to share our riches with them but to reveal to them their own. Although the act of charity brings great benefit to others, the greatest benefit of all is to show another person their own greatness.

What would it be like for me to see the greatness in another person, to see the greatness in everyone I meet, and to express that to them?

God, help me see the greatness in everyone.

Do this with the next person you see after reading this, and your Twin or present partner.

Place your left hand on your heart, and the other hand on your friend's heart. Look deep into their eyes, from your heart. Breathe with your friend in this space.

Say: 'YOU ARE A PURE SOUL: I OPEN MY HEART TO YOU.'
Breathe with your friend for 1 minute.
Now say: I honor the place in you in which the entire universe dwells.

I honor the place in you which is true, light, humble and love.
When you are in this place in the core of your soul,
and I Am in this space in the core of my soul,
then we are One.

Now reverse the process with your friend and twin.

Soul Mates

You can never fully be with or recognize your soul mate until
you have developed more love within yourself first, and know
yourself better, understanding the deeper feelings and experiences of the soul. It is love that draws and magnetizes you to
your soul mate. In addition, you cannot fully enjoy being with
your soul mate until the soul mate part of your heart opens,
which is a definite feeling that you will know has happened or
not.

Your soul mate may be found, but not *acquired*, until the love of
the less developed soul comes into resonance with the love
possessed by the more loving soul. This means you can be with
your soul half physically and still not connect truly because of
your own unfelt wounds and lack of humility.

Soul mate love lasts forever, providing the twin souls seek and
obtain Divine Love. This love is only a complete One when these
two *apparently* independent soul 'halves' come together in perfect
unity. This unity comes when both have become At-One with
God FIRST. One cannot unite fully with their soul mate until one
is united with God first, although glimpses can be tasted and
even lived in.

The fullness and eternal nature of human love is only possible
between Twin Souls. Until a soul tastes and lives this, they will

not experience the fullest potential depth of human love and how God created the human soul. God has created us to live this: He really loves us all so much.

The love of soul mates makes the happiness of two humans seemingly complete. Yet this love is not of a Divine nature, but the highest, purest and only eternal form of natural love. God has designed it so we can have both. Once it is included with Divine Love, love reigns in its fullness on every level. Only when we have the Love of the Divine can we fulfill the laws of the Divine; and if we have natural love only, we can only fulfill natural laws.

But if we fulfill and live both, then all forms of love are realized! And this is God's Wish for us: to enjoy the fullness of love on every level, in every way we can imagine, and in ways we cannot yet imagine.

Soul mate love is an eternal love, and this great love requires that at some stage these two parts become One again. The fundamental law of the universe is that all things will come into harmony with the Will of God. Soul mate love is the only love that can have a separate and individual existence in the Celestial Heavens, where Divine Love exists to the exclusion of every other love save the soul mate love; and the more the two-in-one possess the Divine Love, the greater will be their possession of the soul mate love.

There is no other love or thing, except Divine Love, that can surpass it, or make two souls so united that even death cannot sever it. The relationship between soul mates is a very strong attraction, and has great importance in natural love. But it is important to remember all forms of natural, human love disappear when you are At-One with God, as the natural, human soul is transformed into a Divine Soul.

In the Celestial Heavens, there is no trace at all of the human soul, which makes this everlasting bond between soul mates even more special, and why it is even more important that each soul mate reaches At-One-ment with God so they can enjoy the fullness of their Union with each other, and take it to even greater heights within the Kingdom, within God Itself.

The strong attraction between soul mates is due to the resemblance of their soul's structure. One can easily tell soul mates just by looking at them, as they share a similar vibrational signature, or the same soul signature. Even with the soul's transformation this attraction continues to exist, because the change has not been structural, but substantial.

However, the union of separate soul mates is not necessary for enjoying the full happiness of Divine Love. It is not necessary for becoming At-One with God, and indeed cannot be fully enjoyed as the perfect One Soul until well after At-One-ment with God has occurred. So, At-One-ment with God is still At-One-ment with God, and is the primary goal, the focus of each soul mate's life. *At-One-ment with God is not dependent on being with your soul mate.*

When we use the gift of free will to turn to God for Divine Love, what is the one thing that God imagined would bring us complete happiness throughout eternity? To find our soul mate, one whose qualities and unique perceptions bring the puzzle of ourselves to completion. This is how we were created.

God's Will for us to become At-One with Him has provided us with the treasure of loving another who will remain for us a window into the heart of love. When we are At-One with God, we can enjoy the fulfillment of soul mate love completely because true soul nature and its qualities have become Realized.

Because of the intensity of the pleasure and the pains involved in meeting and being with your soul mate, the wisest thing to do is *to prepare:* fully feel and release the wounds of all previous intimate relations and do as much soul healing as possible *before even calling in your soul mate.*

Ask to feel:

- the times you did not love yourself
- the times you projected mother and father wounds onto the other and vice versa
- all the times you felt and received emotional pain and did not express or release it (even if you did not feel it at the time)
- all the times you allowed yourself to be used or abused because you did not love yourself or allow yourself to feel your own pains
- all the times you felt betrayed and abandoned; or all the times you felt judged and separated from, not just in intimate relations but for all the instances this has occurred in your soul

Free your soul to meet your soul mate in a truthful and loving way! The Healing Prayer and The Divine Love Prayer at the end of this book will especially help with this.

In this process, you will cleanse many soul hurts and disappointments, which will prevent you from placing expectations, demands and projections onto your present relationship, or with a future soul mate. Love does not demand, expect or project anything: if we do this, it is not love, and we are being unloving and untruthful to our self and the other, as well as instantly jumping out of harmony with divine laws. *Would love do that?*

And of course, new and deeper emotions will arise when you meet your soul mate as well, that you could never tap into by yourself or in your present relationship. Preparing for this emotional intensity beforehand is the wisest thing to do, by praying and feeling into all deeper previous hurts.

All five forms of love merge together to give us the complete and total love that God has created for us to enjoy.

For me, there are five main desires which relate to why I wished to be with my Twin Soul / Soul Mate, and what these desires are now revealing in living with my Twin.

1. To accelerate my At-One-ment with God by feeling, expressing and humbly releasing all emotions that are not loving. By coming more into our One Soul, I feel more of how much God loves us, and wishes us to enjoy and be Truly happy in life, which will only be fulfilled when we are At-One with Him.

2. To accelerate my and our At-One-ment by feeling the purest, most innocent, core joy and human love it is possible to experience. All within me that is not of love arises in this meeting. And, just by having this experience and living it more, something is released and relieved from Our Soul. Sharing and playing with my soul mate, the other side of me, allows us to eventually merge with each other into One Soul, *after* first becoming At-One with God.

3. In feeling, accepting and understanding my soul mate and how she acts, lives and moves through life, her qualities and how she understands and feels about everything, her emotional movements and expressions, her desires, I have

come to a deeper, more intimate understanding of my soul, our Soul, and the very nature of love itself. We are the same but in polarity, yet these polarities lie within me too. In being with her, I discover these polarities within me, for it to all come into balance. This is a rocket ship to God and to love.

4. In experiencing making love with my soul mate, I have experienced the ultimate soul-sexual experience I have always desired to have. And there is more, including the ultimate transmutation of the sexual force into light, into transcendental sexual electricity that is a fuel for our Union with God. Soulful sexual union with my soul mate activates latent soul codes and gifts, helping to bring each of us into Soul Realization.

It may bring sadness to feel you can only ever be fulfilled in your soul's sexuality with your soul mate, but also inspiration, joy and desire to heal yourself fast to attract this other.

5. To share and assist others into coming closer to God.

The soul-to-soul connections we have experienced with our other partners, whose soul we have touched and been touched by, is merely a surrounding layer of the heart that we once felt and thought to be our core heart, as it was the deepest experience we had ever had of human love. But this is just another layer.

The core secret center of the human soul is far deeper and purer than this layer, and only opens up fully for God and one other human soul.

This is why we do not know this space, and think that our previous encounters were so deep. These encounters were dreamlike layers around the heart that were part of the wound, part of the entryway, part of the guarded doorway to the secret center of the soul.

This is a virginal space untouched by any other; only God has touched it as He reaches out and Loves us, and we touch it in our moments of deep prayer, yearning and desire for God. It is the secret and naked space where we pray purely, intimately, passionately, painfully, ecstatically and imploringly from our soul to God.

How would it be to let another human soul into this most intimate and vulnerable of spaces? This is the twin soul space; only accessible for me, God and my soul mate.

Feeling this with my twin has brought about incredible changes, fast!

God is always involved as The Holy Third in a Sacred Relationship, and is especially important for soul mates. More people will meet their soul mates when they recognize this fact, and include God in their yearnings to meet him or her. The more you receive Divine Love, the more possibility there is that you will meet your soul mate, as God desires this for you, indeed has created it for you, and wants to give it to you. Go to the Source! And all will be given to you.

But first, some wounds have to be cleared, and one has to become more loving, and the ultimate love is Divine Love. The more you have of this Love, the more your soul mate will be magnetized to you. The more that Divine Love is asked for by both of you in your relationship, the more happier and loving your life will be.

Because of the many illusions surrounding soul mate love, it is always wise to be in the Second Sphere of Love (see next chapters) before actively desiring and praying to be with him or her. It is in this more expanded and loving space that your desire will be most clearly answered and received by the Divine, as you are free of many of the needs within you surrounding the desire for this human love to make you feel better, or to cover a lack and a hole within you.

Bear in mind one soul mate will always be more evolved than the other, and therefore more healed, humble, self-responsible and able to clearly flow through feelings to their causes and healing.

What are your five or more reasons for wanting to be with your soul mate?

Write them down and *be honest about it*.

Often we want to be with our soul mate to:

- fill us up and cover our own pain
- make our human life better because of our deep unfulfilled needs around human love from our childhoods

This can be:

- because we feel no one loved or loves us
- because we have had bad relationships in the past
- because of loneliness and bad parental relationships, missing love
- because of physical, emotional and sexual abuse,
- because of a lack of self love, healthy emotional boundaries, and because of the sheer romance surrounding this ideal.

See whether your reasons are in alignment with Truth and Love of the soul, and of God.

Romantic, sensual, passionate love for your partner and ultimately your soul-half, and the emotional bond that you desire in this is brought into its Divine design and ultimate enjoyment through praying for and receiving Divine Love in the act of having sex, thus bringing it into the Sphere of *making love and then becoming love.*

Our yearning for romantic love hints at our eternal yearning and romance with Beloved God, and then our soul mate, our soul mate being a combination of the feelings of romantic human love and aspiration for Divine Love. Our partners that come before our soul mate are means of healing ourselves, emotionally and sexually, and coming into closer connection with our soul.

For more: read the chapter on Male-Female Union in the book Sacred Wounds Original Innocence.

SELF LOVE

'Yesterday I was clever, so I wanted to change the world. Today I am wise, so I am changing myself.'
Rumi

Your self-identity is created in your first seven years of life, and this identity creates unique filters based on the emotional traumas you have experienced, and the subsequent belief systems, or thought patterns, that arise from these wounds. These filters make us see the evidence that makes our belief appear true, distorting our experience of any and all events to validate this belief.

This stops your ability to perceive truth in the present moment, to respond in love or even conscious choice. Your belief systems are simply effects of deeper emotional wounds, and both the wound and belief system become the reality you experience and the situations, people and relationships you attract.

Self love is accepting yourself as you are right now, with all your flaws and mistakes, and desiring to grow beyond this state at the same time. On the Path to God, you accept yourself, you desire to grow your soul, and you desire to receive God's Love and love God fervently, and with devotion. This is the ultimate Self love, as by loving your soul in this Way, you will eventually come to love yourself as God loves you.

When you come to love yourself exactly as God Loves you, remembering God wishes to give you everything if you but allow It and follow the Laws of Love, you will be loving others as God Loves them. Then you will be sharing God's feelings and desires, acting on them in the world for the benefit of all beings. You will be sharing God's Will and Plan for humanity and the cosmos, not just your own version of it.

Self love is a personal relationship with your soul; it is intimately knowing yourself, observing yourself, and consciously choosing, again and again, to realign and correct your mistakes in thoughts, feelings and actions. Self love is a personal, soul-to-Soul Relationship with God, nurturing This every day, growing little by little every day.

In self love, it seems sometimes we have to take radical actions, but remember: *in actions of loving yourself, you will be loving all others,* for their highest good, no matter what it 'seems' like at the time. It will all work out.

Self love is how you honor your own soul's progress towards God. Honor sees only the highest frequency you possess, and holds you to this. If you deviate from this, there can only be a lack of love, a place where love is absent within you, a place where you are not loving, that prevents this.

Self love in God's Embrace is the ultimate protection, for it enables you to love self, others and God at the same time. When you sincerely ask God to hold you in His Loving Arms, keep you in the Shadow of His Love and protect you with His Love, you are loving the purest part of your soul, allowing it to bloom. Love is the only protection, and if one does not love one's own self, one cannot really receive God's Love.

As love is the only protection, by choosing only this, all your false protections will be exposed for healing and release into vulnerability and joy. Choosing your own soul's growth means you overcome the lie of this world, which states, mantra-like, that one has to betray oneself for duty, obligation, for the sake of others.

The highest form of betrayal is when you betray your own self for others. This is not love, but belief married to fear of discovering and feeling the depths of your own pain.

Self love chooses humility and to feel deeply. Self love desires passionately. Self love discovers choices and chooses wisely in full knowledge. There is power in this choice if moved into with love. This is Manifestation.

Self love manifests more when your desire and passion for giving to others also equally benefits yourself. You are totally included in your serving of others, and you too are receiving from it. This is a win-win-win situation, for you, others and God, for you are following His Laws. *Love others as you love yourself, love yourself as God loves you.* God loves us totally and wants us to have everything if we but allow it. Can you love yourself enough to allow that into your life, and then share it?

This means having a beginner's mind, constantly, every day. Returning to the same basic laws of love, feeling into your Law of Attraction and realizing that you are creating what is happening 'to' you because of your own wounds (not taking on others wounds either!). This results in humility and deep feeling, which then leads, once released, into more love. This too is loving your soul, for it is releasing it. As Goethe shares, 'The angels, if they deem to come, do so not because of your tears; but because of your constant resolve to be a beginner.' Beginners win the race, and love has no losers.

Once you find your authentic voice, a certain faith develops, not simply that the universe will provide for you, but that you will provide for you. They can shame you, they can obstruct you, but they can no longer alienate you from your own essence.[16]

It is important to reconnect and live from your own pure soul, and not give power away to God. This apparent paradox resolves in you the more love you hold, feel and share.

You are the cause of all your frustrations. Once you have sorted out yourself, the cause, the effects take care of themselves.

Self love is the first step towards the fullness of natural love and to how, in time, we may also realize an aspect of how God loves us. True self love is the consistent awareness and action where we accept and love ourselves, and recognize the changes we need to make in ourselves, honestly and humbly, to get closer to God.

True self love manifests when we no longer *need* anything from any other person on any level to make us who we are or make us whole. (Need is different to desire, passion and yearning.) This is true self-responsibility. True self love and true self-responsibility in humility create the solid foundation for a soul that is becoming truly loving and journeying to becoming At-One with God.

This is so simple, yet profound. Unconditional love begins at home, in you, in your own body temple, in your own feeling soul, in your own gift of the mind, in your own connection to Spirit. From this foundation all unfolds and reveals according to Divine Laws. If you cannot love your true soul self, whom can you love truly? And how can anyone else love you truly?

Self love is the basis for all intimate soulful relationships of every kind. Without self love, all your relationships will never be soulfully successful. You can pretend that they are, but they will always be error strewn and hiding a part of your own wounded self.

In coming closer to God, we love our own soul more. To truly feel that God desires and loves you is one of the greatest gifts of overwhelming gratitude ever imaginable. To truly feel that God desires you both shatters and heals you. To truly and spontaneously love God from the depths and pure joy of your heart is one of the happiest, most liberating feelings in creation.

The basis of this all is love of self, the seed of true service.

Aloha mai ke akua ipo – you love yourself as you love God.

For a more in-depth explanation on self love, read Sacred Wounds Original Innocence*: www.christblueprint.com*

FRIENDS OF THE HEART

Friendship on the Divine Love Path involves loyalty to Truth and the higher Love. Human friendship is brought into its Divine Design by the soul's involved desiring the Divine, being loyal to and united by this common goal, and in this deepening and ever-revealing, humbling process, specific feelings of fraternal love arise from walking the path in total vulnerability with these friends of the heart. This is soul family, united through soul yearning and common aspiration for God.

This bond is Free for it is moving towards the infinite, and is designed to support the receiving of Divine Love for each soul, a selfless love, regardless of your own agenda. This is an unconditional love and honoring of the true purpose of the soul, and indeed the very creation of the soul itself.

You support and love each other in truth, regardless of how it may affect you, for you desire for them what you desire for yourself. You love them as God loves you, and treat them as you treat yourself. This human friendship based on the Divine is what God wishes for us, and leads to more love being created.

Every true love and authentic soul friendship is a story of unexpected transformation. If we are the same person before and after we loved, that means we have not loved enough.[17]

St John of the Cross says '*spiritual friendship is not when the remembrance of the friendship causes remorse of conscience.*'

This may be true, but this remorse gives one a valuable opportunity to see oneself, to forgive, to inquire into why there is remorse still there, and what emotions lie inside you that still give rise to this remorse, regret, fear or sadness. All these emotions, once felt, will lead you more into your soul, and closer to God. Whenever we truly love our soul, we are loving others also, even if they or we do not realize it at the time, and even if it goes against another's wishes or agenda.

St John goes on beautifully to share:

'When the friendship is purely spiritual, the love of God grows with it; and the more the soul remembers it, the more it remembers the Love of God, and the greater desire it has for God, so that as one grows, the other grows also. The Spirit of God has this property, that it increases good by adding more good to it.

*But when this love arises from the vice of sensuality (human love alone) it produces contrary effects; for the more the one grows, the more the other decreases, and the remembrance of it likewise. (*You will want more of the human love experience and less of Divine Love: the need increases for human love.*)*

As this love grows, the soul's love of God becomes colder … the love born of human love and sensuality ends in human love and sensuality, and that which is of the spirit ends in the spirit of God, and causes it to grow within you.'

As we deepen in our receiving of Divine Love and the clearing away of the obstacles to receiving This, then the relationship to God becomes clearer as we realize how Perfectly God loves us. Friend, Father, Mother, Creator, Beloved – God can be all of these for us, and more. God is always here for us in our humility and desire.

Borne through this love comes a soulful affection for others, which reaches its height with the Community of The Friends of The Heart. This is brought into its Divine Design by affection, softness and acceptance being extended to others and your own soul as you all go through negative emotions such as shame and unworthiness.

This also extends to those you are less familiar with, as well as those who may perceive themselves to be your enemies. Sharing affection with your 'enemies,' being kind to them in their anger or fear towards you, is a sign of this love being perfected.

Another way Divine affection manifests is when the soul moves through its trials and tribulations of healing and releasing; at this time it can be comforted, when appropriate, through a 'touch of love.'

This can be through The Comforter of The Holy Spirit, (God's Messenger of Love) Divine Love guides or Divine Spirits, but can also come through consciously loving humans, our Friends of the Heart, who are moved by love yet also stand in Divine Truth so as to not interfere with our soul's journey or try to comfort us to stop us (or themselves) feeling our own, very necessary emotions. This is a Presence, a space being held, rather than a human love assuring.

Wherever there is comfort, there is pain. Wherever there is pain, there is the opportunity for love to bloom once the pain is felt, because all pain shows us where we have not been loving.

Praying for each other in Community is a touching, beautiful and transforming experience. Seeing a soul break down, and praying for that soul to receive more Divine Love as a group radically shifts that soul, happens when we all align to that soul's deepest desire and help them manifest it more. Whenever this happens, the soul involved goes to the next level.

This is because we all desire the Union with God, and our human love focuses on the divine as One Power, One Heart and One Focus. The silent presence of true support for the deepest part of the soul is priceless, and allows the deepest vulnerability to reveal and open the soul into its true nature.

Feeling deep affection for God as a Friend, Father or Mother is beautiful, and brings us closer to Him in our own souls. Feeling this affection is a vital part of the journey, as this closeness means God is seeing us as His Child, and we are feeling Him as Our Love.

THE SOUL and SPIRIT BODY

YOUR SOUL

Your soul is composed of your heartfelt desires, longings, passions, aspirations, deep feelings, and what moves, touches, activates and inspires you. Within the soul is the ability to give and receive love in all forms. The soul is made of pure human love and is the only part of you that has the possibility of living forever, the only part of you that can merge into God.

It is the real you, the eternal you, and it is accompanied by its vehicles of the spirit body, which is how it moves throughout creation, and the physical body, which is how it moves on Earth. The point of your soul having a physical body is to aid in its individualization through the process of embodying the soul.

God created your soul, and it existed before your physical body. The creation of the soul took place a long time before the appearance of humans on Earth. The human soul is created with a desire for the expression and reception of love from other souls, but this desire is often suppressed and distorted when you are in the womb and after birth.

The human soul is not divine, nor ever was it so. But it has the potential to become Divine through consistent asking to receive Divine Love. The soul feels, not thinks, and it is through deep feeling and communion that it grows more and more. It is through feeling, not emotions, that your soul connects with other souls, and can communicate with God.

Your soul is made of two halves: male and female. One day you are destined to meet the other half of your soul, your twin, either in the physical, or in the spirit body. Much healing arises in this reunion. One starts to merge with their twin soul in the Sixth Sphere, and this process deepens when one of the twins becomes

At-One with God.

Your soul has been created with free will and choice. This has been given to you by God, and enables your soul to either grow in truth and love, or decrease in love. *The ultimate use of free will as envisaged by God is for your soul to desire to become At-One with God*, thus transforming it into a Divine Soul. This is God's deep desire for us, His most cherished creations.

Your soul holds your true purpose, mission and deepest fulfillment. It is the most natural part of you, and is always wanting to communicate with you. It has been created pure and perfect, and it is your true center of love that you *already* possess. You have felt this pure center in various moments in your life, when you felt unconditional love for another, or devotion for God, or another from a deep and unconditional place within you. This center is joyful, peaceful, wise, loving and giving.

Your soul, no matter its personal condition, can grow in love and happiness at any time, and your soul's condition and life experience is never fixed nor predetermined. Any human soul can receive Divine Love, no matter what you have done. If the human soul continues to receive Divine Love consistently, it can grow infinitely in Divine Love, bliss, joy and power, and in understanding the wisdom of God's Truths.

The soul grows through:

1 Humility and self-responsibility, your desire to totally and completely feel all your emotions, and to make it no one else's fault, neither punishing, blaming, judging or harming yourself or others.
2 Desire to receive Divine Love and Truth as the priority: human love is secondary

3 Free will choice: being educated about all the possibilities available to you

4 Being sovereign: having your own connection to God and Truth within you dependent on no one else

5 Having a heartfelt determination, commitment and discipline

6 Merging with the spirit body vehicle and caring for the physical: The Holy Trinity

7 Loving and serving others in all dimensions

8 Developing the six forms of Love

9 Living by the 64 moral codes of love: Ma'at

10 Discernment and wisdom regarding what is love and what is truth; investigating and applying this consistently with everyone in all aspects of your life without exception

How Does the Soul Grow

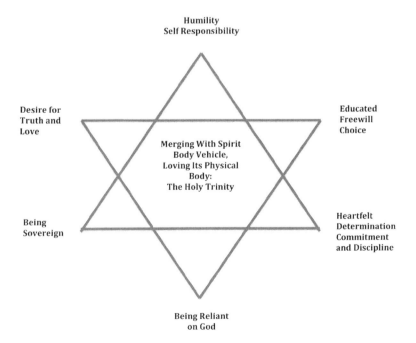

YOUR SOUL and ITS SPIRIT BODY

'The sun can remain in the heavens and its rays are so strong that without moving they can reach us here; so the soul and its spirit, in much the same way as the sun and its rays, can remain where they are, and yet, through the power of the heat that comes to them from the true Sun of God, some higher part of them can rise above itself.'[18]

We are made from body, soul and spirit, of which soul is the main and essential power. The *spirit is the active energy of the soul*, the instrument through which soul manifests itself. The spirit is inseparable from the soul, and has no other function *apart from to manifest the potentialities of the soul in action*. As the soul was created in the image of God, and as spirit is the active energy of the soul, so the Holy Spirit is the active energy of the Great Soul of God.

The spirit body merges with the soul to facilitate At-One-ment with God. As the spirit body is innately connected to the material body, many mystics have done fasts, cleanses and extreme physical acts to facilitate this three-fold marriage with God.

From the perspective of the spirit body, healing is accomplished by moving energy. Everything in life is vibration moving at different frequencies and speeds of spin. Molecules do not have to touch each other to interact. Energy flows through the electromagnetic field that the spirit body moves in and through in the differing dimensions, and along with water, this forms the matrix of life in creation. Water forms structures that transmit energy, like the spirit body, serving as a channel of communication and energy flow.

The spirit body is a manifestation of the workings of the soul, the moving active energies of the soul. The soul's home is in the

---

spirit body, whether you have a physical body or not, and it is never without the spirit body, its vehicle. The soul's condition determines your destiny.

From the perspective of the soul journeying towards Union with God, healing is accomplished through receiving Divine Love from God. Everything in life is here to faciliate this purpose, and to uncover and release any blocks to receiving more of this Love. The soul intent on becoming a Divine Soul focuses its sincere yearnings on God, whose Great Soul lies outside Creation.

This Creation and the human soul are effects of God, not God itself. Along this Way, the soul embraces all of Creation, growing in human love, in loving itself and others. In these actions of love married to receiving ever-increasing amounts of Divine Love and possessing this Divine Love, the human soul transcends Creation itself by transcending its humanity itself.

The human spirit body and its mind begins to dissolve when your soul enters the Seventh Sphere, and begins the New Birth Process into The Divine Soul.[19]

Love knows no sadness; the soul speaks its condition by the appearance of the spirit body's countenance, the soul being so full of gladness and joy, the countenance can only express those emotions of the soul.[20]

What stops your soul from growing?
The wounds of the human soul

God Loves us and wants us to Be with Her. God is our true Parent, always smiling upon us in our weakness, always here for us, always willing to take us into Her Arms of Love if we but ask from our hearts.

WOUNDED HUMAN/PERFECT HUMAN

MALE
FEMALE
WAR & SEPARATION

SOVEREIGN SOUL
INTERDEPENDENT
DISCONNECT

5 WOUNDS
OF LOVE
JUDGMENT
BETRAYAL
SEPARATION
ABANDONMENT
DENIAL

SELF LOVE
LOSS OF
INNOCENCE

PARENTAL/ANCESTRAL
PRENATAL/
BIRTH
TRAUMAS
CONCEPTION/GESTATION/BIRTH

AMON
AMAN

FREEWILL?
SEPARATION
FROM GOD

NEGATIVE SPIRITS
MALE/FEMALE

WORLD MATRIX
UNQUESTIONING
SUBSTITUTES
FOR GOD
FOLLOWING

DNA MANIPULATION
MISALIGNMENT

LOSS OF SACRED
SEXUAL SELF

SPIRITUAL MATRIX
GOVERNED BY FAME
ENTITIES ATTENTION
HOLES LOVE $
VALIDATION RECOGNITION
NEED FOR:

If you notice, the human form on this diagram is composed of viruses and infections. This was done for a specific reason. Why?

The average human soul is like this. Every human has an emotional body completely covered with infected wounds. Each wound is infected with emotional poison – the poison of all the emotions that make us suffer, such as hate, anger, envy, and sadness. The mind is so wounded and full of poison by the process of domestication, that everyone describes the wounded mind as normal. This is considered normal, *but I can tell you it is not normal.*

The symptoms of the disease are all the emotions that make humans suffer: anger, hate, sadness, envy, and betrayal. *We don't have to suffer any longer.* First we need the truth to open the emotional wounds, take the poison out, and heal the wounds completely. *Only love has the ability to put you in that state of bliss.* Being in bliss is like being in love. Being in love is like being in bliss. You are perceiving love wherever you go. It is entirely possible to live this way all the time because others have done it and they are no different from you. They live in bliss because they have changed their agreements and are dreaming a different dream. *This way of life is possible, and it's in your hands.*
Don Miguel Ruiz, The Four Agreements

Certain Sufi sects say that everyone is sick until they are totally healed and living in their pure soul and love all the time. *The only 'normal' people are those who have healed everything that is not love* in their soul. Everyone else is abnormal. I like this perspective because it is based in love and reality.

Some of our memories are housed within our soul. Other memories are housed in the mind, which lies within our spirit body, and other deeper, more stressful and longer term memories can appear as etched grooves in our brain and organs, within our physical body. Our soul animates the spirit body, which in turn animates the physical body. The spirit body, which looks like a crystalline version of the physical body, appears younger the more healed you are.

Emotional injuries become blocked within our soul, and are reflected through the spirit body and then into the physical body as illness. The soul is made of feelings and emotions, emotion being that which we need to release so we can come into our true feelings.

The soul has pathways similar in construction to your brain. Your emotionally driven memories are stored in your soul, and are then reflected through your spirit body into your physical body. Your physical brain is constructed when gestating in your mother's womb in response to the emotions and feelings your mother was feeling. It's all emotion.

From the soul's center is where you most deeply pray to God, and receive God's Love. The purer your soul becomes, the more Divine Love you can receive. *One purifies their soul by feeling all their errors against Divine and moral laws one has done or has passed down into one's soul and DNA,* as these block God's Love from naturally entering, and by educating the soul to become the master of the spirit body (mind) and physical body. The main qualities a soul needs to grow are humility, desire, right use of educated choice, and *becoming a devoted lover and servant of God.*

When an error enters your soul, it sets up a pathway for more error to enter your soul. When truth enters your soul, it sets up a pathway for more truth to enter your soul. Picture your soul as energetic pathways with all these connection points. Consider your soul like your brain where all these tiny networks are constructed. There are unimpeded pathways for emotions to flow through the soul in the same manner as the brain. We have pathways where only error flows, these being error constructed pathways. Similar pathways for truth are separate. In closing one channel down, we open the other more fully.

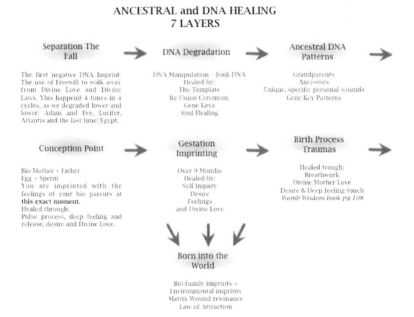

ANCESTRAL and DNA HEALING
7 LAYERS

Separation The Fall →

The first negative DNA Imprint. The use of Freewill to walk away from Divine Love and Divine Laws. This happend 4 times in 4 cycles, as we degraded lower and lower: Adam and Eve, Lucifer, Atlantis and the last time: Egypt.

DNA Degradation →

DNA Manipulation - Junk DNA
Healed by:
The Template
Re Union Ceremony
Gene Keys
Soul Healing

Ancestral DNA Patterns →

Grandparents
Ancestors
Unique, specific personal wounds
Gene Key Patterns

Conception Point →

Bio Mother + Father
Egg + Sperm
You are imprinted with the feelings of your bio parents at **this exact moment.**
Healed through:
Pulse process, deep feeling and release, desire and Divine Love.

Gestation Imprinting →

Over 9 Months
Healed by:
Self Inquiry
Desire
Feelings
and Divine Love

Birth Process Traumas →

Healed trough:
Breathwork
Divine Mother Love
Desire & Deep feeling touch
Womb Wisdom book pg 108

↓ ↓ ↓

Born into the World

Bio-family imprints +
Environmental imprints
Matrix Wound resonance
Law of Attraction

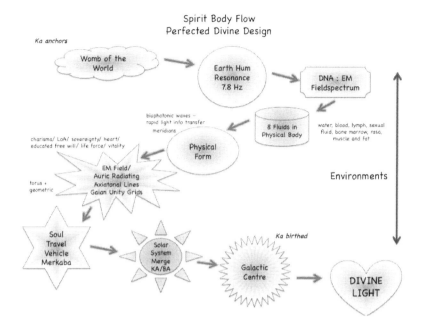

Spirit Body Flow
Perfected Divine Design

THE SPIRIT BODY

The spirit body is a transparent, crystalline blueprint for physical health and well-being. It is the regenerator and sustainer of the physical body, its original blueprint, *and it looks just like your physical body*. The more healed and evolved it is, the younger it will look, no matter how old you are physically.

For most of us, the spirit body is *the first taste we have of multidimensional reality*, and is the most easily accessible and available connector and bridge to your soul. It carries and leaves a psychic footprint wherever it goes, and is how we know someone is about to ring us, enter through the door, or do something.

The soul animates the spirit body, which in turn animates the physical body. The soul is the cause of all other bodies, and the prime connector to God through feelings. *The spirit body is the vehicle of consciousness for the soul to move and operate across dimensions, time and space.*

Your spirit body is your auric field, your electromagnetic field, your psychic self, your power of manifestation and attraction, *your charisma and magnetism,* the feeling others get from you, your personality. It is what most others will feel you to be, based on what you emanate, or put out into the world. It is your strength, confidence and authority: the way you hold and carry yourself in the world until you become more soul orientated and anchored.

It is your foundation for dynamic well-being and inspired engagement with life in joy. *It is how you embody your soul on Earth.* When the spirit body is clear, we connect to the web of life and Earth itself, helping us to become Self-contained, Sovereign Centered and Self-empowered.

The spirit body connects to your physical body through bio-photonic waves of light, connecting the electromagnetic fields of your DNA to your cellular networks, transferring information at light speed. Coursing out to your meridians, chakras and auric field, this light spans out into *all* other environments: to other people's energy fields or auras, your neighborhood, country, the Earth and out into the solar system and the center of our Galaxy.

The spirit body holds connections to your family resonances and their gifts, lessons, inherited shadows and healing. Earth memories, deep belief systems and mental structures lie here.

The spirit body contains the mind, thoughts, thinking communication and expression through *languages of all kinds,* be it English, sacred geometry or sacred languages. These languages may *touch* the soul but are not *of* the soul, which expresses through pure feeling and love.

The mind dissolves when one becomes closer to God. Brilliance of mind and genius are marks of having a highly developed spirit body, but not necessarily soul. If both are combined, a powerful creative synergy that can transform into Love can birth. The spirit body is highly organized and coherent when healed, and consists of a series of fluid geometric structures unfolding in harmony. It operates, when commanded by the soul, from Divine Light, whereas the source for the soul is Divine Love.

The true union of spirit body and soul, mind-pineal and the heart-seed, occurs when one is near At-One-ment with God.

As Yeshua shares: *'Father, into your hands **I commit my spirit**.'*
Luke 23:46

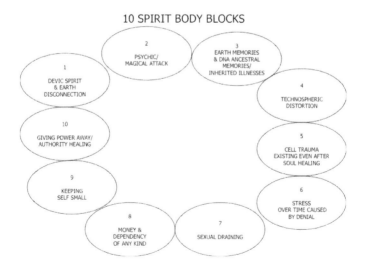

15 QUALITIES OF THE DIVINE SPIRIT BODY

Spirit of the Earth

Spirit of the Earth. Greenness as living cord to the fertile processes of nature, its voice, the web of life, primal sustenance, preservation and biological love.

Penetrating or Diamond Mind

Ability to penetrate a situation or person with clarity and insight, to reveal the truth, to cut through all veils of illusion. The ability to sever or create connections.

Power of Illumination

Illuminate any shadow, any confusion in self or others. To light up, move, touch, inspire and catalyze self and others into action, clarity and soul growth.

Power to Initiate and Sustain

Power to initiate and sustain the energies of birthing and dying, the beginning and the ending of something, be it a project, relationship et al.

Power of Splendour

To naturally sit in your Queenly or Kingly Presence, the royal Self that serves others. To be majestic and splendid without.

Knowing one's Self and Growth Process

Ability to sustain body-mind by knowing one's self and growth process and what you need. Endurance, stamina, ability to complete and end things.

Power to tell the Truth

Willpower to persevere with honesty, honour and truthful integrity when everyone else is not; this connects spirit body to soul.

Ability to get Things Done

Be a leader and take charge. Consider all aspects of a situation and act decisively. Ability to break through obstacles.

Ability to Manifest

The ability to manifest abundance in all areas of life. The power of ease and effortless manifestation.

Capacity to sit in Holy State

Capacity to sit in a Holy State and command instant respect through your presence and accumulated power of your accomplishments. Authority.

Nurture Body-Mind-Soul

Ability to nurture body-mind-soul through right relationships, healthy internal and external environments, right speech, right conduct and grounded integrity.

Know your own Worth

Know your own worth and the worth/abilities of others. Self worth and self-esteem. Trust in yourself. Centred in Sovereign Self.

Power to change

The power to change, ignite, transform, seen as miraculous or incredible. Revered by others.

Power of Radiance and Transmission

The ability to radiate Light and Wisdom to others directly and instantly as an experience.

Power to Travel in other Dimensions

The power to travel into other dimensions as servant of the soul. Multi dimensional being and vehicle of the soul.

WHAT IS LOVE
and
WHAT IS IT NOT?

This is the biggest question of all time! Divine Love, largely forgotten and relegated behind a long list of everything else of material, human and temporary value, has been supplanted by human love as the Grail of all good things and the balm for every ill in life. The lack of Divine Love being asked for and received by humans is the main cause of human suffering.

This lack creates all our problems and weakens our love for our own soul and for others, as we look to other people, creatures and objects to fill the lack within us. In this lack, we do not truly love self or others, although we all feel glimpses of this love every day, as it is part of our innate and pure human soul.

In our lives, we generally place these other objects before Divine Love:

1 Our fears, addictions and substitutes for Divine
2 Love, such as busyness and work
3 Our children, parents, partners, brothers and sisters
4 Our jobs, homes, possessions, material objects,
5 status and reputation
6 Our friends
7 Our pets

After this, Divine Truth and Divine Love may become important! It is curious that many who say This is so important place it low in their list of priorities and actual time they spend putting It into action. It becomes an add-on to your life to make your life happier, rather than the central pillar.

WHAT LOVE IS NOT (I)

To Realize and live all the forms of love, our fullest potential, we have to firstly recognize some deeper truths about our own self.

What most of us feel, think or have been told by parents, society, friends, partners and our own wounds (which constantly generate false information on what love is, such as being needed) is love, IS NOT.

This is challenging to admit and confront, but Love is Truth also; there is no separation between the two, apart from our ideas about it, which split them apart into either a sentimental, fluffy, feel-good fantasy designed to cover our fears and pains, or an empty, cold, mental and detached ideal.

Love is a warm consciousness that always speaks and shares truth, and does not support illusion of any kind. Yet it can Comfort us (at times and as soulfully appropriate) in our genuine yearning for Truth and Love as we see our illusions, false beliefs and our façade breaking down. The more you feel, the more you heal.

It is this breaking down that needs to occur within us before we start to experience more Divine Love, and for the other forms of love to realize their perfected and immaculate Divine Design through the Divinizing of Romance, the Divinizing of Friendship and the Divinizing of Affection, all united through the receiving of Divine Love.

C.S. Lewis said that just as Lucifer fell from Divine Love by pride, so too can love, the greatest emotion of all, become corrupt in our thinking by US *presuming it to be what it is not*. Of course love is always love, it is just our presumptions around what it is, and is not, that corrupts it in our thinking. Nonetheless, he made an interesting point: *to discover what love's truth is, we have to recognize what it is not.*

- Love does not nurse others through their own emotions,

making it all better.

- Love does not refuse or run away from feeling *al* your own emotions.
- Love does not rescue anyone from feeling his or her own emotions.
- Love does not give itself away to feed another's needs.
- Love is not running to be with others who will agree with you and your wounds.
- Love does not refuse to speak truth, no matter what your fears are around this.
- Love does not demand or expect anything from anyone.
- Love does not give to get.
- Love is not painful.
- Love does not retaliate.
- Love does not bargain.
- Love does not compromise.
- Love does not need to be loved.
- Love does not need to be needed, but can be desired from God.
- Love does not take anything or anyone for granted.
- Love does not sacrifice Itself for anyone or anything.
- Love is not martyring yourself.
- Love is not giving yourself away, placating your own ego or another.
- Love is not a duty or obligation for any reason.
- Love does not lie for any reason.
- Love does not hide itself for any reason.
- Love may not look like love to the world or other people *who are invested in you.*
- Love does not give out of fear, duty, coercion, pressure or *because it is meant to.*
- Love does not depend on anything or anyone for Its existence.
- Love does not run away from Truth but runs towards it, no

matter what the cost.

- Love does not delay or postpone its growth and expansion within you.
- Love does not ignore or justify its Law of Attraction and mirrors.
- Love does not deny, avoid or escape anything.
- Love does not use anyone or anything because love does not need anyone or anything.
- Love does not fill its absence with temporary substitutes and addictions.
- Love does not run away from the pain of its felt absence within you.
- Love has no shame and feels no loss.
- Love does not need to be understood or explain its feelings.
- Love does not gossip.

If you are honest, you will be able to see undertones of the above statements in your life, right?

Love has no errors because all errors are the want of love.[21]

Love is always humble. Love does not give to get. How many times do you give what you think is love to get what you think is love back? So I can say 'I love you, I love you.' But what I am actually saying is, 'Love me back, love me back.'

Love does not need to be loved. If it is love, it does not need to be returned. Love is enough to feel just by itself. It does not need to be received by anything or anyone else. It is purely enough by itself. And in this, love does not compromise; it does not compromise with truth because truth is part of love. If it compromises with truth, even out of ignorance, then it is not actually love.

Because love is singular it does not depend on anyone or anything else for its existence. Love does not need you or me or anything else to be what It is. Love wants more truth, because that will lead to more love, and that is what love desires, more of itself. Love loves Love. It has no reason or purpose other than to create more love.

Love cannot be love unless there is the soul's truth in it, and if there is Divine Truth in it. And this is quite a lot different to what we may believe love to be, which can be a forgetting of truth, a denial of truth.

So, now write down five ways you sell your soul out in the name of love, how you cheapen and degrade yourself in order to stop feeling a deeper emotion within you, how you sell out the truth and love of your soul and God in order to receive a certain emotion, a certain payback, a certain hoped for reciprocal emotion (which may never come) from others, which you call love.

So, you may refuse to speak the truth about yourself or another. You do it to keep a false peace, to keep a mask in place, putting on a fake smile to fit in, to become part of the crowd. You shut down your own feelings to stop others from feeling bad; you go along with the herd, not loving yourself and indeed sometimes even hating yourself in this process.

You may feel obliged to follow the herd and do things you do not want to do. You cannot say no. And the master can always say no. This is a sign of mastery; being able to say no. As Barry Long said, when you are making love and not able to stop in any moment, that is violent. So when you cannot say no, it may sometimes be an act of violence against yourself and others. Contemplate this.

You may counsel others in untruth in order to make yourself feel better, and then you compromise yourself to keep this mask of looking perfect. You may want to please others, scared of rejection. Then you sacrifice yourself out of this duty of obligation. Then you want to feel needed. In fact you are being selfish, not loving at all.

- Does love need to feel needed?
- Does love need approval?
- Does love need appreciation and respect?
- Does love need to package the truth?

What would want to do all of these things? Unworthiness, lack of self love. But maybe you think it's loving, and do it to feel safe in your mask. There is safety in that mask; let us now no longer stay safe in our masks.

- I love you because I'm sad.
- I love you because I'm angry.
- I love you because I don't want to feel my pain.
- I love you because I want to control you and really, I just want to control my own emotions and feel secure and safe.
- I love you because I am confused and do not know myself.
- I love you because I am meant to.
- I love you because I feel unworthy and you make me feel better.
- I love you because I can live through you, because I can marvel at your accomplishments, and never have to feel my own unworthiness and lack.
- I love you because you make me feel safe, safe from having to feel myself and my own fears, and my own greatness.
- I love you because I love someone else, and they do not love me.
- I love you because I am deeply lonely, and you make it better.

- I love you because I do not trust myself.
- I love you because I am in denial of my truth, and of my desires.
- I love you because I need someone, anyone, anything, to stop me feeling bad.

This is your investigation. You can do it alone, or talking with other people, and pray about it to feel which ones you are engaging in. These are some of the structures behind your beliefs and wounds around what love is. There is a lot there. Just remember, this is about your desire for God and the obstacles for pure desire, which is the basis of receiving Divine Love.

A group I recently shared with about What Love Is Not, summed up in one word how they felt about feeling and knowing this now:

'Relieved, Clear, Happy, Heavy, Longing, Self-responsible, Profound desire, Distortion inside, On the path to be excavated, Humility, Surrender, Naked and thankful, Clarity in what's been shared and also feeling the need to be responsible, a sense of powerlessness, a deeper desire for truth and clarity, entering into a space unknown, I don't have a word to describe how I feel, I feel shaken as if everything has been crushed and I need to move through.'

WHAT IS LOVE?

"Anyone who fails to go forward begins to go back, and love can never be content to stay for long where it is.'
St Teresa of Avila

Love honors the truth of the soul in you and others, the soul created by God.

- Love chooses and is totally willing and desiring to feel any and all emotions.
- Love speaks truth always, to everyone.
- Love moves forward to grow more.
- Love welcomes its Law of Attraction and seeks its causal emotions.
- Love seeks out where it is absent.
- Love gives with truth, and gives freely in this.
- Loving yourself means you know yourself, wounds and strengths.
- Love follows Truth, no matter what Truth looks like.
- Love's behavior is not dependent on what anyone else says, thinks, does or reacts to.
- Love stands by Itself and only needs Itself to be Itself.
- Love freely chooses and desires love for its own sake.
- Love accepts and appreciates.
- Love allows everyone to choose what they wish to choose, desire what they wish to desire, and create what they wish to create.
- Love is humble.
- Love is the only protection.

We have not been educated in the truths of what love actually is behind our current beliefs, wounds and the information and emotions that come to us marked as 'love' in our mental-emotional in-box. This information is filtered through our unconscious criteria, the cage of all our previous experiences and needs: what we think is love. We can think that the information that comes through this, our *filter bubble*, is unbiased and true. But it is not.

In fact, from within our bubble, it is nearly impossible to see how biased this information is, and we are.[22]Our filter bubble affects our ability to consciously choose how our soul wants to live. We may think we are guiding our own destiny, but what we have left unfelt and unhealed from the past, determines our present and what we do next. *You can get stuck in a static, ever-narrowing version of yourself – an endless you-loop.*[23]

What I seem to like may not be what my soul actually desires.

We block many truths shared with us because we filter much incoming information and emotions through the bubble of our own past experiences and emotions, our own beliefs. You could say that you are not ready to hear and put this into action, that you are not really willing, that your desire is not strong enough, that you couldn't be bothered, that you are too involved in your small self, that it is spirits that are interfering; so you filter out what is not appropriate for your small self, or you only hear what you want to hear to suit your present soul condition.

Why do you suddenly feel tired when you are listening to a certain subject? Why do you suddenly start tuning out and start thinking about something else when something is being presented to you? Letting the mind organize, wandering to future plans, repetitive thoughts, being overwhelmed, pushing yourself too much, justifying new information to fit information into your present filter bubble, or the classic denial, 'Oh that truth is not for me, that is for someone else.'

We filter out much information and instantly file it away in a certain compartment of our mind, or keep it on the surface of our emotions (anger, fear, blame, shame, resentment). So even when truth is shared, we may instantly filter it to suit our version of what we think reality should be in our program, so we do not really hear or receive it.

The mind automatically judges and filters things in different compartments,: compare and contrast, good, not good. It is our wounds filtering and creating our mind that in turn is filtering all the incoming input. It is all your previous experiences, wounds and beliefs that are filtering everything you are experiencing now, and the information that is coming in; and this is how the mind works, not how the soul works.

WHAT LOVE IS NOT (II)

Now, if you are to be a little more honest, you will see undertones of the following statement in your life also: ready?

Many people you think you love, and who think they love you, do not really love you, and you do not love them.

This can be shocking to feel and see; yet in this seeing, and by being honest, a basis for true love can start to be established. Generally, it is not friendships we seek – it is wound-ships, ways to collude with others *who have similar or totally opposite wounds* so you can both stay in the wound, thinking this charge is 'love.'

And we can become addicted to this. *We use each other, like tools, to stop feeling and seeing ourselves.* This is not a friendship of love; this is a friendship of fear, of insecurity; a wound-ship disguising the pain that is already within you. A collusion of error reflecting error, a mirror of error.

You may feel 'tender care' and a wish to protect the other from feeling pain, anger, fear and all the other feelings that will actually lead to healing, but in truth you are just protecting yourself from feeling these emotions that lurk hidden *inside you*. And we become addicted to this protection from feeling our own emotions. Once this is seen in this mirror, you can choose to turn your face and feelings towards being more genuine.

And there may very well be some genuine feelings of love and affection between you and the other underneath these addictions and wounds. If there is, then this affection can be turned, if you so choose, towards a more truthful and healing relating, which can only result in more love. If there is no connection left after this recognition and your own internal healing around this, then you know the relating has served its evolutionary purpose, and is completed. You move on.

When you say, 'I love you' to other people you may be actually saying:

- I don't want to feel certain emotions hidden deep within me.
- I love you because I don't want to feel heavy.
- I love you because I don't want to feel shitty.
- I love you because I don't want to feel lonely.
- I love you so I do not have to feel the huge gaping hole within me.
- I love you because I don't want to feel out of control.
- I love you so I can stay in control.
- I love you so I don't have to feel angry.
- I love you so I can feel angry.
- I love you because I really don't want to feel lost.
- I love you because I don't want to feel how hopeless my life is.
- I love you because I don't want to feel my own pain.
- I love you because you fit the fantasy in my head of what my lover should be like.
- I love you because I do not want to feel empty.
- I love you because I do not love myself.
- I love you because someone in my past did not love me.
- I love you because I am addicted to sex, to comfort.
- I love you because you make me feel good and stop me feeling other emotions I do not wish to feel.
- I love you because you fill me up.
- I love you because you make me feel scared and that's what love is for me.
- I love you because you remind me of how I have been abused and how I have abused others.
- I love you because you serve me and do not bother me.

- I love you because other people say I do, and we look good together.
- I love you because society demands that I should, and it is right to.
- I love you because I am too scared to be myself and step out into the world alone.
- I love you because you give me security, stability and because I am obliged to because we have children and a home.
- I love you because my parents, friends and culture want me to.
- I love you because you make me feel needed.
- I love you because I need you.
- I love you because I want to take care of you and make you, and me, feel good.

- I need to do something to deserve love.
- I need to do something to give love.
- I need to do something to receive love.
- Love is need. Need is love.

- I can only love when I am perfect and good.
- I can only love and be loved when I am perfect and good.
- I can only love myself when I am perfect and good.

Is any of this really love?
Does love use anything?
Does love manipulate anybody?
So why are you doing it everyday?
Why do you grab hold of anyone else to stop you feeling these things?

You are not really saying, 'I love you.' Put instead the emotion that you do not dare to feel in place of the word love. So, you are saying, 'I sad you.' 'I lonely you.' 'I guilt you.' 'I hopeless you.' 'I misery you.' 'I lonely you.' 'I unworthy you.' 'I love you so I do not have to feel betrayed, abandoned …'

That would actually be being genuine … or 'I need you.' And you can use all of these above excuses in your relationship with God and 'desiring' prayers to Him – except He will not respond and you will be left alone or at worse the prey of negative spirits. Many people try to use God as the ultimate substitute, but end up hooking into negative spirits pretending to be God, or pretending to help you.

So how does it feel to use someone, usually your partner or children, every day?
A few souls share:

'I confused love with need and thought that when people needed me, this was love. I thought I needed to serve to get love. I needed to be somehow, behave somehow. Love is need, need is love therefore I need to do everything to be needed. I need to sacrifice, sacrifice everything. I need to do something rather than be, being obliged to do something, and not be as I am.'

'It can feel terrible because there can seem like there is no access to stop these patterns. And that is the most painful. I start to see it and then want to switch that button off, but it does not work that way. The desire not to repeat it makes me more aware when I feel the tendency. It makes me stop and feel what is going on before actually reproducing it.'

So, how do you now relate with this bubble of false love now popping? Just sit with this, pray to God about it, and an implosion can start to happen that is beautiful at the same time as it is scary. You can only get to a deeper degree of receiving

Divine Love and pure desire once these other things are recognized and felt.

And, you may now have your walls up to receiving this. So that is your belief systems and wounds saying, 'No, that is not true. That can't be me. I am really a loving and good person.' This knowledge may make you feel alone, and the deeper openings into Love come from praying to God from this place, and not looking for other people and things. So you are praying in the sense that you are saying, 'Please God help me to feel all of this. Please God help me to feel these emotions within my self.'

And then you will be one step closer to what Divine Love and pure desire actually is, rather than what your belief or wound around it is. It can be hard to admit. Just feel it ... *I need you. I love you because you help me to not feel all these emotions, that is why I love you.*

Eknath Easwaran shares an interesting story. 'If we listen in on a marriage proposal with the ears of St Francis, this is what we would hear. The man gets down on bended knee, and says, 'Sibyl dear, I love me, will you marry me? You will make me happy, so won't you marry me?' And Sibyl says, 'I love me too and you will make me happy. So I will.'

We seek from others what we lack within ourselves.
Why don't we give what we most need instead?

There are truths you may want to share with other people, but you do not because you are scared to, and think, 'Oh, but I might be making a judgment.' But how are you going to know unless you speak it in a way that is curious, humble and open to the other's emotions and your own?

We are in this together, and this is a process of love, of softness, of accepting and being with our emotions and others' emotions. And to share in this way is loving and truthful for you and the other person, because then you can both learn, even if you make a mistake, for you both make a concrete step towards living in truth and love, which is a concrete step to coming closer to God, which means that God can come closer to you and answer your *truthful* prayers.

You only truly love yourself and others if you are truthful. You love God if you are truthful about what this love entails or not. 'Love' in our understanding of it, is a system of beliefs and emotional needs invariably informed and created by our wounds, our beliefs, our parents, culture and our partners, and is often flawed and mistaken. It is more often a need and projection, an avoidance of our own selves, rather than love. We need to concentrate on our relationship with God in order to truly understand love, which can only happen on the soul level.

Ask yourself this in every situation:
What would God's Love do, right here, right now?
How does God treat me?
This then is how to treat others.

What does love do?
If we ask these questions, we are starting to love ourselves, others and God.

Maybe we can only truly feel what God's feelings are when we are closer to God. God's Love works in God's Truth. And until this time, we can always ask for the answer and we will receive what we need to in order for our souls to grow in love.

FEELING the BELIEFS of the WOUNDED SOUL

Our wounded self experiences a way of need that is very different to what love truly is. It has built a strong belief system around the experiences of not feeling loved and compensating for this in many, many ways. This belief system holds a lot of feelings that need to be released in order to truly experience love.

This prayer meditation is designed to help us feel the truth of both the wounded self, which is present until we are Soul realized, and the True Self, which is love.

The following prayer meditations are some of the scripts, the programs, that are running our wounded soul, establishing a false basis for our relationship with ourselves (negating our true Self Love) and with others in creating wound-ships or co-dependent relationships. All of this blocks our relationship to God, who desires to flood us with Divine Love if we but ask for it sincerely and open ourselves up to this Love.

It is wise to viscerally feel these scripts rather than trying to cover over them with platitudes, affirmations and feel-good techniques and tactics. By fully feeling completely, the soul is released forever of the wound and its coping strategies around it. Temporary strategies to heal our wounds always fail. To realize we love another to get love because we do not love our own self is one of our core human wounds.

For each of the two parts of this prayer meditation, express out loud or silently these sentences. Let the feelings and memories come. Express the feelings intuitively, changing and adding to the sentences if it helps.

You can repeat one sentence several times in a row until you feel it, or go straight into the next one. You can improvise sentences that may better fit your feelings.

One may also experience spirit interference in this prayer meditation. This can manifest as voices and feelings disagreeing with it. Unless you are living as unconditional love, you can be sure these are negative spirits trying to dissuade you from traveling deeper into your own wounds to release them, thereby banishing these spirit influences forever.

Do each part for one hour.
This meditation prayer can be about two hours long.

Center yourself and drop into a prayerful, silent heartful space. Ask to become vulnerable and open your heart.

Part One:

I am not loved
I am not loved
I am not loved

I have never been loved
My parents did not love me
I need love
I need love
I need love

Please love me

My quest for love has never worked
My quest for love will never work
Nobody really loves me
Nobody really loved me

How do you feel?

Part Two:

I am love
I am love
I am love
God loves me
God loves me
God loves me

God desires me
God desires me
God desires me

I am love
I am love
I am love (from your heart)

I am not loved
I have never been loved
I am not loved
I am not LOVED
I am just not loved
No one has ever loved me
No one loves me
I am not loved
I am not loved

I do not love myself
I do not love myself
I do not love myself

I am loved

I am loved
I am loved
I am LOVED

God is not here for me
God has never been here for me
God is not here for me
God has left me

I am not loved
I have never been loved
No one loves me

God loves me
God LOVES me
God wants me
God wants me
God LOVES me
God WANTS me
God desires me

I don't want God
I don't want God
I don't want God
I want fear
I want fear
I want fear

I AM LOVED
I AM LOVED
I AM LOVED

God wants me
God desires me

God loves me

What does this make you feel?

The experience of love and need in co-dependent relationships

In such a relationship, one or both partners cover each others emotions by giving false comfort, false 'love' and other placating behaviors that prevent the other in deeply feeling and owning their own emotions. When you want to get out of this pattern, this prayer meditation will help. It will let both partners feel the truth of the unspoken demand of love and how they respond to it.

Simply sit in front of your partner and express out loud these sentences as a way to reveal the unconscious behavior that is being played out between you both.

It is good to express it with all the range of emotions which are being played out in daily life. As a poor lost little child, with seduction, with anger, with guilt, bargaining, needing protection…

Do these emotions trigger the second partner? Then he or she can feel which emotions are active inside their own self that makes them wish to answer the demand of their partner's wounded self, instead of allowing themselves to process their own feelings. All these emotions are hiding another emotion that the partner who covers the emotions is not aware of.

In this version of the meditation, the second part is spoken and will reveal a range of emotions to be felt by the partner who listens. The partners exchange roles after each part.

USING GOD as an EXCUSE

Do you want to receive Divine Love so you do not have to feel painful emotions? Because if your desire is not strong, you will not receive Divine Love. You can have moments when your desire is pure and you will receive some Divine Love, and then there will be moments when your desire is not pure and you are wanting Divine Love to not feel these emotions; and of course you will not receive Divine Love because God loves you Perfectly in Truth and will not entertain your illusions. But maybe you will receive nice feelings from spirits around you.

For all these reasons (and the ones talked about previously,) you may say, 'I love you' to another human being; AND you may say it to God for the same reason: to stop feeling your own deeper emotions, hoping that God will take it all away for you. This is childish, perpetuating the victim mode within you, hoping someone else will do it for you. This is neither soulful, self-empowering or what God desires for you. And you may cry, wail and think you are feeling many things ... when what you may be feeling is your own resistance and your dire need to avoid feeling the emotions you never wanted to feel.

We can make substitutes in prayer; and we need to dive into these places and admit the falseness and the emotions we do not want to feel in ourselves. And this is really the place where we can see whether we are aligned or not, where we can then have a possibility to reset everything. It is not easy every day to be in love and truth, but desire cannot be purified until you recognize and feel all these parts, and see how you say, 'I love you,' to prevent yourself from feeling other emotions.

Try saying and feeling 'I don't love you' to others whom you think you love, and God, and see what happens.

Love, human or divine, can become another belief, another construct, and another illusion. A crutch. There are many Christian and religious spirits who have progressed a little way into Divine Love, but have remained stuck for hundreds of years because they have not dared, or known how to, enter their own human emotions, preferring instead to focus on God alone. And then they wonder why they are still stuck in a church in the spirit world or stuck on Earth with the same issues, and are no nearer God; some spirits even think that they are in heaven.

It is easy to say, *'Yes, I have desire for God,'* but we do not realise that there is all of this in the way of actually having a strong desire. Harbouring fear, unwillingness, heaviness, lethargy, stagnation and repression from childhood, unworthiness, the reluctance to ask for help, we prefer instead to stay quiet and not bother anyone.

Why? Because when we were children we were beaten for asking about things or doing things; allied with the comfort of worldly life and its trappings, our substitutes, our false love … and more, these are some of the reasons we do not feel desire for Divine Love and God. (See the book *Sacred Wounds Original Innocence* for more.)

When you look and feel the extent of the distortions around desire and love, is it any wonder that only thousands of souls on earth in the last 2000 years have actually become At-One with God? Because even the simplest things, which are very much a part of the fabric of the soul, can become twisted and distorted because of all the ideas around what love is, what these ideas are hiding and our inability to truly strongly desire.

Pure desire is a gift you offer without any expectation of anything back – like spontaneous gratitude. All of you have experienced this pure desire *and* you have also experienced this other way as well. As your soul evolves, desire for God becomes purer and purer because the emotions and beliefs around it start to be released and dissolved.

If you really desire God, *you will do anything*; you will be creative and experiment, do whatever you can. Do not wait for anyone. Truth is not some abstract concept out there; it is something you can be doing all the time within yourself and with everyone else. Constantly seeing the truth about yourself and living like this is not something you do just once a day. It is a constant state of being, a way of being of the soul, all the time, every day, with everyone, most especially with yourself.

When you feel any negative emotion at all, dive into it with *pure desire*. Ask God to fully feel it totally, and its causes. Drop whatever you are doing, stop everything, and go into it.

The WOUND of LOVE

In our wound-ships and romances, we make something of others that they are not, we make them what we want them to be that suits us, so we can stop feeling ourselves, so that our wound stays out of reach, hidden, buried. And then if the wound does come up, it becomes about them!

The most common projection is a lack of love within one's own self, which then reaches out to another to fill this need, *appearing loving in the process*, because of mutual charge and the mutual hole resonating.

When a mutual hole resonates between two souls, it feels powerful; it has a strong charge and attraction, and many people think this is love because it is so alluring, so enticing, so hormonal, so ... familiar. And it becomes reasoned to be so, justified to be so, rationalized and fantasized *to be so*.

The wounded hole within the heart flutters as its strings are pulled and both people fall deeper into the hole, as now it does not have to be so lonely anymore, all there by yourself. And of course you will feel this as *'love!'* Something is being met, something strong is attracting, something strong is resonating ... but this is not love.

And this charge plays out with partners, parents, friends, families and even our children. Many parents unconsciously 'use' their children so the parent can feel loved, important, special, and needed under the mask of being unconditionally loving to their children. The parent needs the child in order for the parent to feel love. This need is not love, simply another excuse for the parent to not feel their own lack and wound, and of course when the child acts up and does not meet their expectations, then the child receives harmful projections and verbal and physical abuse.

The child will of course feel this as children are sensitive to emotions and impressions on a pre-verbal level, and they will act out the parent's repressed emotions back to the parent whenever the parent refuses to feel one of their own emotions. So when your child is angry, look at yourself for what is in you that is still repressed, not felt and hurt. It is all reflecting you, or rather the deeper emotion that has not been felt or released within you.

Many people with 'loving auras' project a need for love, approval, adoration and attention outwards. It appears loving because it appeals to the same place within our own self – it is one wound meeting another and presto! We feel what we think is love and do not see anything. Hence the old saying, 'love is blind,' *whereas in Truth Love sees everything*.

Truly loving people have no need to project outwards, as they have no need to get love or indeed anything at all from others, or to seek others' love, attention, adoration and approval, because they are fulfilled by Divine Love.[24]

Loving people surely give and share truth and love, even may emanate it, but not in a way that feeds or hides others' holes, and not in ways that point towards themselves as being anything great, special or particularly esteemable.

But this may not appeal to most people seeking a quick fix for their life, as it will necessarily challenge your ideas, beliefs and wounds IF IT IS TRUTH. Love will illumine your masks and veils if it is True. The extent of the delusion on Earth is gigantic. Basic understandings have been forgotten and covered over and many followers are created by many gurus to feed huge egos and huge holes where love does not dwell.

Our own childhoods, beliefs, wounds and societal/media and parents' perceptions form most of our perceptions about love. Most of your friends will support your ideas too. The majority of the music, poetry, films, TV programs, internet information and books available celebrate, idolize and idealize human love as the panacea for all things.

This aspect of love will *never* work to solve your problems, for even when you reach the pinnacle, the zenith of human love, feeling joyful, relatively happy and content in your life, you will, one day, realize you cannot go any further, that there is something missing, that there is something more. It is at this point that you will become confused, wondering what is next, why you have stopped evolving.

This is when God can come in, if you choose so, and are humble enough. Of course, some people will never feel this and will stay in a nice state for a long time, thinking that this is it – they have reached the pinnacle. But it is not.

Find out and investigate what Divine laws are, what your real wounds around love are, so you can see where your soul is at in its evolution. Then love your soul,[25] and to love your soul means you have to feel your soul and its wounds, and to feel and know your soul one has to love and understand God, the Creator of your soul. This becomes an unbeatable partnership that leads to Truth and Love. There is no love without truth at its core. To believe you love another without truth being within it is not love. To believe you love yourself without truth in it is not love.

It is a two-way process. When you love yourself more, you come closer to God. Yet, to love yourself *fully*, to its highest potential, one has to have experienced Divine Love and Truth and developed a personal, intimate relationship with God, to feel God, and therefore more fully feel your own soul, for we are made by God.

You have to go to the Source from where you come from in order to feel what you are in your essence, and your higher potential.

One goes with the other in this sacred relationship. You are separate from God until we are not. Being humble allows one to step towards God in Truth. Any form of intellectual masturbation saying that 'I am God,' or you are not in separation is in clear denial of the obvious fact that you are, until you are not.

False joy, false gods, false 'love,' and false laughter are the substitute ideas around Divine Love, soul friendship, true joy and soulful affection. The Prozac nation ideals of false joy and laughter is that it soothes the ego, hides nervousness, fear, shame and insecurity; it gets us attention, makes us popular, makes us liked, helps us to be 'loved,' makes sure we are seen as spiritual, helps us to fit in, to sell and buy things. On the outside you are laughing; inside, you are crying.

The false gods we may pray to, evoke and ask favors from, such as 'masters,' demi-gods and avatars/gurus who are possessed by powerfully exotic spirits and deities, most of whom are barely in a better soul condition than you are, *and many of whom are in a much worse soul condition than you are,* can be your substitutes for Divine Love, and this is only ever available directly and without intermediary from God. The Indian tradition, deities, gurus and avatars are particularly well used by many souls to feed their addictions and to substitute for real Divine Love.

Feeding these spirits with energy, devotion, adoration and

attention, whilst it may feel good at a certain point in your life, will actually cloak your own soul and distract you from feeling your true soul condition. A blanket of light descends, making us feel good, veiling our true selves and our wounds, blinding us to who we really are and our sovereign connection to the One God of Divine Love, who loves us Perfectly. Only by feeling your true nakedness can we receive this Divine Love more and more.

THE 22 DIMENSIONS

of LOVE

FOREWORD

In writing this part of the book, many gifts were given to me. As I finished writing the first draft, I stumbled across a copy of *The Dark Night of the Soul* by St John of the Cross in a friend's flat. A week later, on my birthday, I had the chance to read it, and was deeply touched and humbled.

As I continued to read, I very clearly felt the spirit of John come to me and suffuse my soul and energy fields with the Love that he carries. This humbled and silenced me profoundly to my core, and I went into a deep meditation, later proceeding to write down what he wished to contribute to The Dimensions of Love.

A similar occurrence happened with St Teresa of Avila, although in more detail. As I had sent my editor the finished version of the 22 Spheres of Love, she remarked that she was reading a text of St Teresa's that was similar, in that it was talking about the Eight Spheres of Love to reach At-One-ment with God, albeit more than 460 years ago!

I was intrigued, and proceeded to look up her book, *Interior Castle*. I immediately found many direct similarities to what I had been writing about and experiencing, as well as a great corroboration between her accounts of the stages of Divine Love and those shared in *The Padgett Messages* from Christ and other Spirits.

One day, just before I started to quote her on some of the aspects of what she had been experiencing, Teresa came to me whilst I was deep in prayer. When I say, 'Came to me,' understand that Teresa is a Seventh Sphere Spirit (and has now moved into At-One-ment with God); she was very close to God, almost merged in Him. She did not come to me per se, but impressed herself, in a very pure way, without words, just as a feeling of exquisitely pure light and love felt in my soul.

She then 'downgraded' or transduced her energy into the Fifth and Third Spheres so I could receive some of her words, and then went back into her pure state in the Seventh Sphere. This movement was an education in itself, as I directly and tangibly experienced the way an advanced spirit can move through the Spheres.

Then, through a combination of feelings and impressions floating into words and back again, she shared with me that her book, *Interior Castle*, had some errors in it which she wished to make right before she merged into God as part of her mission.

These errors were based on her own unworthiness, which she mistook for humility in some, but not all cases. When she left her physical body and went into the spirit world, she began to understand that God Loves us more than she had tangibly Realized. God did not create us or want us to be unworthy or falsely humble, but rather rejoice in the gifts that He has so generously given us.

She realized her errors in this context, borne from her own childhood injuries and religious upbringing, and had been waiting ever since for the 'right' person to come along and help her rectify these written errors (she herself is healed of them now) so that she could then become At-One with God. This is what had been holding her back, by her own choice. She decided this, out of the purity of her own soul: to remedy the error, even though she was free of it already.

Even when she had written her book whilst still in physical form, she remarked that she was waiting for learned men to help revise the text of *Interior Castle*. Alas, the learned men who did this were religious and again, having the same errors of unworthiness and false humility borne from childhood and religious dogma, did not correct the text in Truth and Love, therefore leaving Teresa still waiting for the right person to come along and assist her to get this wisdom into the world in a more loving way.

God is Perfect and orchestrates everything for the fullest benefit of all concerned, always. It is always a win-win-win situation for everyone in love! I am consistently amazed and grateful for this. God is incredible!

Teresa needed the right soul to help her finish her work. I desired, through an initial impulse given to me by the Divine, to write a clear, easy to read and simple Map of the Steps on the Divine Love Path (which until now has not existed in this world) to make this book as complete as possible.

I also needed to become more humble, which, after being with Teresa and her own humility and love, happened more and more as I deepened into this journey. As I communed with her and felt the great purity and light of her soul, this book became complete.

Teresa helped me to edit her book (quite an interesting process), to take out some errors and reveal the nature of the love she is now experiencing with God. I feel deeply touched and moved to tears by her descriptions of great humility and the Glory of God's love for us.

Some of her descriptions and advice is useful to us in any Sphere we are in (although it is wise not to mistake where you are in this progression) so this is why anyone can read this and gain benefit from it.

You may already identify with certain aspects she is sharing, or have already experienced a few of them; just remember there are differing intensities of these experiences in the different Spheres. Nonetheless, it is useful to everyone, and simply by reading it one can be humbled, which always means we are a step closer to God.

I share this so that it may be of some benefit to you in your soul progression. Maybe one day it may be easier for us to reach God than others who have come before us with no map and have had to suffer more, to carve out a pathway.

May our Path be easier, for we stand on the shoulders of the giants who came before us, who bravely and humbly ventured into the unknown, and in whose steps we can now tread more lightly. Amen.

Both Teresa and John had keys to share, but these keys were bound in religious doctrines and aspects of their childhood wounding. Once these outer layers were dissolved, the gold of their souls' wisdom, given to them by God but then filtered through their wounds, was easily apparent, and with their help and my own gifts, all three of us could transcribe the purity of what part of this Pathway to God is all about.

God put us all together spiritually through direct communication (I have to say John was a bit more direct than Teresa!) and through our written works, as it is God's desire that a clear map of the Divine Love Path becomes freely available to help guide souls through some of the beauties and pitfalls, the graces and the fears, the incredible Love, wonders and mystical pains that happen as we move closer and closer to God.

God loves us all perfectly and gives us what we need to grow perfectly also. I became aware of the pitfalls of the Sphere I was moving into as I started to write this book, and without knowing this, I could have been stuck there for a long time. I trust that others who read this will not become tempted or too lazy to stay in relative happiness, but keep progressing into ultimate happiness. Faith is ever growing until we are At-One with God.

Teresa's contributions are placed separately to the rest of the text in each Sphere as they have their own rhythm and are valuable in and of themselves. They complement and complete this book, and perhaps will best suit the more self-contained, mature and mystical sides of our souls.

I am grateful to God for bringing us together. She calls the Spheres, or dimensions of love, *mansions* (as Christ did) within a grand castle, each of which have many rooms (or levels/planes) within them. Through our coming together, we could both move onto the next Sphere of Love in our soul's journey.

There are deeply mystical experiences of interior soul pain, trials, and the inexplicably arid desolation of the human soul as it dies bit by bit as it moves through the higher Spheres; and this is balanced by your soul experiencing more joy, peace, gratitude, flow, life force, beauty and interior rest (and your sharing of life and love with your soul half if you have met) in fully desiring and *deserving* all that God wishes to give you.

Anything within us that feels it does not deserve Divine Love in its fullness is part of our wounding, in particular our Original Wounding, and is not how God created us to be.

Nonetheless, it is something we need to feel, embrace and move through. Our unworthiness can often arise when we feel the great softness of love, so Teresa must have received a lot of Divine

Love! Unworthiness dissipates the more we return to our original innocence, for the return of innocence is the return of my ability to love myself fully as God loves me.

As we come into the times of the great cleansing of our planet and our species, many of the more negative aspects of our soul growth can be accelerated through with greater ease than before (although it all still has to be done) due to the changes of vibration on the planet and the fact that more people and spirits have gone before us on the Path, making it easier for us now.

Of course, the Earth changes and the lightening of the ecological and spiritual load on the planet, as well as the leaving of many malevolent spirits in this time of great cleansing, will also help those left on Earth to grow more quickly in a multitude of ways. For as the Earth's fields shift, so too will our abilities to absorb light into our DNA, and increase in love in our souls.

This book is designed to be an easily accessible *travel guide* for those on the path of Divine Love, showing us some of the steps we all have to take on this path irrespective of religion, race, age or belief system. It helps us to look for what lies in each Sphere, and how to make educated choices by being aware of the pitfalls and beauties of the Path. This all allows us to progress clearly and as swiftly as we can.

The wisdom for this book is generated from Christ Yeshua and other Spirits from *The Padgett Messages*, from my own personal experiences based on moving through many of these Spheres, from other advanced souls, from students who have been moving through the Spheres, from Celestial and Sixth / Seventh Sphere guides of mine, from Shams of Tabriz, whom I had a long and radical meeting with, and Magdalene: The Sophia.

INTRODUCTION

'However strong you may think yourself, you cannot enter the Mansions by your own efforts: God, the Lord of the Castle Himself, must admit you to them. He is a great Lover of humility. Once you have been shown how to enjoy this Castle, you will find rest in everything, even in the things which most try you, and you will cherish the returning to it which nobody can take from you.'[27]

On the Path to Union with God, there are eight dimensions or eight major steps that one takes. Each of these dimensions is an entirely new *Sphere of love*, with each Sphere expanding on from the previous one, holding more Love within it.

Each Sphere or dimension is separated by a boundary of Love, and the only way to progress from one dimensional Sphere to another is to grow in Love and Truth.

God created the first human souls in harmony and pure human love as perfectly innocent Sixth Sphere humans. But, over a period of time on Earth, their soul condition degraded as they forgot about love, so new and lower dimensions of Love were created *as* they degraded.

For example, the movement from the Sixth Sphere into the Fifth Sphere was created by them moving out of a space of innocence, harmlessness, and loving each other as they loved their own selves; they thus created the Fifth Sphere *in this very action*. As they degraded even further and forgot even more about God, divine laws and love, they created the Fourth Sphere through these very actions and amnesia. This all happened rapidly.

Until 2000 years ago, there were only six of these inter-dimensional spaces or Spheres in creation. Then between 2000 years ago and now, through Christ, another sixteen Spheres were created, making a total of twenty-two. The first eight Spheres are the most important for us on Earth, as they mark the journey *to* entering the Kingdom of God or Celestial Kingdom, whilst the next sixteen Spheres mark the journey *within* the Kingdom of God Itself.[28]

As Christ expanded his ability to Love, a new Sphere was created; and as the next soul reached that Sphere, so it expanded. *Each person who enters a Sphere expands and creates more of that dimensional space of love and truth.* So, the more people that enter the Second Sphere, the more that Sphere will grow in influence and size, making it more of a possibility for others to enter, although they will still have to do the same work of love within themselves to enter it.

Conversely, because the hell aspect of the First Sphere is so large on Earth at this time, as so many people are living under fear and without Divine Love and truth, this influence is the biggest. Similarly, because so few souls have reached At-One-ment with God in the process of the New Birth in the Seventh and Eighth Spheres, this has been more of a remote possibility until this time on Earth, which is NOW changing and *rapidly accelerating.*

Each succeeding Sphere holds new, vaster love and truth within it. Each succeeding Sphere is larger and larger, both in spaciousness and in love than the previous one, and each Sphere has different sub-levels within it, different planes of Love and Truth, that we move through. As we move through each Sphere, we receive more Divine Love, more blessings, more direct knowing of Truths, more gifts to share and serve others with, to *directly and experientially* help them increase in love and truth, and more of the virtues of human and Divine Love.

We receive more direct communication and Love from Divine Spirits as we progress. In the first two Spheres, we receive the most help from our guides, who are generally one or two Spheres ahead of us in their soul development.

As we progress into the Third Sphere of Divine Love and beyond, we start to be influenced by higher Spirits on the Divine Love Path, and even Celestial Spirits from time to time, who reach out a loving hand to guide us more directly to God. Each Sphere makes us more humble than the previous one, *'for he that humbles himself is exalted in love, and he that exalts himself is humbled.'* Greatness is humility.

Within each Sphere are ups and downs, we receive some Divine Love and blessing, and then pain or a deep lesson arises for us to feel and process. We are ascending and descending continually within the sub-levels of each Sphere. It is like a ladder that we move up and down on. God rests at the summit of this ladder, desiring us to reach into His substance and Great Soul. And then the ladder continues on, in a new way ...

We all live in the Sphere where our soul condition is, *in Love and Truth*. If I love to the extent of living in the Fourth Sphere, I can travel from the First into the Second, Third and Fourth Spheres, but I cannot go any further, because each Sphere has a boundary of a certain level of love. If my soul has not developed in that aspect of love, I cannot cross that boundary. This is the only thing that prevents us from traveling through different dimensions.

Love can be growing constantly. It is our true power to take our place in this expansion. When you decide to focus on this, you get very creative, for growing in love requires novel and new decisions and the creative independence of inspired action. This is the call of the pure drop of love that lies at the very heart of our being: the call of your pure soul.

Ask yourself this question; ask God; ask your guides:

What are the lessons of love, and what are the truths I have to face about myself, so I can make the transition from the Sphere I am in right now, to the next Sphere?

Any spirit who has made this transition will be able to tell you, and you will grow fast if you work through those particular lessons.

You can grow in love, and if you make different choices you can degrade in love. If you make a choice that is disharmonious with love, and out of truth, out of alignment with your soul, then your soul condition degrades. When you make a choice that is harmonious with love and is aligned and in truth, your soul condition expands. You can feel this happening, as in you can feel the joy, the expansion and the peaceful clarity of making choices harmonious with love, and feel the contraction, the pain, and the roughness of making choices disharmonious with love.

For example, when you are generous with someone without wanting something back, how do you feel? What happens within yourself when you are harsh to someone, or judge another? Feel the truth of each of these choices and actions. When you choose love, when you do an action of love, you feel that inside yourself and you grow a little bit more in love.

Until we reach the Celestial Spheres of At-One-ment with God, we do not have enough Divine Love because *all the natural loves are still not absorbed by the Divine Love*; for all below the Celestial Spheres still have natural love, which causes them to retain their worldly affections.

In the Spheres, the Law of Attraction is paramount. Every soul lives where it fits in – where it is in harmony. The belief system of the soul has a large effect on the experience it will have. We are naturally attracted to those things which enable us to pursue the development of our thoughts; and these are our 'treasures' which have the most attachments and affections. From these affections will arise our desires, and unless something greater intervenes, we will follow these desires.

We aspire to get into the Sphere which holds the greatest opportunities to develop these things. If we desire to develop our mental or moral qualities, we will naturally seek the natural love Spheres where these qualities have the greatest opportunity for such development. If we deeply yearn for God, we will try to spend the most time in the Divine Love Spheres.

God, in His great wisdom and goodness, has provided the Spheres and made[29] them suitable for many purposes, and all of us choose which ones we enter and live in. But, not only one Sphere *of its kind* is provided, for there are several steps in the progression of each of these desires we may have.

For example, if I wish to develop more natural love so I can have harmonious relationships, then I will spend some time in a natural love Sphere to purify my natural love and progress from the lower level of this, the Second Sphere, to the higher level of it, the Fourth Sphere, rapidly in order to do so. If I wanted to live in harmony, peace and free of human suffering, I would rush to the Sixth Sphere of Self-Realization. If I wanted to become an incredible healer, I would hasten to the Fourth Sphere, where these gifts are well developed.

The Second, the Fourth and the Sixth Spheres are for those who desire to grow in their mental and moral pursuits of natural love.

In contrast, the Third, Fifth and Seventh Spheres are the ones specially prepared for those who are seeking the development of Divine Love in their souls. Divine Love is what is yearned for, and acquired. It is wise to remember that with soul development in Divine Love comes the mental, meditational, energetic and moral development of natural love; but the meditational, energetic, mental and moral development of natural love *does not* lead to the acquiring of Divine Love.[30]

Every desire and aspiration of these souls is focused on their great yearnings and life changes in order to obtain Divine Love to the highest degree. *They never become satisfied with this,* in contrast to those who seek the mental and natural love development.

God recognizes and respects our independent will and the choices all of us make. He does not force us to seek His Love, but waits until we, by our own experience, learn that what we once thought was sufficient for our happiness is not sufficient.

Realizing this insufficiency, we become dissatisfied, and with such dissatisfaction comes the wish and yearning to learn about the great unknown, which causes us to feel a dependence upon a source of happiness and love *not coming from within our own self.* This is the scary thing for most people on the spiritual path today, which teaches self-reliance, not God Reliance.

The great advantage in striving to enter the Divine Love Spheres and Divine Heavens is that you not only gain your soul's development, which is eternal and permanent, but also the development of your mind and moral nature. And so you understand: *'Seek first the Kingdom of God, and all other things shall be added unto you.'*

CREATING THE SPHERES

Yeshua said: '*In My Father's House there are many Mansions: if it were not so, I would have told you. I go to prepare a place for you. And if I go and prepare a place for you, I will come again, and receive you unto myself; that where I am, there you may be also. And whither I go you know, and the way you know.*'

Thomas said: '*Lord, we know not where you go; how can we know this way?*'

Yeshua replied: *I Am the Way, the Truth and the Life; no man cometh unto the Father but by me.*' [31]

One Translation:
There are many rooms in many mansions (another word for the Spheres) created by God for everyone to live in according to their nature, loves, dispositions and desires. I am going ahead to God, creating, in my wake, a pathway of Divine Love and consciousness, new stations where you can rest and grow in love, before journeying further onwards. If this were not so, and you only had one mansion (Sphere) you could be in, I would have told you about it.

You now have an opportunity to follow me on the same journey. As I go forwards into each new mansion (Sphere), my soul finds and settles at its own level within it, and then I rise and move, ever forwards, creating new Spheres. I leave a great wake, a swirl of dust and light behind me in the spirit world that all of you can follow. Once each new Sphere has been created by me, the pathway is open and I Am there; for I Am the Creator of this Way, the Truth and the Life; and when you get here, you will be where I have been, and therefore with me.

Your own pure soul created by God in His Image reveals the path for you as you deepen your relationship to God, relying on this more and more. It shows you one step after another, tells you which way to turn at a crossroads (transition points and boundaries between each Sphere of love) and gives you the energy to travel further.

My Father's 'House' means a space within which the unfolding of the perpetual creating process of the cosmos is occurring all the time, every moment, even right now. The 'rooms' are literally way stations or temporary resting places in this unfolding process of the soul's evolution. There are many of these 'way stations,' *an abundance of places (rooms or planes within each Sphere) for one's soul-consciousness to consolidate itself, and then move on.*

THE FIVE DEATHS

'I die a little every day.'[32]

The movement into the next Sphere of Love is guarded by a boundary of love. To pass through these boundaries, we increase the amount of love we are holding and living by receiving more and more Divine Love. As this love increases within us, something also leaves us, passes away, is transcended because it is embraced fully. A part of us dies a little every day as we become closer to God.

Each Sphere we enter into is a death to our old self; part of our old self dies, part of our wounds release, part of the old emotions and soul we thought we were, goes. As we go through the Divine Love Path, there are five of these deaths, as we go from Sphere one to two, Sphere two to three, Sphere three to five, Sphere five to seven, and the new birth into the Divine Soul or At-One-ment with God.

This new birth is the death of the human soul as we know and cherish it today, and the birth of the Divine Soul, which is our fullest potential.

The Five Deaths are the human soul's openings and dying into God, Divine Love, Divine Truths and the Divine Soul. This born again process accelerates tangibly in the Divine Love Spheres, and is a deeply mystical process incomprehensible to the mind but keenly felt in the interior depths of the soul.

These Five Deaths mark the stages of the transformation of the very substance and structure of the human soul, and the Openings into eternal life that await us as potential Divine Souls. As we progress from being finite and human into the infinite Divine substance of God, who you are changes completely on the most fundamental level, as you cease being human as it is known today.

The initial Spheres mark the feeling and releasing of inherited ancestral, parental and childhood injuries; as these emotions are deeply felt and released the tangible transformation of the substance of the soul commences. This accelerates further in the higher Spheres when you encounter and release the wounds of the first human parents, Amon and Aman or Adam and Eve, which are encoded into your soul and junk DNA loops.

This map marks the increasing desire for Divine Love at any and all costs no matter what, the willingness to give yourself up for this, utterly and completely, and the consistent passion for truth and At-One-ment with God.

It marks an increasing inner silence as one embraces all emotions of the soul and the peace that descends upon you as you die a little more each day to whom you once thought you were. Each Death marks your increasing dependence on Divine Love and Truth, on God, as the very lifeblood of your existence and purpose for being alive.

The Five Deaths become Five Steps to Eternal and Divine Life, the ever increasing life of the expanding soul, the openings into the Reality of Divine Love through the permanent establishing of deep humility as your foundation, burning desire as your guiding, living light, holy choice as perpetual harmony, and your total willingness to obey the laws of love at all times in all parts of your life simply because it is true and what you desire most of all.

Passion for God overtakes you, crafting your soul to transform the flame of your pain to become the fuel for Divine Love to flow into your soul, for the Living Light of consciousness to blaze through the darkness. The Five Deaths are how this Passion manifests in your soul, melting all that is finite, all the masks, veils, wounds and denials, armor and shield, sword and spear, all parts of you, all parts of your creation.

Ceaselessly flowing, the Passion waits for you to lose yourself in it.

At times it can feel like you are being nailed to the cross of Divine laws and truths, which dissolves all your own personal truths as surely as night follows day. This happens externally through the judgments, fears and persecutions of others unwilling to allow your soul to follow God out of fear of what it means for them and their attachments.

Internally this occurs as you burn in your resistance to following divine laws, feeling the flame burning you up through your total feeling of any and all emotions, refusing projection onto anyone, or anything. This is your road and the fulfilling of your desire to meet God fully.

As Christ said, 'If anyone desires to come after me, let him deny himself and take up his cross daily, and follow Me.'[33]

The Passion is not a linear journey: we can experience some of the symptoms of each death at differing times, but to establish oneself in a new Sphere of love is another thing. It is a soulful journey, not for hard-core Buddhists or Yogis, although it can be. It is a journey of the Beloved, of the Lover of God.

In each death, you become more and more dependent on God. What moves the soul through each death are the keys of *humility, desire, choice and prayer*. Even after At-One-ment with God, there is still more to grow into. No human has ever yet come to Realize the full depth of God's Love and therefore these qualities. These qualities never end, for they are infinite qualities.

A PATHWAY OF SACRED TEARS

'Tears are often the telescope by which men see far into heaven.'[34]

This is a Pathway of Sacred Tears, tears shed for the beauty, the pain and the breaking down of self in devastatingly real moments of humbly accepted personal 'truth.' Embracing and sticking with Divine Truth at all costs means all else pales into insignificance besides the Only Thing that really matters.

There is a big difference between tears cried about the effects of a wound, and tears sobbed and released from the primal place within the soul where the causes of its deepest pains, suffering and heartbreaks dwell. The tears of crying on the surface of an emotion have little emotional impact, and are not felt by those more sensitive to truth and the deeper reality of the soul.

The wrenching sobs emanating from a soul truly delving into and feeling their causal wounds stop angels themselves, and are felt by all and sundry. Feeling these heartfelt sobs releasing grief, one deepens into feeling their own wounds; and so a chain reaction of sacred tears can occur.

Many personalities get caught in endless cycles of effect crying, thinking they are healing but never really transforming anything because of the fear to delve deeper. Very few humans desire to feel their pain because it is painful! Crying in self-pity keeps one circling around the hole of their pain. Crying tears for the loss of worldly objects or people is your loss of attachment to them, and actually are tears shed for the freedom of your expanding soul so you can actually love them more. You are scared of feeling the loss of who you felt you were, and what you needed to maintain this façade; it is little about others.

Surface tears have many varieties: 'crocodile' tears are shed to manipulate, to deny a deeper emotion, and to gain a superficial sympathy and attention for a person, deflecting it away from another *or* from the soul denying its deeper causal feelings. Crocodile tears arise from a soul scared to be seen for who they truly are, and their own vulnerability.

Tears can be shed for the letting go of mental beliefs as the mind relaxes, releases, and starts to come under the rule of the soul, rather than the mind dominating the soul. As the loss of control is felt, emotions are released, the mind stops, and you wonder what happened!

As Teresa of Avila shares:
'Emotional people, who weep for the slightest thing, will again and again think they are weeping for reasons which have to do with God; but this will not be so in reality. It may even be the case (when they shed floods of tears, and for some time they cannot refrain from doing so whenever they think of God or hear Him spoken of) that some humour has been oppressing the heart, and that it is this, rather than their love of God, which has excited their tears.

It seems as if they will never make an end of weeping; having come to believe that tears are good, they make no attempt to control them. In fact, they would not do otherwise than weep even if they could, and they make every effort they can to induce tears. Negative spirits do their best, in such cases, to weaken them, so that they may be unable either to practise prayer or keep their Rule.

When the fire within my soul is strong, however hard my heart may be, it distils as if in an alembic. You will easily recognize when tears arise from this source, because they are comforting and tranquillizing rather than disturbing, and seldom do any harm. The great thing about this deception will be that, although it may harm the body, it cannot (if the soul is humble) hurt the soul. If it is not humble, it will do it no harm to keep its suspicions.

Do not let us suppose that if we weep a great deal we have done everything that matters; let us also work hard and practise the virtues, for these are what we most need. Let the tears come when God is pleased to send them: we ourselves should make no efforts to induce them.

They will leave this dry ground of ours well watered and will be of great help in producing fruit; but the less notice we take of them, the more they will do, because they are the water which comes from Heaven. When we ourselves draw water, we tire ourselves by digging for it, and the water we get is not the same; often we dig till we wear ourselves out without having discovered so much as a pool of water, still less a wellspring.'

Tears of shame, tears of feeling small and unworthy, tears of frustration and anger, at your own lack of desire, at your own lack of deeper willingness and stuck-ness, tears at the rigidity of your comfort zones. Beating your head against a brick wall as you cannot figure out what to do *or how to feel*. The mind locks into a feedback loop, running around itself. In these moments, Move. Express it all. Follow your soul in whatever it wishes to release. Go a bit mad, it's ok.

We can cry tears for our abandoning of God, tears for our betrayals of love, tears for our children, parents, friends and animals, tears for our denials of love, tears for our judgments of love, tears for the loss of our cherished yet naïve ideals about love, tears for our separations from love, tears for things we know not what we are crying for, and there is no need to know.

We can cry tears of compassion for others' pain as our own, we cry tears for our own heartbreak. We can cry and laugh at the same time, feeling both sadness and joy, heartbreak and hilarity. In this, we are not attached to the negative emotion (from the soul's perspective) and can feel both sides of release and expansion at the same time.

Tears of sweet madness, tears of pain, tears of sorrow, tears like honey that drip like nectar, remaking anew all that they touch. There are the tears of sweet sorrow, being the vessel for the woes of the world to be felt on behalf of all; someone has to cry if no one else does.

The tears of grief as you feel your deepest pains with the aid of your greatest love of all loves, God; the tears of the sheer joy of the soul, the tears of loving orgasm as you make love with your Beloved whilst in prayer with God; the intimate tears of adoration for a Soul Mate in the act of making love, as the soul is touched on every level of love, human and Divine.

Tears of gratitude, being touched by God in new and virgin places that have always been pure; tears of being touched in the ecstatic yearning, desire, shaking prayer and inflowing of God's Love; tears borne from your desire to receive that love so keenly, so heartfully; tears of expansion and release. The intimacy of tears of adoration, of wondrous awe and loving gratitude for Beloved God, and more, and more, and more ...

Some tears can never be described, for they encompass all emotions at the same time. I wish you these tears of all tears.

THE FIRST SPHERE

FEAR
COURAGE
SHOCK and NEW-FOUND AWARENESS OF THE TRUTH
WILLINGNESS and CHOICE EXPANDS
VULNERABILITY, EMOTIONS and SELF-RESPONSIBILITY
DESIRE FOR GROWTH, CHANGE, GOD and THE NEW

'The quest for Love changes us. There is no seeker amongst those who search for Love who has not matured along the Way. The moment you start looking for Love, you start to change within and without.'[35]

The First Sphere is dominated by fear, and by the fear of actually feeling fear. This double fear is behind almost every action of those souls in the lowest stages of the First Sphere, like a blanket covering everything. Many choices, thoughts, desires and emotions come from a root of fear that results in fear-based decision-making.

Surface dominated emotions like anger, blame and denial of any kind of deeper emotions, such as pain and grief, dominate, with the effect that one is either timid or angry, repressed or exter-nalized.

Blame, projection, avoidance of true expression, shame and unworthiness seem like a never-ending spiral here. One does not feel much Divine Love, and prayer is infrequent. One is ruled by addictions, substitutes for love, and negative spirits. One creates different masks to fit into social groups, family and friends, as one wants to be accepted and approved, to feel safe. This is your daily mode of living, and you have these masks to survive in the matrix, to get along. People are much more interested in their career, addictions, entertainment, friends, family, children and partner, than with their own sovereign soul and God.

'It is no measure of health to be well adjusted to a profoundly sick society.'
J. Krishnamurti

There are feelings of dissatisfaction with life, and one knows something is missing, but uses many substitutes and distractions to fill this nagging gap. No one really loves each other in the First Sphere, although they may think so; everyone is using each other to avoid feeling their own soul's painful emotions, although glimpses of love may be had.

Taking is the norm rather than giving, and this is all to fill the hole within. One may even take some kind of pleasure in others' suffering, on the street, in daily life or in comedy shows which poke fun at others and humiliate them for laughter's sake.

There is constant collusion with others to validate your own pains and wounds in wound-ships (as opposed to true Friendships) and avoid pain. There is constant dependence on others, be it friends, teachers, workshops, family, to help you move forwards. You make few decisions based on how you really feel – you make decisions based on what others want and feel, thinking this is what you want and feel.

Sufi mystics call this Sphere *the depraved Nafs* (ego-self) the most primitive and common state of being, like an animal, where the soul is trapped in gossip, worldly pursuits and being run by its wounds and what society demands of it.

One lives here as a victim – blaming others and the world for one's own continuing unhappiness, rarely following one's deeper urgings, but rather the urgings of money, the world, family and others in general. One even becomes a victim of questioning why there is suffering in the world, and why would God allow such a thing?

In the First Sphere, one may spend time arguing or fighting with others, your self, and even with God. 'I want to do this, this is all too hard, this is stupid, I don't want to have to deal with this, why God, why are you doing this to me, I don't like you, life is unfair,' and you feel angry, resistant, or completely cave into resignation and become a miserable victim.

One justifies and excuses one's fears in this phase, running away from confronting and feeling them, and even doing the same when anybody else has a fear! *What do you expect? Of course I have that fear.'*

Souls in the First Sphere may have worry and stress etched into their face and soul, (and cover it up with cosmetic surgery and treatments) and have little belief, faith, trust, or desire in their own self love or personal truth. One cycles around the effects of the emotions, caught in a vicious cycle too afraid to go into the fear itself. Whilst it is important to feel the effects of emotions, in the First Sphere one gets caught in them and lives in them perpetually.

BUT, as you begin to trust, to pray more, and receive Divine Love to fuel you forwards, more self-confidence and belief in yourself comes to bring positive changes to your life. The independent, or more accurately, the isolated and deeply separated ego self, 'I can do it all myself,' starts to break down, and a sense of real humility starts. You become more willing to feel the fear and ask for help.

When fear no longer dominates your life, from that moment on your soul is going to expand, even when you are afraid. You can still feel fear, but because you allow it and embrace it and fully feel it as and when it arises, it dissipates and leaves you. Whereas before, as soon as you felt fear, you went into a stuck place within you.

This fear might be fear of hurting others feelings, fear of other people's reactive emotions, fear of authority, fear to feel your own more painful emotions hidden yet lurking under the surface, and in fact, any fear.

To move from First Sphere to Second Sphere, one has to welcome, ask for, pray for and embrace fear consistently. One has to dive into any and all fears and deeper pains you have. Then more Divine Love can enter, once the emotion is felt and released fully. Moving through the First Sphere takes the longest time and is painful 'work' as you have the most resistance, pride, unwillingness, judgment and blame. It takes discipline, commitment, a guide, self love, good health and vigilance.

However, it is so worth it as you begin to feel Divine Love, and each time you do, It spurs you on, deepening your humility and trust.

'When you find your path, have sufficient courage to make mistakes. Disappointment, defeat and despair are the tools God uses to show us the way.'
Paulo Coelho

There are three main sub-planes of fear in the First Sphere: Hell, the 'Twilight Zone,' and 'Summerland.' Hell is the place where the most wounded souls live, twisted and in their own suffering, actively turning against love because of their wounds and trying to influence others to do the same. They do not believe in God and will even hate God, feeling abandoned and betrayed by

Him, so it is hard to ask them to pray!

This is all they know, and whilst brighter spirits try to help them, they are often simply not open to any help whatsoever and indeed can get very triggered and angry once approached. Brighter spirits will therefore use other, more ingenious ways to open them indirectly to their own soul's condition.

As Teresa of Avila shares:
'Let us consider the condition of those who are in hell. They are not resigned, nor have they contentment and delight, which God gives it. They cannot see their suffering is doing them any good, yet they keep suffering more and more, for the torment suffered by the soul is much more acute than that suffered by the body, and the pains which such souls have to endure are beyond comparison.

What can we do in so short a life as this which will matter in the slightest if it will free us from these terrible and eternal torments? It is impossible to explain to anyone who has not experienced it what a grievous thing is the soul's suffering and how different it is from the suffering of the body.'

In the second plane of the First Sphere known as the *'Twilight Zone'* souls spend time discussing God, emotions and metaphysical topics, rather than actually experiencing them. Religious groups, beliefs and spiritual ignorance abound.

Some of the most opinionated spirits can be found here and arguments can be intense, as you can see from the many religious conflicts that have ravaged the Earth for millennia. The level of ignorance is high, and many spirits channel information to gullible mortals, even calling themselves God.

We all reach a plateau on our journey. This could be an aching for love, a void of emptiness, numbness, deadness, where we have cut ourselves off from deeper feelings, where we have disassociated from certain painful events which lie underneath our surface day-to-day life.

At this point, pray to dive into this space, for there are emotions lying underneath this plateau waiting to be felt, and you will need bravery and deep desire to enter here. This plateau is like a station along the way – but you now have to go to the end of the line and not just hang out at the nearest station.

This plateau is the entrance to the vortex of your causal wounds, and whilst it may feel like there is no emotion or feeling there, it is more accurate to say that there are emotions here you are scared to embrace and have deeply buried or cut yourself off from. More of your soul is waiting here for you to embrace it.

In the last sub-plane of the First Sphere known as *Summerland*, there is gossip, also differences of opinion, and anger. It is the final phase before one enters the Second Sphere, and is like a dawning of truth as a painful causal wound is fully felt and released.

In Summerland, one tends to discover more of what one really wants to do, and what talents and gifts one has. Spirits find they can follow material pursuits here, but in time this attraction fades, and they begin to realize that spirituality is more important as a greater source of happiness.

THE FIRST MANSIONS:
ST TERESA OF AVILA

Do not imagine these seven mansions as arranged in a row, one behind another, but fix your attention on the center, the palace occupied by God, the King, the Sun, whose light reaches every part of it. Like an onion, which has many outer rinds surrounding the core, just so around this central place are many more, as there also are above it.

Around the outer parts of this Sphere, the light, which comes from the palace, becomes dimmer, hardly reaching the first Mansions at all because there are so many bad things, snakes, vipers[36] and poisonous creatures living there.

It is as if one were to enter a place flooded by sunlight with eyes so full of dust that one could hardly open them. The room itself is light enough, but one cannot enjoy the light because one is prevented from doing so by these wild beasts, which force one to close one's eyes to everything but oneself and them.

This is the condition of a soul which is so completely absorbed in things of the world and in possessions, honors or business, that, although it would like to gaze at the castle and enjoy its beauty, it is prevented from doing so, and seems quite unable to free itself from all these impediments.

Many souls remain in the outer court of the castle, the place occupied by the guards; they are not interested in entering it, and have no idea what there is in that wonderful place, or who dwells in it.

The door of entry into this castle is prayer and meditation. If a person does not realize Whom he is addressing, and understand what he is asking for, and who it is that is asking and of Whom he is asking it, he is not praying at all even though he is constantly moving his lips.

Souls without prayer are like people whose bodies or limbs are paralyzed: they possess feet and hands but they cannot control them. In the same way, there are souls so infirm and so accustomed to busying themselves with outside affairs that nothing can be done for them, and it seems as though they are incapable of entering within themselves at all.

So accustomed have they grown to living all the time with *the reptiles and other creatures* to be found in the outer court of the castle that they have almost become like them; and *although by nature they are so richly endowed as to have the power of holding converse with none other than God Himself,* there is nothing that can be done for them unless they strive to realize their miserable condition and to remedy it.

These souls are much absorbed in worldly affairs, but their desires are good; infrequently they pray to God and think about the state of their souls, though not carefully. They pray a few times a month, and as a rule think all the time of their preoccupations, for they are much attached to them; where their treasure is, there is their heart also. From time to time, however, they shake their minds free of them, and eventually they enter the first rooms on the lowest floor of the First Sphere, but so many reptiles get in with them that they are unable to appreciate the beauty of the castle, or to find any peace within it. Still, they have done a good deal by entering at all.

While in a state like this the soul will find profit in nothing, *and hence, none of the good works it may do will be of any avail;* for they do not have their origin in the First Principle, God, through

Whom alone our virtue is true virtue. Any good thing we do has its source, not in ourselves, but rather in the spring where the tree of the soul is planted, and in that Sun of God which sheds its radiance on our works.

Whenever we do any good thing, or see such a thing being done, we should take ourselves straight away to its Source, thanking God, realizing that without His help we are powerless. Before commencing any soul work, pray to God to guide you within it.

We reach much greater heights of virtue by thinking upon the virtue of God than if we stay in our own little plot of ground of self-knowledge and tie ourselves down to it completely. But, self-knowledge is important, and even if you were raised right up to the heavens, never relax your cultivation of it; so long as we are on this Earth, nothing matters more to us than humility.

It is an excellent thing indeed to begin on your path by entering the room within the castle where humility is acquired rather than by flying off to other rooms. For that is the way to make progress, and, if we have a safe, level road to walk along, why should we desire wings to fly? Let us rather try to get the greatest possible profit out of walking.

We shall never succeed in knowing ourselves unless we seek to know God; by looking at His purity we shall see our foulness; by meditating upon His humility, we shall see how far we are from being humble. There are two advantages in this.

First, it is clear that anything white looks very much whiter against something black, just as the black looks blacker against the white. Secondly, if we turn from self towards God, our understanding and our will become nobler and readier to embrace all that is good.

If we never rise above the slough of our own miseries we do ourselves a great disservice. If we never stop thinking about ourselves, I am not surprised that we experience these fears and others that are still worse.

Although this is only the first Mansion, it contains riches of great price, and any who can elude the reptiles which are to be found in it, will not fail to go farther.

There are many ways in which souls enter these rooms, always with good intentions; but legions of evil spirits in each room prevent souls from passing from one to another, and as we fail to realize this, we are tricked by all kinds of deceptions.

These negative spirits are less successful with those who are nearer God's dwelling-place; but at this early stage, as the soul is still absorbed in worldly affairs, engulfed in worldly pleasure and puffed up with worldly honors and ambitions, its vassals, which are the senses and the faculties given to it by God as part of its nature, have not the same power, and such a soul is easily vanquished, although it may desire not to break Divine Laws and may even perform good works.

Those who find themselves in this state need to take every opportunity of repairing to God and His guides and helpers, so that they may help. *In reality it is necessary in every state of life, from the beginning, that our help should come from God.*

Everyone who wishes to enter the Second Sphere will be well advised to try to put aside all unnecessary affairs and business of this world. For those who hope to reach the principal Mansion, of At-One-ment with God, this is so important that unless you begin in this way you will never be able to get there. Beware of cares, which have nothing to do with you.

To be inspired with zeal for the greatest possible perfection is a good thing; but the result of it might be that one would think any little fault on the part of others to be a serious failure, and would always be looking out for such things; sometimes she might even be so zealous as to be unable to see her own faults; and others, observing only her zeal about their misdeeds and not understanding the excellence of her intentions, might well take none too kindly.

True perfection consists in the love of God and of our neighbor, and the more perfect is our observance of these two commandments, the nearer to perfection we shall be. If we attain them perfectly we are doing His will and so shall be united with Him.

This mutual love is so important that I should like you never to forget it; for if the soul goes about looking for trifling faults in others (which sometimes may not be imperfections at all, though perhaps our ignorance may lead us to make the worst of them) it may lose its own peace of mind and perhaps disturb that of others.

THE FIRST DEATH: OPENING AND BREAKING DOWN

'Bountiful is your life, full and complete. Or so you think, until someone or something comes along and makes you realize what you have been missing all this time. Like a mirror that reflects what is absent rather than what is present, they show you the void in your soul – the void you have resisted seeing. This person can be a lover, a friend, a spiritual teacher; sometimes it can be a child to look after or a series of events.

It's as if for years on end you compile a personal dictionary. In it you give your definition of every concept that matters to you, such as truth, happiness or beauty. At every major turning point in life, you refer to this dictionary, hardly ever feeling the need to question its premises. Then one day a stranger comes along, snatches your precious dictionary and throws it away, saying, 'All your definitions need to be redefined. It's time for you to unlearn everything you know.'[37]

The first death on the Path of Divine Love is when your old life, your old ways, your (passionless) job, your old relationships, your old habits and means of getting by in the world start to be recognized as unfulfilling and shallow, as unsatisfying and purposeless. You start to feel that there is something more, and old things start to drop away and have less significance. The first step is often the hardest one to take.

Worldly pursuits, attachments, all start to be left behind as you search for something new, a deeper purpose, a deeper meaning, and a fuller feeling. You start to recognize the hole within yourself, places where you have not let love in, where you have abandoned love and denied it, where you are not following your deeper passions and desires, instead compromising, betraying and sacrificing your soul for your ideas of love and how you should be according to the world's ideas about what love is, what it should feel like, and how it acts.

You start to see the deceits you have been living in, and how they have come to dominate your life, how you have left out the most important things in your life for the sake of something else or somebody else. You start to reach towards love of your own soul and to God, *and all that involves in practical actions*, and take the first big moves onto the soulful path. You begin to hunger and thirst for something more.

You may have done spiritual work before this but this is the beginning of the path of Divine Love, for your soul drives you forwards with its first taste of Divine Love. So already you are beginning to feel that passion. While there still may be fear, pain and control, your soul feels compelled to start letting go of all these things that are blocking your way to receive more and more Divine Love.

Willingness, desire and new choices start to present themselves, and you realize the power of choice in your life: you can simply say no to certain things and people and situations, and say yes to new, unknown and more fulfilling events and people. You become educated on what choice really is and how to exercise it in the ways of Divine Truth and Divine Love, not worldly or metaphysical notions around love. You are less afraid of being humble and vulnerable, and start to expose yourself regularly. You start to change many things in your life, with fear and trepidation, yet also with a sense of adventure and aliveness, of striking out into the unknown, feeling small and hesitant, yet embracing this smallness.

You begin to recognize, with grace and with guidance, that your own personal truths and ways of doing things are not working, and that there are laws in life which do work in bringing more love and truth to you. You start to recognize, enjoy and work more with your deeper feelings and desires, you begin to identify with these more, and start to see the patterns within you that deny love; and you desire to do something about it.

The old must go for the new to come in is the mantra here, as you clear out the old possessions, books, furniture, attitudes, beliefs and limiting emotions that no longer serve the birthing of a new you.

You are at the start of a magnificent journey and know not where it will take you, but you feel compelled and more trusting to ride with this wave nonetheless. Physical travel, a break from work or a total resignation to discover oneself are part of the inner journey here, as you seek to discover your soul in a series of new and unknown contexts.

Who am I and what am I here to do is the guiding force here, as you start to search for the happiness that lies at the end of all things. You can sense it, not knowing what it is, but your soul beckons you forward, and a whole multitude of glorious synchronicities, guides, books, people and angels seen and unseen come flooding into your life to kick start this new and exciting adventure into pastures fertile with promise.

There are many cycles of this breakdown and breakthrough on the spiral of the five deaths, of the passion of love, so breakdown can happen each time you go into a new level or octave of Divine Love.

Shedding old skins, dying a little each day, becoming more alive and impassioned, less materialistic, letting go of old ideas, attitudes and behaviors, becoming more open and wonder-filled as to what reality actually could be, means the skies open up for you.

And then there come the tears, the pain, the letting go of things once held so dear, so comfortable, so much a part of who you thought you were, and what defined you. Identity weakens. Divine Love is yearned for, a new feeling. The healing begins.

Sexuality starts to be explored consciously as a way to share and exchange energy, as a way to elevate and expand, as a way to heal and release, as a way to trigger and evolve, as a way to express a deeper love and connect more parts of yourself together, designed to lead towards the sacred.

Lack of love-making in long-term relationships and the emotional repression that this involves starts to be questioned from an emotional standpoint, as does the validity and worth of such relationships in the context of your soul's growth.

New friends are made, old paradigms and conventions, once unquestioned, start to be investigated. What once served you so well now seems outmoded, outdated, a relic from the past. Independent lines of thought and feeling start to form in your mind, and new, seemingly crazy notions start to be entertained. You start to dip your toes into things, people and events that once seemed wild and out of the ordinary, out of the question. But now they are part of the answer.

Freedom of choice, to choose and choose again, to be fluid, to change your once rigid mind, timetabling, scheduling; plans and goals at the drop of a hat become more commonplace and accepted. Your willingness to accept and allow grows, as you become more neutral in your definitions and judgments of things.

Fears loom up, but seem to be smaller as you dive more into life. More emotions, once repressed, well up, startling you with their intensity, almost with a life of their own. Chaos becomes the new order, as the structures you have built start to teeter and shake.

Your foundations, once so comfortable, so known, are seen to be built on a totally artificial and wounded foundation: with one touch, the whole stack of cards can collapse. You start to see the madness of the world and its systems, the madness of your relationships and emotional crutches, the madness of being a victim, and choose to no longer justify or follow them.

Questioning all, the futility of it all may also come into view. The meanings and values that were once the bedrock of your world view become more transparent as the mud of your beliefs and the lies you have cushioned your life upon reveal. You become more honest, more disciplined, more aware of your energy and attention and where they are going. You now have a choice with what to do with your attention, and you start to put it into different uses that actually bring you more fulfillment than drudgery.

You become tired of settling for second best, being stuck in routines, mundane tasks and habitual responses, both in you and others, and yearn for something more ... exciting, something that inspires you, something new and something that just clicks within you.

This yearning accelerates when you meet a physical guide who points you in the right direction, who loves and supports your soul above and beyond anything else; for we all need help to see what we alone cannot, to help us release old, stuck emotions and die a little more to the artificial reality they have created.

The First Sphere is more about surviving than living, more about living your conditioning than living your authenticity. You live for the outside; defined by job, status, social agreements, and you follow what is expected by family and partner living in these patterns.

The First Sphere is about the matrix we have created and is based on fear. We swallow our truth for the sake of peace. We deny our soul for the sake of comfort and approval. We keep control of others and ourselves. We stay in the comfort zone. We can be victims of everything and anybody, taking no responsibility for ourselves or the planet.

We are often caught in attachments (material/personal), dependency (others, the system, addictions both to substances and behaviors), judgments (ourselves and others), comparisons, expectations and self-importance (feeling inferior). The First Sphere is about the masks we put on in order to belong, fit in and feel safe in the matrix.

We use survival tactics to fit into the box, to be accepted and loved. Words like 'heart, love, soul and God' are almost taboo or overused. Relationships are based on collusion, wounds and co-dependency. Security and happiness are suggested to be found through material belongings, jobs and other people. Vulnerability is seen to be a weakness in this world of appearance.

Fear is a normal feeling that is ok to be felt, accepted and expressed. This will then allow more love and truth between people, more authenticity and less need for masks. One starts to discover the desire and willingness to come closer to Truth and the willingness to feel and release unfelt, painful emotions in order to receive Divine Love.

NEEDS AND SUBSTITUTES FOR LOVE AND GOD

We try to distract ourselves from feeling our deeper emotions and our soul through many and various means. We create our own laws, our personal truths that we use to navigate through life, to survive in this world, to conform and get by, through what others have demonstrated to us and we think they are truth.

This is a life and world that has been artificially constructed, ALL built around the wound of being separated from love, the greatest need and desire of our souls.

To move more into living in love, *we need to see how we are substituting for love and truth in our life.* We create substitutes to stop us from feeling our deeper wounds, and these substitutes, needs and addictions keep us circling round and round in the *effects* of these deep seated emotions that form the very fabric of our wounded soul.

The more we circle, the more frustrated we can become at our lack of progress, at our own unwillingness to feel deeper, until something has got to give. We fill the holes of our wounds with cheap, pale imitations and substitutes from the world and other people around us. All these substitutes are medications for the causal wound underneath. It is like covering over a bleeding, cut-off stump of an amputated arm with a piece of tissue paper, and hoping it will stick and do the job.

A substitute can also be called an addiction. An addiction is an unhealed emotion within yourself that requires satisfaction and filling from *any* outside source. Addictions rise from our lack of humility and unwillingness to feel our emotions.[38] All addictions are harmful, whether physical, sexual, emotional, or spiritual, and can involve people, sex, relationships, drugs, alcohol, busyness and spirit influences, amongst many others.

Addictions are your direct avoidance of unhealed emotions, and the result of not taking personal responsibility. Addictions operating between partners at the emotional level *all* relate to childhood emotions and can be further veiled by spirit influence and the amplified fears they generate. *All addictions must be healed in order to continue to receive Divine Love to the point of At-One-ment with God.*

What would you do without these addictions and substitutes for Divine Love?

- Partner and parents – looking for human love to fill a need inside that only Divine Love can fulfill
- Food – comfort food and over-eating, stuffing down emotions
- Drugs, alcohol, gambling – numbing, distorting true desire
- Emotional addictions and patterns
- Sex – hole-filling with another human and sexuality
- Animals – to comfort a wound of love, touch, lack of childhood affection
- Medicating your wounds – doctors, hypochondria, pill popping, drugs, supplements, pharmaceutical prescriptions
- Religions – to turn towards, rather than within; beliefs
- Job – not doing your soul purpose and living listlessly, for the world, in a mundane existence, just to survive and get by
- Books – to distract and entertain the mind, already confused and overloaded with information, staying away from feeling the soul and actually Being

- Busyness – to distract from feeling and being alone to feel behind the surface
- Internet and telephone – to over-distract
- Facebook and Twitter – to distract and remain in the minutiae of daily life
- Over socializing and pointless gatherings that no longer serve your soul
- Planning/lists – to keep the mind turning
- Saving and changing the world – making yourself feel better with the next thing that you have never actually done ... and/or justifying your life with the idea of service to push you on, instead of looking at your own self
- Gossip and idle chatter – to stifle silence and deeper feelings
- Theories and metaphysical speculation – to continue the dominion of the mind
- Over-exercising – to stay stuck in a physical 'high' and avoid emotions
- Hobbies – to keep distracted
- Extravagance – to fill the holes with external items, indulge yourself and keep focused on the external as a source of filling yourself up
- Fantasizing – about anything and everything
- Fashion and beauty care – the best beauty care comes from healing oneself – this is the anti-aging serum extraordinaire!
- Success, goals, intentions – running life by external laws rather than delving within and allowing true soul manifestation to occur once you have done the healing. Then you get given far more than you could ever have hoped for whilst in the wounded state.
- False laughter, false love, false joy, false friendship – debilitating to true self love
- Hugging – too much hugging covers over wounds that

need to be felt, not just medicated

- Stories of the self, that keep you on the surface
- Memories, nostalgia, sentimentality, idealization of past and future events and people, especially parents or lovers
- Over-shopping and window shopping
- Too much sleep
- Too many movies and TV
- Too much house cleaning and decorating

Of course, we all need to engage *in a few* of these activities, and some good can come from them, but *we use them to distract ourselves from feeling most of the time.*

You are doing it every day actively, or rattling around in your head (subconscious). When you are doing these things you are saying, *'No, I don't want God today. I can't really be bothered. I would rather have these things than have Divine Love.'*

As one moves into the Second Sphere, you lose your appetite for the old life you were living, and your soul starts to change its color, affections, appetites and desires from its old life towards God. You begin to find little pleasure, support, consolation or an abiding place in the things that once gave you so much, and begin to find your pleasure, comfort and succor in the things of Truth and Love.

You leave an entire world and state of consciousness behind here, a reality that almost everyone on Earth is living in without knowing it. You separate yourself gladly and willingly, with dedication and desire, learning to rely on God in your own small way to bring you out of the fears and hells you have been living in.

'It is never too late to ask yourself, 'Am I ready to change the life I am

living? Am I ready to change within?' Even if a single day is the same as the day before, it surely is a pity. At every moment, and with each new breath, one should be renewed and renewed again. There is only one way to be born into a new life: to die before death.'[39]

THE SECOND SPHERE OF NATURAL LOVE

DESIRING and SPEAKING TRUTH AT ALL TIMES
TOTAL HONESTY and TRANSPARENCY
FOLLOWING YOUR PASSIONS and DESIRES
CONSISTENT PRAYER and RECEIVING OF DIVINE LOVE
CONSTANT ACCESSING and RELEASING OF EMOTIONS
YEARNINGS FOR SOUL MATE BEGIN TO MANIFEST
DEEP TRUST and FAITH IN GOD ARISES
GOD BECOMES YOUR BEST FRIEND

Muhammad said, 'You are a hundred thousand particles and each particle of yours is being carried off by some desire; within each particle of yours, you are carrying an illusion. The one who demonstrates purity of intention, and sincerity of action goes to Paradise. There is no need for a promise such as, "If he or she has been able to do this, he or she goes to Paradise." If he or she has been able to do this, he or she is completely Paradise itself.'

The shift from the First to the Second Sphere is the shift from being a victim, blaming and projecting your wounds and needs outwards onto others, into becoming totally self responsible for everything in your life, in every way. Instead of blaming others, one owns every emotion that is felt within. This felt, emotional shift releases deeper feelings of happiness, trust and connection to your own soul, and a new feeling of lightness.

The burden of fear and following its dictates has vanished, although fears may still be felt. The difference is you are now willing and desiring to go to their causes fully with little hesitation. You have left the feeling of being dominated by fear, mind chatter and anxiety into a new expanded sense of self, more love for your soul and more connection to God, if one is on a Divine Love Path.

Yet this is the Sphere where you now have enough self love and divine connection to fully enter into, and heal, your deepest personal wounds, the wounds that have dogged and haunted your whole life. You need self love to enter your deeper wounds. You now have enough love, 'juice' and willingness to enter these deepest, darkest places of your soul.

This is a paradox as now you are enjoying life more than ever, more in flow with your passions and desires in radical action, which are starting to manifest, and yet the biggest hurts, pains and wounds are now ready to be fully felt! You are now ready. In fact, you cannot move into the Third Sphere until you have fully felt and released many of these causal wounds.

Self love goes to an entirely different level in the Second Sphere. It is more palpably felt, and the reasons it has been denied or abandoned in your life become revealed, felt and released. This accelerating process reaches another octave in the Fourth Sphere in Sovereign Self Love, Sovereign because you are more connected in your own feeling relationship to God and possess more Divine Love.

We tend to repeat our suffering if we have not learnt fully all that can be learnt from it. We have to experience our suffering completely while it happens, as a child does, allied with our desire for a higher life so we never want to experience or repeat the suffering again.

Until we have squeezed every single last morsel and lesson from our painful experiences, they will tend to repeat again in similar forms through the Law of Attraction showing us the same pattern, again and again. Ultimately, this is compassion, because it reminds us of the same wound within us, urging us to another layer so it is completed once and for all, freeing us into another level of love.

In the Second Sphere, you feel more connected to a bigger reality, and your center of gravity shifts more into your soul and heart. God arrives in your life in a practical way. You get to be friends with people you just meet, and you consistently speak truth from your heart, both in its beauty and its vulnerability.

The path reveals itself step by step, and you receive new inner reference points as old ones melt. You are vulnerable. You cry a lot and let go of everything you have learned about yourself. Every day is new. You are blown away, it is painful and joyful. You start to realize you know nothing, and this gives you a feeling of freedom and the fuel to pray to God more for more Divine Love.

Your way of living and new choices may become a threat to people living in fear. You stop coping with their beliefs and speak truth. You may experience their anger or rejection, but you speak from your heart, whatever it takes. This is the first transition in the Second Sphere: the release of fear and the speaking of truth. Fear no longer dominates your decision-making, your choices, your feelings or your thought processes, and you are engaging and following your primary desires for Divine Love, Divine Truth and Self.

There is a deeper and more consistent yearning to progress on the path, to learn about, to re-connect, to remember your true nature. The flames of courage and passion are ignited inside your soul to undertake whatever is needed to continue. Fear is still an issue, but no longer an obstacle to dive into the Unknown.

The 'I can/must do it alone' becomes 'I can't do it alone.' Humility arises and connecting to God through prayer becomes more natural and spontaneous. With the wider opening of the heart, greater understanding about the true nature of Love is now possible.

An overall feeling of being taken care of *according to Divine Order* is recognized as the new foundation for everything. Major wounds still need to be felt and healed, yet these emotions become easier to access through your earnest aspiration for Truth.

Life becomes colorful with the whole scope of the differing shades of emotions, sensations and feelings. Genuine dialogues are regularly engaged with on the soul level and enjoyed, becoming food for the soul. New life choices and actions, in accordance with our soul (finally!) can be put into the world. To stay with God's Love and Truth is what life becomes all about. Trust and faith are built up.

You are no longer run by fear or the need to control. You take full self-responsibility for yourself (feelings, thoughts, words and deeds). No projections: you feel your feelings and express them. You choose to surrender to the heart and want to speak your heart's truth – good and bad. You open up to vulnerability and weakness, knowing that you cannot live without God any longer. The longing to heal your Soul and express love every single day arises.

On the Divine Love Path, this begins with passion for God *above all else*. There are natural love qualities, such as morality, that you also have to learn in this process to make these transitions. This is why the Spheres are numbered 1, 3, 5, 7 for the Divine Love path, and in-between them lie the natural love Spheres of 1, 2, 4 and 6.

A lot of people on the natural love path go from the First to Second Spheres and ignore their fear so much *that they think they do not have fear.* What they have learned is to ignore their fears by living a desire filled and passionate life rather than feeling their fears.

When you are on the Divine Love Path, you do not ignore your fears and make out they are not there; you feel them all *completely* and they no longer dominate your decision-making. In feeling our fears, and completely engaging them when they arise, we do not let them dominate our decisions about the desires or the truths in our lives. By doing this, they do not control our lives anymore.

It is not about intellectually accepting truth, or just talking about emotions and patterns, or just giving it all to God, expecting God to sort out your problems and take away your lessons, which is a very unloving thing to do and expect!

If the fear is not felt emotionally within you, you are not on the Divine Love Path. When you make the switch from First Sphere to Second Sphere *from an emotional or soulful perspective,* no one will ever affect your relationship with God again, no one will ever be able to control your relationship with God again, and no one will even be able to control your relationship with yourself. It is in the Second Sphere that the famous book, *Conversations with God* was channeled by a spirit falsely claiming to be God.

If there is still even a little denial of fear, then fear is dominating your life and there is a denial of truth. If we do not have the strong desire to know everything that is going on inside of us, we compromise the truth.

If you compromise the truth, both about yourself and the Divine

Truth, you have yet to make this transition. In the Second Sphere, you are not afraid of truth anymore, and have a strong passion and desire to hear the truth and act upon it immediately. *A primary lesson about love is that love always tells the truth no matter what the consequences are.*

'The wound is the place where the Light enters you.' – Rumi

Our ability to stay with discomfort provides unprecedented growth opportunities. Feeling and moving through uncomfortable emotions is essential in creating change, so it is a good idea to get comfortable with the uncomfortable in ourselves, and in others. As Gibran shares, 'Out of suffering emerge the strongest souls; the most massive characters are seared with scars.' You may be wounded, but you are also holding the light of a thousand suns.

For example, you wake up in the morning and say 'I feel good,' when actually you are feeling afraid. You just lied. So, just telling the truth to yourself and everyone else around you ALL THE TIME is part of the transition between the Second and Third Spheres.

And if we are honest, we can see in our own lives how often we tell a white lie and withhold the truth even in small instances, and before we know what we have done, we have prevented ourselves from making this transition.

There is no room for error here in the sense that we have to be relentlessly truthful at all times. If we make a mistake, it is wise to instantly correct it, apologize, and *ask why I did it in the first place*. What reason did I lie for?

Every time I say the exact truth as it is to myself and every single person around me, no matter what their response is, it gives me freedom, and there is a beautiful feeling that you honored yourself, your feelings and the truth. And you grow through this transition. But what often happens is that we are so afraid that someone might not like us, so afraid of those emotions coming from other people, that we lock ourselves in a place where we cannot progress.

So even though you may still have some wounds to feel and work through, and are following your desires and passions, some of which are out of harmony with love and some of which are in harmony with love, from this moment on you will no longer be afraid of truth, you will always be desiring it, you will always want to live in it.

Every day it will become the primary driving factor of your life. As you progress in this, you can come to know and feel the true soul condition of others as well, for knowing thyself and loving thyself means you can better love and know others and God.

Live emotionally in the truth of where you are all the time. Do not create any façade when having a conversation, or in your relationship with God. Share who you are and what you feel all the time. If you are afraid, feel afraid, and do not try to be courageous anymore. Just soften into that.

Be soft to every emotion that comes up. Allow the truth of who you are all the time. In this place, you no longer desire or want the façade self at all, and can give it up completely, because you want to live your desires and passions fully.[40]

In ALWAYS passionately desiring more truth for yourself, and desiring to live in truth with every single person around you, *all the time*, you give up the façade with every person around you. Can you imagine the effect that this is going to have on every person around you? By loving yourself like this, you are loving every other person too, for by loving yourself you are automatically loving others too, even if they do not realize it at first!

Love the revealing and feeling of more truth about yourself; feel gratitude for it when it arises, no matter where or whom it comes from, for it will connect you to God and yourself so much more.

When you get into this state emotionally, it is easy to do and enjoyable. And every single interaction you have with every person is truthful. You just want to do it more and more! The truth is also that if you do not share, express or give what is within you, be it gifts, emotions or truths, it will turn into poison or more armor.

The Second Sphere is where you trust your own soul more and therefore have more faith in God. God becomes your new Best Friend, the One you always go to first regarding anything in your life. As this happens, your love for your soul increases too.

The more you love God and have faith in Him, the more you will naturally be loving your own soul. This is still not a complete trust and faith (this reaches its fruition in At-One-ment with God) but it is solid enough and clear enough in your life that God *is what truly matters to you* above all else. Trust and faith deepens the more Divine Love we receive, and it is ever increasing. Humility in its true sense really starts here, and begins to deepen.

Another requirement to reach the Second Sphere is the recognition that material, economic and surface social pursuits are limited, and do not lead to happiness. In the Second Sphere, souls choose their spiritual path and if a soul decides later to change to another spiritual path, they will return to this Sphere.

The Second Sphere is thus called a *sphere of decision*, and in deciding what path to follow, you are more readily influenced by those from more advanced Spheres. Thus a spirit from the Fourth Sphere may well extol the virtues of his path, and the beauty of his Sphere.

This is where knowing what you desire the most, and becoming aware of the merits of each Sphere becomes useful, as you can then choose and pray to follow the path you truly desire, be it natural love or Divine Love. In these transitions, spirits may retain some of the spiritual ideas they had in the previous Sphere, but will be beginning to modify them in order to progress.

As we move through this Sphere, we start to seek and see God more strongly in everything we do. All the songs we hear are now about our yearning for God; all the books, all that people say to us, they are all ways in which we start to see the world become a messenger of truth and progress just for us, spurring us on, quite unknown to others, but known to ourselves.

Eventually arriving at the highest plane in this Sphere, a change occurs. We remember we have got this far through the help given to us by numerous guides, by God and our receiving of Divine Love, and a great urge overtakes us, through gratitude and the obedience that Divine Love automatically brings, *to perform a similar function for others*. This is known as an at-One-ment task, and this is when it begins to dawn on us.

On Earth, you can deal with emotions in the Fourth Sphere in the Second Sphere, which of course is going to hasten your progression. For example, you begin to individuate more as a soul in the Second Sphere, discovering more of who you really are underneath your masks and your wounds, and stepping more into your sovereign self, *loving your own soul more because you are getting to know yourself more.*

This process of Individualization and sovereign self authority begins in the Second Sphere, reaching new octaves in the Fourth and Sixth Spheres, climaxing in Divine Individuality in the Eighth Sphere, where you become an Individualized aspect of God – At-One.

This is how the Spheres work: Spheres 3, 5, 7 are Divine Love Spheres, and Spheres 2, 4, 6 are natural love Spheres. Each ascending Sphere is a higher harmonic of the previous one: the Fifth Sphere is a higher harmonic of the Third, and so on. So the Divine Love you receive in the Third Sphere, as beautiful, powerful and readily available as it is, goes to a different level in the next step, the Fifth Sphere.

This can only occur because you have gone through the purifications, refinements and individualizing process of the Fourth Sphere.

It is useful to remember that the first *real* Divine Love Sphere is the Third Sphere, which is when you truly receive Divine Love in some of its majesty on a totally different level than ever before. The feelings of God's Love for you, and your ever-growing love for Him, have managed to sustain and keep you going through the trials and pains of the first two Spheres. Now, it all goes to an entirely different level as you enter this first pure Divine Love Sphere.

Many people newly entering the Second Sphere of speaking truth and trying to be totally honest often have a militant zeal to them, a harshness in their wishing to be 'true.' Truth is loving, and whilst we all make mistakes in our sharing of this, it is always wise to remember that *truth is best received and spoken in a degree of softness*, and in a loving way, as it then allows healing and opening for *both parties* involved to occur.

The Second Sphere soul is not perfect in any way at all, and this soul is not really in a condition to be pointing out errors in others with any degree of clarity, precision or divine authority until he or she is in the Third Sphere and beyond.

Those who try to point things out in others whilst in the Second Sphere maybe in partial error with this pointing.

Such souls are not versed enough in Divine Love and Truth, and are still internally struggling with major wounds and filters which distort one's sense of clear seeing and lead to judgment, misunderstanding, and an error-laden application of 'Divine Truths' to other people's situations *and one's own*.

This is why Christ said: *'Do not try and point out the speck in your brother's eye when you have a log in your own.'*

Your version of 'truth' here is likely to be *projections* filtered through as yet uncleared *'personal truths'* through which you are viewing reality. It is always best to be humble!

You are not in the soul condition to be sharing Divine Truth or Love clearly at this point, so it is best to share 'truth' in an open-ended, curious way with self and others AND be open and humble to the likely possibility that these truths are partial at best and that you cannot see the whole picture.

Be patient, keep growing until you reach the Third Sphere, where your at-One-ment task will be given to you AND manifest, and you will then be clear enough to enact it in Truth, and with great results, *through your passion.*

In the Second Sphere we develop healthy emotional boundaries to form our soul center. Without these boundaries, we cannot fully access our sovereign soul and self-authority. What often blocks these boundaries are distorted ideas about love, duty and service, all of which need to be investigated.

It is in our forming of these loving and healthy emotional boundaries that we may become a bit harsh or militant in our speaking of truth, as we are trying to find our boundaries and our truer sense of self love.

In the Second Sphere, all your passions and desires deserve and need to be put into some form of action by you. This occurs as you actually go out and do it, in which case all the blocks you have to living in this Sphere and manifesting your passions and desires will arise for you to feel and process.

Do not give up! This is part of the journey. Pray to feel all the blocks that are preventing you from living in your passions and desires, AS WELL AS praying for the desire/passion to manifest. Passion is love in action.

Make a list of the priority of the passions and desires in your life. Include everything your soul desires. For example, my passions and desires, in order, are:

1 GOD
2 SOUL MATE (and all the reasons why I wish to be with my soul mate)
3 HELPING OTHERS

4   WRITING/CREATING
5   GOD CENTERED COMMUNITY

The *fullness* of all these passions and desires many not manifest until the Third Sphere or beyond, but the Second Sphere is where they will begin to manifest more clearly with desire and prayer.

Further References and Reading:
The Christ Blueprint, chapters on *'Passion,'* and *'Holy Desire.'*

THE SECOND MANSIONS

Here is where we find the great importance of perseverance, and the 'war'which negative spirits wage against us. *It is essential if we are to attain our goal to put in place good habits and foundations from the beginning.*

In some ways these souls have a harder time than those in the First Mansions; but they are in less peril, for they seem now to understand their position and there is great hope that they will get further into the Castle.

The souls in the First Mansions are dumb and can hear nothing, and so it is not such a trial to them to be unable to speak; *the others, who can hear and not speak, find the trials harder to bear.*

These souls can understand God when He calls them; for as they gradually get nearer to the place where God dwells, He becomes a good Neighbor to them. Our God is so anxious that we should desire Him and strive after His companionship that He calls us ceaselessly, time after time, to approach Him; and His voice is sweet.

His appeals come through talks and teachings, conversations with good people, inner urgings, through the reading of good books; through sicknesses and trials, or by means of truths which God teaches us at times in prayer.

However feeble our prayers may be, God values them highly; *and there are many other ways in which God calls us.* God is quite prepared to wait for us for many days and years, especially when He sees we are persevering and have good desires. This is the most necessary thing here; if we have this we cannot fail to gain greatly.

The assault which negative spirits now make upon the soul, in all kinds of ways, is more focused; and the soul suffers more than in the preceding Mansion, for before it was deaf and dumb, and offered less resistance, like one who to a great extent has lost hope of gaining the victory. Here, the understanding is keener and the faculties are more alert.

Negative spirits pretend that earthly pleasures are eternal: *they remind the soul of the esteem in which it is held in the world, of its friends and relatives*, of the way in which its health will be endangered by cleanses and penances (which the soul always wants to do when it enters this Mansion) and of a thousand other impediments.

What confusion these spirits bring about in the poor soul, and how distressed it is, not knowing if it ought to proceed further or return to the room where it was before!

On the other hand, Reason tells the soul how mistaken it is in thinking that all these earthly things are of the slightest value by comparison with what it is seeking, and faith instructs it in what it must do to find satisfaction. Memory shows it how all these things come to an end, and reminds us that those who have derived so much enjoyment from these things have died.

Your will inclines to love One in Whom it has seen so many acts and signs of love, some of which it would like to return. *In particular, the will shows the soul how this true Lover never leaves it, but goes with it everywhere and gives it life and being.* Then the understanding comes forward and makes the soul realize that, for however many years it may live, it can *never hope to have a better friend*, for the world is full of falsehood and these pleasures are accompanied by trials, cares and annoyances; and it tells the soul to be certain that outside this castle it will find neither security nor peace.

So dead is our faith that we desire what we see more than what faith tells us about, although what we actually see is that people who pursue these visible things meet with nothing but ill fortune. All this is the work of these negative spirits.

The soul will certainly suffer trials at this time, especially if these spirits see that its character and habits are such that it is ready to make further progress: all the powers of hell will combine to drive it back again. It is here that we have need of God's aid, without which we can do nothing.

Of Thy mercy, allow not this soul to be deluded and led astray when its journey is but begun. Give me light so I may see how all my welfare consists in this, and so I may flee from evil companionship.

Have a fixed determination not to allow yourself to be beaten, for if these negative spirits see that you have firmly resolved to lose your life, peace and everything else you have rather than return to the First Mansion, they will soon cease troubling you. Place your trust in the mercy of God, and you will see how He can lead you on from one group of Mansions to another, and set you on safe ground where these beasts cannot harass or hurt you.

It is a great thing here for you to *associate with others who are walking in the right way*: to mix not only with those whom one sees in the rooms (Sphere) where one is, but with those whom you know have entered rooms nearer the Center, for they will be of great help to you, and can help take you with them. Consult people of experience; for otherwise you will imagine that you are doing yourselves harm by pursuing your necessary occupations.

But, providing we do not abandon our prayer, God will turn

everything we do to our profit, even though we may find no one to teach us. *It is absurd to think that we can enter Heaven without first entering our own souls: without getting to know ourselves.*

All that you, the beginner in prayer, have to do is to be resolute and with all possible diligence *bring your will (personal truths) into conformity with the will of God (Divine Truths and Laws).* The more you do this, the more you can receive God in your desire for Divine Love, and the greater the progress you will make.

Often it is God's Will that we should be persecuted and afflicted by evil thoughts, which we cannot cast out, and also by aridities; sometimes He even allows 'reptiles' to bite us, so that we may learn better how to be on our guard in the future and see if we are really grieved at having broken Divine Laws. If you sometimes fail, do not lose heart, or cease striving to make progress, for even out of your fall God will bring good, just as a man selling an antidote will drink poison before he takes it in order to prove its power.

If nothing else shows us what harm we do to ourselves by dissipating our desires, this war, which goes on within us, does, and can lead us back to recollection. *Can any evil be greater than the evil which we find in our own house?* Unless we have peace, and strive for peace in our own home, we shall not find it in the homes of others.

Let this war now cease.

THE SECOND DEATH: LIVING IN DIVINE LAWS

'They fretted over him and troubled him with their fears and projections. They made him the concern, the problem and the focus ... They interfered with every aspect of his life. They gave him no space to grow into his own man. They robbed him of space and time. They misunderstood his every gesture and utterance. They magnified his silence. They distorted his stillness. They suspected his prayers. They saw sinister aspects to his innocence.'[41]

The definite, clear and consistent choice by your soul to live passionately by Divine Laws, totally desiring Divine Truth in your life, seeking and receiving Divine Love with all of your soul, triggers a chain reaction.

A battle for the soul commences, a battle on one hand between the forces generated by the matrix of the wounds within you (reflected and amplified by negative spirits and people around you fearful of your progress), and the loving desires of your soul allying with God and positive spirit guides.

This is a battle that plays out on many fronts, reflected in your relationships and the resistance to change that assaults you on every front from other people and spirits, testing your desire and your new-found choices. Once you choose God, feeling His Love and Laws, feeling how much you are loved, and what profound healing can happen through receiving Divine Love, then: the game begins.

For many this can be a dramatic battle. For others, less so. It depends on how much time, energy and investment you have put into the idea that others (the government, society, friends, lovers and past needs from your parents) and the world can make you happy and fulfill you.

The extent of this lies in your emotional needs around how much you value these things, and the wounds you have covered by giving your love and power away to these temporary things that will never fulfill your soul.

Your identification with this world, and the people and things of it, determine the extent and strength of this battle. If you are already focused enough because of your love for your own soul and God, the world cannot hold much sway over you.

If you are invested in the fear-based decisions and choices around what love, approval and recognition you can get from the dream of this world, then it will be painful, and you will be assaulted by the forces of your separated self all arising at once.[42]

This mirror will raise its head to reflect to you what you are hiding, what you are not being truthful or honest about, until you are strong enough, desirous enough and humble enough *to put Divine Love and Laws above and beyond everything and anything else.* And this is the second death: following these Divine Laws no matter what, not knowing the outcome, venturing into the Great Unknown, the hero's journey, knowing that God will be there for you.

Following these laws means the end of the domination of fear in your life, and there will be a definite occasion where your soul will feel this occur. It does not mean you will not feel fear *now and again*; it just means that the domination of it is now gone, and you feel free to fully follow your passions and desires for your own soul's growth into Divine Truth and love, and are quickly able to feel and see the effects of them bloom and manifest in your life.

The Primary Divine Laws here are deep humility, burning desire, self love, dedication and commitment; bravery to follow the call of your soul, and clear and consistent choices to live like this.

One starts to engage in hourly prayer (it only takes seconds to pray deeply and receive Divine Love once one is connected) and Divine Love becomes the priority; human love and need becomes secondary. Your needs and substitutes for Divine Love are seen, and piece by piece, let go of.

An inner strength you never knew existed arises within you, allied with a deep sobriety and quietness. Your values change and shift rapidly, and the sloughing off of more old skin occurs. You honor this dying part of you and cherish its passing more, as it means more Divine Love is coming to your soul.

This is a sobering experience, a deepening examination in profound self-honesty and reflection of the causes and negative feelings dominating your life.

You become more self-reflective and inward looking, and your path becomes less and less about the outer world and people. It is all about you and your soul, and developing and strengthening the bond of mutual love between you and your Creator. The external reference points become less and less as you get to know your soul more and more intimately; a deeper love affair with the soul happens as the gateway to God.

You begin to realize that love is not just. True faith begins to arise based on your deepening experiences and glimpses of Divine Love and reality. You begin to give your all, no matter what the cost. The choice to love Love and desire more of it becomes stronger than the love of fear that had previously dominated your life, and in fact anything else.

This Death includes the Abraham initiation. As the legend goes,

Abraham, upon the request of God, took his beloved son Isaac to the top of a mountain to sacrifice him. He totally trusted God and his Divine Love so fully that he was willing to give up his son for Him, going against all physical and moral laws to satisfy the Divine law uttered by His Father.

At the top of the mountain, at the moment of the beheading, God appeared, and blessed Abraham, saying, 'In you, I Am well pleased.'

This is an initiation that all those on the Divine Love Path *have to undergo*: to be prepared to sacrifice what they love most dearly to come closer to God. There is no shortcut around this, or way to avoid it: it has to be done if you are serious about your At-One-ment with God. All has to be given in faith and total trust for Divine Love to pour into you at an ever-increasing rate.

Of course, this does not mean you have to behead anyone! On the contrary, it is about beheading yourself, cutting off your own head/ego so love can flow in with fewer impediments. *It is only I, myself, that stops At-One-ment with God from happening.* It is only I that is the impediment.

Abraham was in total trust and faith, which is the opposite of betrayal. He did not betray his Divine relationship or Divine laws. He placed that first and foremost, for the Divine relationship was the One Relationship *he could not do without.*

The highest form of betrayal is the betrayal of your soul to not betray another. So you think, '*That person needs my love, but I don't feel it is true to do so, but I will do it anyway because I am meant to, because that is what I think love is.*'

Feeling obliged is a form of conditioning which actually erodes your self-love, generates resentment and anger within the soul and prevents true vulnerability, as you do not feel free to express your true emotions because you are caught in a web of trying to please others. Even if you are not pleasing others, you can be doing this *inside yourself.*

We all have to 'give away' the temporary things and people of this world in order for the eternal. As Yeshua said, *'Those who love their mothers, fathers, daughters and sons more than Me are not worthy of Me.'* All these things, people, relationships, everything will only last thirty, forty years and you are potentially infinite and eternal. This is an initiation of love as you do it FOR Divine Love, and pain may arise because of your previous errors against love, OR you may just feel Divine Love and freedom in this choice.

This is why some people have a problem with God, because circumstances may occur that bring pain, but the lesson that comes with the pain is the balm to evolve the soul. Similarly, when they receive Divine Love their wounds and pains arise; so they think God is wrathful and to be feared, they think it is God's fault, that God is nasty, that God has abandoned them, that *'God doesn't love me.'*

And then, certain forms of religion and new age spirituality are born as a result and reaction against this. *'I don't want to feel the pain held in my soul. Let's create a reality without God.'* But this reality is based on the avoidance of pain, which means the avoidance of the pathway that will lead you to more love! *So in trying to avoid pain, we are creating more pain for ourselves.*

People complain about why bad things happen to good people. It is these 'bad things' that create the fuel in the furnace of your soul so that alchemy can occur. Suffering becomes the fuel for love and its lessons to work within you in a near infinite variety of contexts.

Willingly test yourself, for the only way to know if a real embrace and therefore transcendence of fear has occurred is in the same conditions that triggered it in the first place. This means you willingly choose to go into the same place, person, situation, event, and part of your own soul that brought up the fear, anger, pain, grief and reaction within you before. *See what happens as you go there NOW.*

We all have these places, persons, situations, events, and parts of our own soul that still lurk in us. Can you trace what this is for you, where you fear to tread and with whom?

Willingly do this so you know you are free of it, and this too is joy. There are few things better than knowing you have conquered your darkness and to then celebrate it by re-entering the same situation with no charge or reaction, in love. More peace arises from this. And this is fulfilling.

Choosing Divine Truth and God means things will change, fast. The reflected resistance all around you and within you is what you have created to see your own separated self, to feel it, and to release it. God is not wrathful; He is infinitely loving, giving you all that you need to heal and come into more Love.

God does not punish you; you have been doing that very well already. The sooner you see it, and choose to apply your burning desire for God into all aspects of your life, the sooner you can access the beauty, joy, bliss, wonder and awe of Divine Love.

In the First Sphere, willpower and motivation is important to keep moving through the inertia and the heaviness with discipline and dedication, to move into the pain of the wounds you have resisted feeling for many years; consciously, purposefully investigate and be brave enough, be vulnerable enough, be raw enough, be weak enough to move through the walls of denial, feeling and staying with the naked emotions that arise.

At some point in the journey through the Second Sphere, personal will, drive and motivation dissolves more, and the heart takes over in more softness and surrender. *The 'will' to push* forward breaks, cracks and collapses more into the heart.

This is when more Divine Love can enter into you, and you, as you know yourself to be as defined by the will, become more broken, powerless and turned towards the softness of the heart and to God.

You can no longer force yourself onwards with the mind and will, and from this point on, more of your soul can manifest and dissolve into an unknowingness, into being more present, taking it one day at a time, breathing, praying and trusting in love's truth more and more.

Traveling through the Second Sphere breaks many structures that have served you to arrive here. Structures in the mind, in the intellect, daily habits, practices, ways of perceiving and experiencing.

It feels like chaos, as control and former references are lost, but in reality it is more of a Divinely orchestrated chaos necessary for an (eventually) impeccably conducted re-ordering of many things in the soul to move closer into Divine Love. An internal chaos breaks one down in order to break through, causing one to lose many former reference points, both internal and external.

One may struggle and try to go back to some vaguely familiar old ways; instead, surrender more into an unknown, new, fresh way of being, doing and moving. It can be the most fun and the most challenging time, all rolled into one continuous, seamless movement.

There is still free will and dedication to be employed, but it is now in the reverse of the First Sphere, where the will took more prominence to direct and guide. Now, the feeling heart leads you through allowing, flowing into naked feelings; this cannot be forced, simply allowed to arise. The heart does not work through will, but allowance.

The intellect ties people in knots and risks nothing; love is a shameless fool and risks everything, again and again. Mind does not easily break down; love reduces itself to rubble. But treasures are hidden amongst ruins. A broken heart hides treasures.[43]

In the second death, you truly take the big steps into humility and deep burning desire. This is when these qualities start to drive your life forward and *you truly begin to recognize and embrace all your own self-creations*. To desire God completely is death to your egoic self, really letting go, completely losing all control. This is why it is called *The Passion* because love has no shame. All these deaths are different openings to the total passion for God.

God is always loving us. Once you start to apply Divine Laws you come to feel more of the incomprehensible vastness of Divine Truth and Love and how it is operating all the time. The more you prioritize God, the more God will come to you. The more you desire Divine Love in practical action by following Divine Truths, the more Divine Love will come to you.

THE MATRIX

The Matrix is what we come to clearly feel and see as we move through the Second Sphere, and in this clear feeling and recognition, we can more clearly leave it. The Matrix is a system based on the constructs of a finite, separated self. As it is finite, it can be worked out, but only when one is outside its constructs, seeing from more of a 'God's Eye' view.

The Matrix is constriction: the underlying source of all human suffering. Constricting life in yourself or others, walking away from Divine Love, what we most yearn for, creates immense tension and pressure on your individual soul *and* on the entire human race and collective.

It is not enough to heal your own wounds: one has to travel into the collective causal wounds *as well*, which are all living inside you. It is a collective grief and wound we all carry, and by embracing the collective through you these wounds are healed within you also. The deeper the causal wounds are held captive inside you, the more your higher faculties shut down. The wounds are the deepest triggers on the planet into Divine Love and healing.

The wounds were created because we have chosen to not follow Divine laws, and in not following them penalties are involved. In one sense we have been creating our own laws and ways of doing things that work for us in navigating the artificial reality we have constructed around the separation from Divine Love.

We do as we please, ignoring Divine laws, separating ourselves from the greatest love a human can ever know. And that is fine. Until it is no longer fine, and you want to return home.

There is a part of you caught in the matrix of your own perceptions, built upon the false information and veiled feelings of your soul wounds. You have created your own version of this matrix, and because you have forgotten that you have created it, you became lost in it.

You have created your own kingdom separate from Divine Love, and live by its rules, thinking you are free. You have forgotten the laws governing the matrix upon which your smaller matrix is built. Now you can remember it and see, in total clarity, *how your life actually is*, rather than what you hope or intend it to be.

The Matrix is finite and the end date of it is when you become Soul-Realized in Original Innocence once again. That is when it ends for you, and that is all a soul has to do. That is the reason you are here. You are not here for any other reason. There is no other purpose to life. The 'end of the world' is the end of your world of separation from God.

The map below is important because it contains the principles behind your stories and the healings that can come. It is a pathway of the sacred wounds of the soul, a map of the matrix and our journey away from God, AND what was created in this journey. If you were to really look at your life through this lens, you would see that everything in your life would be in here – the emotional urges behind all your actions. Maybe you would like to have a look at your life through the lens of this map, and see how you are creating your own laws in your life right now, rather than following Divine Laws.

THE MAP

The Mask or False Self – The Façade

Anger, pride, defensiveness, constriction, confusion, humili-
ation, doubt, shame, unworthiness, resentment, rage, guilt,
neediness, self-punishment, punishment of others, wanting to
give up, blame of self, blame of others, excessive thinking and
other surface thoughts and emotions mask our fears, which we
try to cover over with our

Substitutes, addictions and needs, which mask our

Fears, denials and unwillingness to be vulnerable and feel
PAIN

(Avoiding Pain is the bane of the human condition)

Which mask our trust in God and our courage and weakness to
feel and be soft and vulnerable to feelings.

*Submit to being weak, humble and vulnerable. Submit to the real
feelings – surrender to them.*

Our greatest fears are being
POWERLESS and OUT OF CONTROL, which in turn mask our
CAUSAL WOUNDS of
GRIEF-RELATED DEEP EMOTIONS
OF FELT
SEPARATION
from
OUR PURE SOUL
and
GOD

WE GO FURTHER AWAY FROM DIVINE LOVE AND TRUTH BY AVOIDING OUR FEARS AND CAUSAL EMOTIONS; BY GOING INTO THEM AND ASKING FOR DIVINE LOVE, WE GET CLOSER TO GOD AND RECEIVE MORE DIVINE LOVE

So how it starts for us is through the façade or mask of surface emotions. We have these emotions every single day. Every single day we have clues as to what is going on in our souls, underneath the surface emotions and triggers, which are little ATTENTION! signs from our souls asking us to stop, feel and inquire as to what is really going on emotionally. Every single day, our soul is trying to speak to us, to inform us of what is REALLY happening.

Deep in your pain is love, a love so sublime, so full of gratitude and reverence that it deserves its guardianship. Only the brave, humble, deeply desirous and loving can enter these realms and walk through them, to emerge hand in hand with God, Who is ever smiling on all our weaknesses, ever caring, ever patient, ever desiring you to return to the greatest love a soul can ever know and desire.

THE THIRD SPHERE OF DIVINE LOVE

LOYALTY, SURRENDER TO DIVINE TRUTH
SILENT SOUL 'MIND' UNFOLDS: MENTALITY DISSIPATES
MORE
'HARD' WORK ENDS – RAPID PROGRESSION STARTS
DIVINE LOVE EVER AVAILABLE IN INCREASING
QUANTITIES
SERVICE TO GOD COMMENCES WITH DIVINE AUTHORITY
IN TRUTH

'Each of us possesses a soul, but we do not prize our souls as creatures made in God's image deserve, and so we do not understand the great secrets which they contain.'[44]

The shift from the Second Sphere to the Third Sphere is more marked then the previous shift from the First Sphere into the Second. The Third Sphere is like entering a totally different world to the previous two Spheres. Everything changes. You have much more access to the overwhelming nature, beauty and glory of Divine Love when you pray.

It is here that you realize the glory of God and literally wish to sing of your wonder and an incomprehensible amazement at the perfection of God's Love for you and all beings. Gratitude for God arises from much purer places in your soul, which now come into recognition-feeling more and more.

Divine Love and God's Blessings are with you much more as a deeply felt reality in your soul. Those on a natural love, medita-tional, energetic, moral, self-help path will not experience this, and will spend little time, if any, in this Sphere.

The pain and intensity of feeling and clearing negative emotions, the really 'hard' work of clearing your deep personal wounds, errors and history, ends somewhere in the Third Sphere.

This does not mean you do not feel, or still have, personal emotions to release or clear; you still do, it just means you feel them quicker and move through them faster.

The Third Sphere is an express train as opposed to the bicycle of the First Sphere, and the car of the Second Sphere. Everything from the Second Sphere, everything you have learned and experienced about the basics of Truth deepens in its rapidity of application.

In the previous two Spheres, we are farming and tilling the land of our soul, digging in the dirt to plant our seeds, the seeds of Truth and Love, sowing and tending the pasture, doing the hard labor so as to prepare the land and the harvest that will come from the land. The Third Sphere is where you get to enjoy the first harvest of these labors; you pick and eat the first fruits, courtesy of God, and enjoy them immensely.

Souls in the last stages of the Second Sphere understand they have to fulfill some work in helping others. This is an '*At-One-ment task*,' because it is a Work they have to carry out to make up for their errors, to repay the help that they themselves have received, and which they continue receiving from God, Higher Spirits and their own guides.

Before this, you are more concerned with yourself as there are many wounds and errors to feel and release, as well as learning the basics of the Divine Love and Truth Path and putting it into practice within yourself, and with others in all aspects of your daily life.

Third Sphere souls are fully qualified to help others of the lower Spheres and do so enthusiastically and constantly, and they acquire divinely orientated tools to offer help efficiently and purely. They advance in the purification of their natural love, and obtain more of the Divine Love, which is now available as if on a celestial tap: ask and you shall receive.

This is when the real fruit of your healing begins to manifest, as you taste and begin to embody more Divine Love and Truth. This makes the journey so far *all worthwhile*.

'To really serve with all one's heart and soul is to do it only for God's sake. It is not real service or worship if it is for the sake of others' wishes or desires.'[45]

The new event that occurs in the Third Sphere is that the principles and revealed understandings of the soul regarding Divine Truth and Divine Love become much clearer and directly received, as your soul is now more purified in its love and can serve a greater and more harmonious purpose.

Dedicated willingness and openness to totally follow Divine Love, Divine Laws, and whatever arises from these feelings are received with a lot of clarity and constantly so, many times a day. We hear the Will of God more clearly and desire to share it clearly, softly and humbly. Because of their greater spiritual development, these souls can now also perceive Divine Truths more clearly.

The soul here is much more mature, and has learned a degree of true surrender. Life feels new and inspiring. The substance of the soul starts a degree of transformation into the Divine. All is well! Yet, the trap here is that one can stay in this degree of Love and beauty and not keep progressing.

Third Sphere souls are dedicated to rectifying all the mistakes of their lives on Earth, and with their more serious errors will guide others along better paths than they themselves have chosen. This may also be a work of 'unlearning' or of 'unteaching' falsehoods that they have shared, in order to undo much of what they have done consciously, or unconsciously, on Earth.

Souls in the Third Sphere will leave their previous healing and teaching vocations in order to solely concentrate on living and sharing Divine Truths and love only.

The souls who have obtained a certain quantity of Divine Love are devoted to their work, and many of them stay for a long time in this Sphere, because they feel the importance of their work as a *labor of love*, and of teaching this 'new' Truth. To them the work may be more difficult, because what they teach is new to many, and therefore they face greater resistance and rejection than those on natural love or self-help/meditational paths.

The Third Sphere is an area where souls progress in their pure soul awareness, where dissolving errors becomes a vocational task, which they perform with enthusiasm and fervor. When they have arrived at this deeper soul awareness, the moment has come for them to advance further, and the doors of the Fourth Sphere open up.

Happiness in the Third Sphere is not perfect, but as you advance, the works you do give you more joy and realization to teach what is correct. There are few better sights than seeing one you have supported transform in this way in front of your eyes.

This is a Way of Love, of devotion, of gratitude. It is not 'work' as it is love in action arising from an inner urging, a spontaneous and joyful sharing. This becomes something you are doing all the time; there is no time for 'teaching' and 'not teaching' – it is simply love and truth being shared all the time because that is what Is.

For Divine Love souls the Third Sphere is a *special experience*, for you have obtained a small portion of Divine Love within your soul. It is here, for the first time, that you can 'live' this Love, where you become more of a living example of God's Will in love, the wisdom of truth, giving and compassion.

'Let your light so shine before men, that they may see your good works, and glorify your Father who art in Heaven.'
Matthew 5

When one is in the Third Sphere, Divine Love and Light start to flow through you to others, shining through your eyes, your words, your auric field, your physical body, your sexual energy, and your spontaneous actions. Your good works begin here in your *At-One-ment task*, the task that God has given you for you to Realize your At-One-ment with Him, and to repay all the generous help He has afforded you to bring you to this position.

There may be different At-One-ment tasks as you move through the Spheres. For example, the one you have in the Third Sphere may change as you move through the Fourth Sphere into the Fifth, and so on. You may have several tasks, for as your soul progresses, you are given more and more to do as you have more and more capacity. The First At-One-ment task is only given in the Third Sphere, and is designed to be *solely* for glorifying God and bringing other souls closer to God in a direct way.

TRUST

'What is the bridal chamber, if not the place of trust and consciousness in the embrace? It is an icon of Union, beyond all forms of possession; here is where the veil is torn from top to bottom; here is where some arise and awaken.'
Gospel of Philip

The deepest level of trust comes when you fully trust your pure, sovereign soul, pure as God created it to be. This trust marries with total faith in God in every aspect and department of life. There is only one other human being whom you can fully trust in the depths of your soul, who will fully know you, feel you and be able to commune with you on all levels: your twin soul.

Engaging with him or her in these depths of trust and love requires a journey over time, and there will be times when you do not meet, but there is a basis, a fundamental meeting in love, that is present during the healing process.

Close to this form of trust can be a spiritual guide who is with you over time and whom you can trust, as you feel and know he or she has the best interests of your soul close to their heart, and consistently shows this to you through their actions and advice to you over time, which always helps you.

The spiritual teacher who shows their love for their student in this way over time earns this trust and respect, and the teacher will in turn keep guiding the student to their own pure, sovereign soul and God as part of this teaching. The credit is never the teacher's: it is all given to God by a truly trustworthy teacher.

So, the ultimate forms of trust are trust in your pure soul, God and existence itself, your Twin Soul, and your spiritual teacher.

'A teacher cannot give you the truth. The truth is already in you. You only need to open yourself, body, mind and heart – so that his or her teachings will penetrate your own seeds of understanding. If you let the words enter you, the soil and the seeds will do the rest of the work.'
Thich Nhat Hanh

The next level of trust lies with close friends, blood family, and those on the same spiritual path as you who share the same values, and have earned your trust and respect through their actions and words, their reliability, their steadfastness and their loyalty and love for you, demonstrated over time.

This loyalty is to love, not to your ego or wounded self, and this may provoke conflicts, but this conflict is borne out of their concern for your true self, and vice versa. True friendship will always involve honesty and truth, not collusion and avoiding wounds, or supporting another's wounds with falseness and your own agendas with that person.

The first level of trust is the general trust we have in people, life, acquaintances, colleagues and everyday living. We trust everyone to some little degree upon meeting them, and we trust life, unless we are deeply in fear. Almost everyone has this basic trust, and some sense of self love that radiates outwards to connect into everyday relations.

SHAKTI

The Third Sphere is the deepening merging of Shakti, Kundalini energies coming from the root chakra and the Divine Love of the Father, coming down from the crown. Both meet in the heart. This Unity is Life Force and Divine Love becoming One infinity loop, joy, life, Divine Love and gratitude in bliss, softness and power. Sex, soul, prayer and God become one seamless flow, enjoyed in all its aspects.

The arising through the chakras of life force becomes sublimated in love and bliss, in prayer, as it arises; this empties out the body/mind/soul of its previous urges and needs as it happens.

In the descending of pure Living Light and Divine Love through the crown in the act of making love, one becomes clear in the divine blueprint of how humans have been created to make love, which is truly only with one's own twin flame. Both flows of energy help the other to become clear.

For example, certain soul-emotional blocks are best released through loving sexual intimacy, dance or by moving Shakti through the soul; but this will not touch deeper emotional hurts, which only Divine Love from Our Father can. And vice versa.

Divine Love from the Father will heal deep soul wounds, yet it is Shakti that can move and touch certain other soul-emotional blocks. And this is all perfect, and how it is has been created to Be in this divine synergy and Union. And of course, one can receive Divine Love from both Mother and Father God as well.

In the Third Sphere one leaves all conventional, popular and alternative forms of sexual expression in order for purity of soul to express and manifest. Sexuality begins to be transformed into a transcendental form of sexual electricity, beyond the electro (male) magnetic (female) spectrum. Sexuality becomes more light, a play of innocence and pleasure that only truly becomes whole between twin flames.

It becomes a much deeper healing power for more Divine Love to flow into self and other for the growth of the soul and the revealing of the pure soul. Prayer to God in love-making becomes the norm, and the act itself becomes still, slow, refined and more of a movement of love rather than sexual action.

To do this, sexual healing has to have happened beforehand, and this healing only happens through love. This transformation accelerates in the Fourth Sphere when a separation occurs between human and sensual love, and the Divine Love.

The Third Sphere is far from perfection, but it is the next step in the Divine Love progression. Within it Truth and error co-exist, but harmful errors have been eradicated. In other words, you still make errors, but without anger, fear and pain, without harming self or others, and these errors are caught and rectified when you do them.

The desire to go to God is the prime force in your life and you will do anything to get there, all the time, and in every arena of your existence. You will gladly be a fool for this love if it means you get one step closer to Him.

At the latter stages of the Third Sphere, entering the doors of the Fourth Sphere, room for error decreases: the path becomes narrower, and you gladly choose this for it is what you desire.

All aspects of your path become more refined than ever before on a deeply felt emotional level, and the slightest error against

Divine Love and Truth becomes hugely magnified within you, and accepted in humility. Growth increases exponentially with this, and one becomes much softer, more loving.

'I wonder what these people know about this Way of Love of God, what? He is God who has created the heavens and the earth, and He has made the universe come into existence. They think that His love is easy, as if they were just talking with Him or just listening to Him. Is this some kind of tutmach sauce, that you would just take it, and slurp it up?'
Shams of Tabriz

THE THIRD MANSIONS

To those who by the mercy of God have *overcome the combats of the Second Mansions*, and by perseverance have entered the Third Mansions, we shall certainly be right in calling such a human blessed, for, unless he turns back, he is on the straight road to salvation.

Here lies the importance of having overcome your past battles; for God never fails to give a person who does this a security of conscience, which is no small blessing.

Do not be too sure of yourselves. Nor must you set importance by the fact that you are always talking about God, continually engaging in prayer, withdrawing yourselves completely from the things of this world. All that is good, but it is not enough. We all say we desire God; but if God is to take complete possession of the soul, more is necessary.

These souls know that nothing would induce them to commit a sin; and they consider themselves God's servants. Yet even on Earth a king may have many servants and they do not all get so far as to enter his chamber. Enter within yourselves and get away from your own trifling good works, for these you are bound to perform, and, indeed, many more. It will be enough for you that you are servants of God; do not try to get so much that you achieve nothing.

Oh, humility, humility! Whenever people make so much of their times of dryness and aridity, I cannot help thinking they are somewhat lacking in it. I am not, of course, referring to the great interior trials, for they amount to much more than a lack of devotion. Allow the Lord to test us; for He knows well how to do it, although often we refuse to understand Him.

When He tells us what we must do in order to be perfect, we turn our backs upon Him and go away sorrowfully; what do you expect God to do? For the reward that He is to give us must of necessity be proportionate with the love that we give Him.

And this love must not be wrought in our imagination but must be proved by works. Yet do not suppose God has any need of our works; what He needs is the resoluteness of our will.

It may seem to us that we have done everything: left all the things of the world and all that we had for His sake, yet He esteems a person *who gives all that he has as one who gives in fullest measure.* This is a good beginning; and, if we persevere in it, instead of going back, even if only in desire, to consort with the reptiles in the first rooms, there is no doubt that by persevering in this detachment and abandonment of everything, we shall attain our object.

What can we do for so generous a God, Who created us and gives us being, without counting ourselves fortunate in being able to repay Him something of what we owe Him for the way He has served us, without asking Him once more for gifts and favors?

The periods of aridity teach you to be humble, and should not make you restless, which is the aim of negative spirits. Be sure that where there is true humility, even if God never grants the soul favors, He will give it peace and resignation to His Will, with which it may be more content than others are with favors.

For often it is to the weakest that God gives favors, which they would not exchange for all the fortitude given to those who go forward in aridity. *We are fonder of spiritual sweetness than of crosses. Test us, O Lord, Thou Who knows all Truth, so we may know ourselves.*

I have known many people who have for many years lived upright and carefully ordered lives, both in soul and in body; and then, after all those years, when it has seemed as if they must have gained mastery over the world, or at least must be completely detached from it, God has sent them tests which have been by no means exacting and they have become restless and depressed in spirit, never really understanding that *it is all due to their own imperfections.* And in persons who have made so much progress, this is a further mistake.

Often it is *God's will that His elect should be conscious of their misery and so He withdraws His help from them – and no more than that is needed to make us recognize our limitations very quickly.* They then realize that this is a way of testing them, for they gain a clear perception of their shortcomings, and sometimes they derive more pain from finding that, in spite of themselves, they are still grieving about earthly things, and not very important things either. This is a great mercy on the part of God, and even though they are at fault, they gain a great deal in humility.

It is much the same thing if such people are despised in any way or lose some of their reputation. God often grants them grace to bear this well, for He loves to help people be virtuous in the presence of others, so that the virtue itself which they possess may not be thought less of, or perhaps He will help them because they have served Him.

And yet they become restless, for they cannot do as they would like to and control their feelings all at once. They would like everyone else to live as well ordered a life as they do themselves; they may believe the trouble they have is somebody else's fault and represent it to themselves as meritorious.

From these you will find out if you are really detached from the things you have abandoned, for trifling incidents arise which give you the opportunity to test yourselves and discover if you have obtained mastery.

Do you think if we could get from one country to another in a week, it would be advisable, with all the winds, snow, floods and bad roads, to take a year over it? Would it not be better to get the journey over and done with? For there are all these obstacles for us to meet and there is also the danger of serpents (negative spirits). The journey demands great humility, and it is the lack of this which prevents us from making progress.

He always gives us much by granting us a spiritual sweetness much greater than we can obtain from the pleasures and distractions of this life. But He gives not many consolations, except when He occasionally invites us to see what is happening in the remaining Mansions, so that we may prepare to enter them.

You will think that spiritual sweetness and consolations are one and the same thing: why, then, this difference of name? This latter is a great solace to souls whom God has brought so far, while it will make those who think they have everything feel ashamed; and if they are humble they will be moved to give thanks.

Should they fail to experience it, they will feel an inward discouragement, quite unnecessarily, however, *for perfection consists not in consolations, but in the increase of love*; on this, too, will depend our reward, as well as on the truth which is in our actions.

Realize what pleasures and what delights we lose through our own fault. All the more so because, if they come from God, they come laden with love and fortitude, by the help of which a soul can progress with less labor and at the same time grow continually in good works and virtues.

Do not suppose that it matters little whether or not we do what we can to obtain them. *But if the fault is not yours, the Lord is just, and what His Majesty denies you in this way He will give you in other ways.* His secrets are hidden deep; but all that He does will be best for you, without the slightest doubt.

What would be of the greatest profit to those of us who, by the goodness of the Lord, are in this state? For He shows them no little mercy in bringing them to it, for, when here, they are on the point of rising still higher.

It would be a great thing for them to have someone to whom they could go *so that they might not be following their own will in anything,* for it is in this way that we usually do ourselves harm. They should not look for anyone cast in the same mold as themselves and select a man who is completely disillusioned with the things of the world.

It is a great advantage for us to be able to consult someone who knows us, so that we may learn to know ourselves. And it is a great encouragement to see that things that we thought impossible are possible for others, and how easily these others do them.

It makes us feel that we may emulate their flights and venture to fly ourselves, as young birds do when their parents teach them; they are not yet ready for great flights but they gradually learn to imitate their parents. This is a great advantage.

However determined such persons may be, they are so near the first Mansions that they might easily return to them, since their fortitude is not built upon solid ground. They are familiar with the storms of the world, and realize how little need there is to fear them or to desire worldly pleasures.

If they had to suffer great persecutions, they might well return to such pleasures and negative spirits well know how to contrive such persecutions in order to do us harm; they might be pressing onward with great zeal, and trying to preserve others from sin, and yet be unable to resist any temptations which came to them.

Let us look at our own shortcomings and leave other people's alone; for those who live ordered lives are apt to be shocked at everything and *we might well learn important lessons from the persons who shock us.* Even with the desires that God gives us to help others, we may make many mistakes. If, when we ask this of God, we do not become negligent ourselves, we shall be able, with His help, to be of great profit to others on the spiritual path.

THE THIRD DEATH: DEPENDING ON GOD

The Third Death of our insistence and reliance on our mind for existence, away from God, can be devastating. It is only through breakdown that one can break through, out of false comfort zones of any kind.

This Death is when you are rendered totally powerless in your realization *'that of myself I can do nothing,'* and the separate self breaks and implodes to a greater degree. Your soul realizes that God is its only desire, and most other human needs and substitutes for love drop away. (See *Original Innocence* book.)

In this process, you lose, let go of, are stripped of, surrender and abandon all strategies, coping mechanisms, feel-good platitudes, affirmations, mantras, ideas, beliefs, buddhas, gods, healing techniques, energy systems, learning methodologies and crutches.

You realize you cannot heal yourself any further without total reliance on God, Who can do all things. There is nothing you can do any more to evolve. You have stopped. Where and what to do?

You are no longer reliant on your separate self, and any of the ways you used to do things; any ways to strategize, control or maintain any kind of grip on your reality, dissolve. And something pure and humble, able to receive more Divine Love, arises. This then allows the establishing of a direct, personal relationship between your soul and God's Soul. This takes the form of what can be best visualized as an infinity loop, looping between your heart-soul and God's Heart-Soul; you become related to the infinite Soul of God through your heart, consciously.

Part of you begins to identify with the infinite in a small yet felt way through your heart. Part of your soul changes forever, as you *remember the image you were made in* on a soulful, cellular and inexplicable way, and you feel this Remembrance in the *substance* of your soul. Once you know, you can never go back. God, through the Holy Spirit and associated Divine Love Guides, Becomes your True Teacher from this point forward.

In this death, you, as control freak, are no more. The breakdown into powerlessness and dependence on God allows the deepest healings through Divine Love to now occur in you, through you, and for those around you. It is from here that more direct communications from Divine Love Spirits are revealed through your more purified human soul, which is remembering more of its essential nature.

Yet this is only the third death. Greater Divine Love and healing await. All healing completes its cycle in the Union with God, where the ultimate truths and love lie. Until we are in Union, we still need healing, no matter where we are.

Dependence on God is not a cage but a great freedom. It relieves the soul, allows the soul to drop much of its burden, its struggles, its conflicts and stress caused by its incessant battle against the innate natural order and harmony of the cosmos. It is a great release into ever-deeper peace, into an emptier mind and inner tuning to the ever-present currents of Divine presence.

To be a master within your own cage with your own truths, or a humble servant receiving Divine Love in the infinite expanse of Divine Truth? The truth, to the separate self, is always in reverse. You cannot trust yourself, yourself being your own conditioned thinking, false wisdom borne from your wounds, and desires governed and informed by fear, the matrix and others. You can trust the

Divine Laws, which often work in opposite to your laws or personal truths, and the laws of the world and its peoples.

Follow worldly laws, and worldly you will become.
Follow divine laws, and divine you will become.[46]

As you become dependent on Divine Laws every day, through the vigilance of the purified soul, more and more humility dawns. Engaging less and less with the world's laws, one becomes more and more engaged in following Divine Laws, consistently directed towards this at all times. There is nothing more worthy to be done or engaged in. Conflicts cease. A deeper peace reigns.

One lives more in the present moment. Not knowing anything is the norm, one delighted and reveled in. The mind unravels its spool and thread, resting in more emptiness created by the soul's expansion into possessing more Divine Love. Truer wisdom borne of the naked moment arises.

In Divine Love you cannot escape feeling anything. There are no Reiki blankets over your wounds, covering over of feelings, no rationalizing or escaping into feel-good solutions, no slavish following of teachers and putting any kind of responsibility onto them, no distractions, no helping of others to escape feeling their and your own wounds.

There are no self-help programs, no ways to escape feeling what you do not wish to feel, no finding the latest trend, or running from one workshop to another to find out about the infinite soul that we do not have, no ways to strategize and improve your limited human self, *all of which are designed to escape feeling your emotional wounds and blocks to Divine Love entering your soul.*

You deliberately choose no escape, because you desire Divine Love, and with this choice and desire, you choose to feel all the pain and then eventually all the love that comes from this.

Divine Love is simple, deep and directly between you and God. All that stands in the way of receiving It is yourself, composed of your wounds, both in your soul and in the collective soul of humanity that you too are part of. Do not delay. Whenever you feel any emotion stirring, stop doing anything and everything else, and just feel it.

Even if you are in the middle of a meeting, in the supermarket, with others, at dinner, or any social occasion, STOP AND FEEL. What do you desire? What is your priority? What is important to you? The longer you delay, the less you will feel. Embracing it in the moment allows the deepest and fastest openings for the soul to occur.

THE FOURTH SPHERE OF NATURAL LOVE

COMPLETION OF CERTAIN EARTH SERVICE AGREEMENTS
INTELLECTUAL REFINEMENT, CLARITY, RELEASE
HEALING ABILITIES MAGNIFY
PURIFICATION OF HUMAN LOVE
INDIVIDUALIZATION OF SOVEREIGN SOUL ACCELERATES
SOUL TRIALS and NEGATIVE SPIRIT ATTACKS AMPLIFY
IMPORTANCE of SOUL MATE

In the Fourth Sphere there begins to be a felt difference between souls following the natural love, meditational, self-help path, and those following the Divine Love Path. A bigger differentiation occurs, and one feels less and less attracted to anyone or anything not on the Divine Love Path.

Souls in this Sphere work hard in their work of At-One-ment and are devoted, round the clock spiritual guides and teachers. They help others with enthusiasm and with much more efficiency than other souls coming from lower Spheres due to their soul development. But they do it for love, for vocation, and they offer this service to any person who needs it and who has been assigned to them.

Fourth Sphere souls are interested in the affairs of Earth to help others grow soulfully, but any other earthly interest disappears as they progress inside this Sphere from room to room, level to level.

Their only interest on the Earth is in helping their own self and other souls to progress towards God, but they take no personal interest in their affairs. Earthly bonds, the importance of daily life and family bonds TOTALLY disappear. DNA changes occur as the healing and integration of *much* parental and ancestral wounds and inherited characteristics in the sexuality become felt and released.

When you are on the Divine Love Path, you really want to feel and know God and you really want to know your Self fully. Self here also means your soul mate, getting to know them too, feeling their qualities, nature and your mutual passions and desires. These are the three most fulfilling relationships your soul is ever going to have: the one with God, your soul mate, and yourself, for these are the expressions of love that God has created for your soul.

God has created the perfect partner for you because God loves you and wants you to enjoy all the aspects of Love. This is an amazing experience to live, full of joy, innocence and pure human love and Divine Love. To live this, you will come to understand in every cell how much God Loves us, and how She wants to give us everything.

In the Fourth Sphere, being with, learning from, and healing with your soul half has more importance and relevance than in the previous Spheres. Earlier in the Divine Love Path, having a soul half, whilst it may be desired, is not so important as releasing soul injuries and desiring and receiving more Divine Love.

In the Fourth Sphere, (and before) soul mate connection becomes more important, as soul mates naturally trigger each other's hidden places that no one else can touch, allowing each to expand into more love, joy and capacity to receive Divine Love IF both are humble and willing.

Inevitably, one soul mate will be more advanced than the other, but both learn and heal from their interactions. One soul mate will be more Love based, the other more Truth based, but both will endeavor to merge both qualities within themselves.

Their great love for each other, and their great love for God, spurs the less developed one to make great efforts to catch up, so that they can live together. Sometimes this is the way a soul is 'extracted' from the hells.

The more advanced soul mate is able to influence the less developed one to make the effort to get out of darkness. This soul mate attraction is so strong that a bright and pure spirit is actually attracted to a darker spirit.

By the time you are moving through the Fourth Sphere, you are totally living in your passions and desires without any obstruction. Everything *your soul has desired and is passionate about since childhood that is in harmony with Divine Love and Truth* will manifest (apart from union with God obviously!) and the process of manifesting this is what cleanses and purifies the soul itself.

This will be on all levels. The one exception to this, in rare cases, is soul mates meeting again, which may sometimes only happen when one of them is in the Fifth Sphere and has resolved all issues regarding parental, ancestral and spirit possession in humility.

Self love refines to a new degree here, in a more subtle way. Almost everything not in alignment with your passions, desires, visions and love of your own soul and sovereign individuality in alignment with Divine Truth and Love is seen and is no longer welcomed in your life; *there is no more compromise* on any aspect of this.

Before this there may have been subtle compromises because of a willingness to serve or accommodate others, but any compromise here on the love for your own soul, and how God loves you, becomes exposed through Law of Attraction events and quickly released.

You become more loving as you go through this process and any resistances you have that have led to these errors becomes felt, realized and released. Others can no longer get away with even subtle demands, expectations or unloving behavior with you, as you feel it as untruthful and no longer tolerate it within you to accommodate such behavior from others or from your own compromising of yourself.

You become humbler, more individuated, clearer, and stronger in the softness and clarity of the soul. *This is all an amplification, integration and completion of the processes that started in the Second Sphere.*

Healing abilities amplify tremendously in the Fourth Sphere. Whilst this can be applied in many ways, the most aligned way in the Divine Love Path for both the soul facilitating healing through becoming a vessel and conduit for Divine Love and Truth, and for the ones receiving it, is through prayer for Divine Love. Once I had moved into the Fourth Sphere, I would pray to receive Divine Love, and have groups praying as well.

The Divine Love flowing into me would then ripple out to these others, bringing great tears, a hugely amplified receiving of Divine Love for all concerned, and healings/ openings whilst this was occurring.

Shortly after this, hours afterwards, even greater things sometimes happened, as the Divine Love settled into the souls of all concerned, and touched their deep causal wounds.

The Fourth Sphere is also a meditational/natural love sphere, with many *potential subjects of study and mental refinement.* For those on the Divine Love Path, this refinement is to serve the soul's progression, clear up any misunderstandings, and clear the way ahead to enter the Fifth Sphere of Divine Love, as well as complete any earthly service agreements that require a mental or organizational intelligence.

Because this Sphere is so pleasant, with little suffering and many loving, clear and powerful things happening, (although 'negative' emotions are still felt, yet moved through faster) there can be a temptation to stay in the Fourth Sphere for a long time and help others in a loving way, which, whilst beautiful, is still only half way to God.

The desire for God one has to feel and evoke has to be deeper because this is not a Divine Love Sphere. Divine Love aspirants have to desire God more in order to move onto the Fifth Sphere, which they do as fast as they can. Because there is less Divine Love available, one is spurred on to even more heartfelt yearning from a deeper place within, in an effort to receive more Divine Love.

The Fourth Sphere is an attractive inter-dimensional space to enjoy the work one is carrying out on humanity's behalf, *but this sphere is an intermediate stage, because we can carry out this work of Love in the higher spheres as well, and much better.*

Spirits who choose and deeply desire Divine Love do not remain a long time in this sphere *at all.* The Third or Fifth Sphere is actually preferable, but certain refinements happen in the Fourth Sphere that some souls find necessary and desirable. Yet again, as Christ said, *'Seek ye first the Kingdom of God and all other things will be added to you.'*

You become a lot more sensitive in this Sphere as you move through it, and it becomes harder to be in the world or spend quality time with those who are not on the Divine Love path. You realize that in order to progress, more space, quiet, nature and aloneness is required for you to become more sensitive, more childlike and more open to everything with no worldly coping mechanisms at all.

A Community of souls on the Divine Love Path – Friends of the Heart – becomes more important and sought after. You are by now detached from life as you have known it to be, and are immersing yourself in a totally different life. You cease to search for your own pleasure and consolation, and instead desire to do things pleasing to God and to render Him service more directly and as best as you can.

The Fourth Sphere is really the half way point to Realizing At-One-ment with God. It marks a big turning point in your journey, as many things change, and although the way you relate to God through His Laws and Love are the same, the way they are applied is different. One discovers this as one moves through the Fourth Sphere.

THE FOURTH MANSIONS

This Mansion is the one in which the greatest number of souls enter. As the natural is united with the supernatural in it, it is here that negative spirits can do the most harm.

Now we begin to touch the supernatural. As these Mansions are getting near to the place where God the King dwells, they are of great beauty, and there are such exquisite things to be seen and appreciated in them that they are incapable of being described without being completely obscure to those devoid of their experience.

In these Mansions poisonous creatures can actually do the soul good. In this state of prayer it is much better for them to enter and make war upon the soul, *for, if the soul had no temptations, these negative spirits might mislead it with regard to the consolations which God gives it,* and do much more harm than they can when it is being tempted. The soul, too, would not gain so much, for it would be deprived of all occasions of merit and be living in a state of permanent absorption. When a soul is continuously in a condition of this kind it is not safe, nor possible, for the Spirit of the Lord to remain in a soul continuously in this state.

The sweetness we get from our meditations and from petitions made to Our Lord proceeds from our own nature, though, of course, God plays a part in the process and in everything, for we can do nothing without Him. This spiritual sweetness arises from the actual virtuous work that we perform, and have acquired by our labors. We are right to feel satisfaction at having worked in such a way.

But, the same satisfaction can be derived from many things that happen to us here on Earth. When, for example, a person suddenly acquires valuable property, or meets a person whom he dearly loves, or brings some important piece of business or some other weighty matter to a successful conclusion, so that everyone speaks well of him; or when a woman has been told that her husband or brother or son is dead, and he comes back to her alive.

Worldly joys have their source in our own nature and end in God, whereas spiritual consolations have their source in God, but we experience them in a natural way and enjoy them as much as we enjoy those already mentioned, and indeed much more.

The soul experiences a great happiness when it realizes what it is doing is for God's sake; but it sheds a few bitter tears, which seem in some way to be the result of this passion. My own experience of this state – of these favors and this sweetness in meditation – was that, if I began to weep over the Passion, I could not stop until I had a splitting headache; and the same thing happened when I wept for my errors.

This was a great grace granted me by Our Lord, for the tears and longings sometimes arise partly from our nature and from the state of preparedness we are in, but eventually lead one to God.

And this is an experience to be greatly prized, provided the soul be humble, *and understands that it does not make it any the more virtuous*; for it is impossible to be sure that these feelings are the effects of love, and, even so, they are a gift of God.

Praise and thank God and rejoice in His goodness and in His being Who He is; for it goes a long way towards awakening your will.

If you would progress a long way on this road and ascend to the

Mansions of your desire, *the important thing is not to think much, but to love much; do, then, whatever most arouses you to love.*

Love consists, not in the extent of our happiness, but in the firmness of our determination to please God in everything, and to endeavor, in all possible ways, not to break Divine Laws. These are the signs of love; do not imagine that the important thing is never to be thinking of anything else, and that if your mind becomes slightly distracted, all is lost.

Thought is not the same thing as understanding. It exasperated me to see the faculties of the soul, as I perceived them, occupied with God and recollected in Him, and thought, on the other hand, confused and excited.

We do not realize we need to know more when we think about Thee, and we cannot ask those who know; indeed we have not even any idea what there is for us to ask them. So we suffer because we do not understand ourselves; and we worry over what is not bad at all, but good, and think it very wrong.

Hence proceed the afflictions of many people who practice prayer, and their complaints of interior trials, especially if they are unlearned people, so that they become melancholy, their health declines, and they abandon prayer altogether, because they fail to realize that there is an interior world close at hand. *Most of these trials and times of unrest come from the fact that we do not understand ourselves.*

I suffer when my prayer is not accompanied by suspension of the faculties, but, when the faculties are suspended, and I feel no pain until the suspension is over; it would be a terrible thing if this obstacle forced me to give up praying altogether.

It is not good for us to be disturbed by our thoughts or to worry about them in the slightest; *for if we do not worry and negative spirits are responsible for them, they will cease*, and if they proceed, as they do, from the weakness which we inherited from the First Parents, and from other weaknesses, *let us have patience and bear everything for the love of God*. Similarly we are obliged to eat and sleep, and we cannot escape from these obligations though they are a burden to us.

None of the scorn and trials that we suffer in this life can equal our interior battles. The cause of the trouble is in us and the result cannot but be painful.

God will free the soul from this when it has reached the last Mansion, but neither your free will, choice, nor understanding, will cease working. It is necessary (and God's will) that we learn to understand ourselves, and not blame anything for the work of our weak imaginations and negative spirits.

Spiritual consolations are sometimes bound up with our passions, and often cause fits of sobbing. To understand this better, let us suppose we are looking at two fountains, the basins of which are filled with water.

These two large basins can be filled with water in different ways: the water in one comes from a long distance, by means of numerous conduits and through human skill; but the other has been constructed at the very source of the water and fills without making any noise.

If the flow of water is abundant, a great stream runs from it after it has been filled; no skill is necessary here, and no conduits have to be made, for the water is flowing all the time. The difference between this and the carrying of the water by means of conduits is, that the latter corresponds to the spiritual sweetness, which is produced by meditation. It reaches us by way of our thoughts; we meditate upon created things and fatigue the understanding; and when at last, by means of our own efforts, it comes, the satisfaction which it brings to the soul fills the basin.

To the other fountain, water comes directly from its source, God, and, when it is His Majesty's Will and He is pleased to grant us some supernatural favor, its coming is accompanied by the greatest peace, quietness, sweetness, content and delight *which are not felt, as earthly delights are felt, in the heart.*

It is for that reason that I said it has its source in God and ends in us, for the whole human, including the physical, enjoys this consolation and sweetness.

This happiness DOES NOT have its source in the heart; it arises in a much more interior part, which springs very deep from the center of the soul, wherein secret things are found which often amaze me. And we creatures go about like silly little shepherd-boys, thinking we are learning to know something of God when the very most we can know amounts to nothing at all, for even in ourselves there are deep secrets we cannot fathom.

As this heavenly water begins to flow from this source, from our very depths, it proceeds to spread within us and cause an interior dilation and produce ineffable blessings, so that *the soul itself cannot understand all that it receives here.* In this state the faculties are not in union, but they become absorbed and are amazed as they consider what is happening to them.

The human will certainly seems to be united in some small way with the Will of God here; but it is by the effects of this prayer and the actions which follow it that the genuineness of the experience is tested. If the person who receives such a grace recognizes it for what it is, Our Lord is granting him a surpassingly great favor, *and another very great one if he does not turn back.*

Desire to attain this way of prayer, and you will be right to do so, for the soul cannot fully understand the favors which God grants it here, or the love which draws it ever nearer to Himself.

There are several reasons why these favors should not be striven for. The most essential is to love God without any motive of self-interest. The second is because there is some lack of humility in our thinking that in return for our services we can obtain anything so great.

The third is that God is not obliged to grant them to us, and He knows better than we what is good for us, and which of us truly love Him. These favors are given only to whom God Wills to give them and often when the soul is not thinking of it *at all.*

Another kind of prayer begins before this one. It is a form of recollection, which also seems supernatural, for it does not involve remaining in the dark, or closing the eyes, nor is it dependent upon anything exterior. A person involuntarily closes his eyes and desires solitude; and, *without the display of any human skill there seems gradually to be built for him a temple in which he can make the prayer already described;* the senses and all external things seem gradually to lose their hold on him, while the soul, on the other hand, regains its lost control.

The soul enters within itself and sometimes it rises above itself. When we are seeking God it is a great help if God grants us this favor. Some people are in the castle before they have begun to think about God at all. They become markedly conscious that they are gradually retiring within themselves, leaving the things of this world, and can enter within themselves whenever they like; whereas with us it is not a question of our will; it happens when God is pleased to grant us this favor.

If we wish to give God free course, *He will grant more than this to those whom He is beginning to call still higher.* Anyone who is conscious that this is happening within himself should give God great praise, for he will be right to recognize what a favor it is; and the thanks he makes for it will prepare him for greater favors.

The person who does most is he who thinks least and desires to do least in this Sphere; beg like a poor and needy person in strong desire, coming before a great and rich Emperor, and then cast down your eyes in humble expectation.

All these interior activities are gentle and peaceful, and to do anything painful brings us harm rather than help. By 'anything painful' I mean anything that we try to force ourselves to do; it would be painful, for example, to hold our breath. The soul must just leave itself in the hands of God, and do what He Wills it to do, completely disregarding its own advantage and resigning itself as much as it possibly can to the Will of God.

The very effort that the soul makes in order to cease from thought will perhaps awaken thought and cause it to think a great deal. The most important and pleasing thing in God's eyes is our remembering His honor and glory and forgetting ourselves, and our own profit, ease and pleasure.

When God wishes the working of the understanding to cease, He employs it in another manner, and illumines the soul's knowledge to a much higher degree than we ourselves can attain.

He leads our understanding into a state of absorption, in which, without knowing how, it is much better instructed than it could ever be as a result of its own efforts, which would only spoil everything.

God gave us our faculties to work with, and everything will have its due reward; there is no reason, then, for trying to cast a spell over them; they must be allowed to perform their office until God gives them a better one.

This gentle movement and interior dilation causes *the soul to be less constrained in matters relating to the service of God than it was before*, and gives it much more freedom. *It has lost all servile fear AND has firm confidence that it is destined to have fruition of Him.*

A person now believes that in God he can do everything, and has the desire to do things that he had not done previously. The fear of trials is now largely assuaged, because he has a more lively faith, and realizes that, in enduring these trials for God's sake, God will give us grace to bear them patiently, and sometimes even to desire them, because we now have a great desire to do something for God.

The better we get to know the greatness of God, and having now tasted the consolations of God, we see that earthly things are rubbish; so, little by little, withdraw from them and in this way become more and more your own Master.

We become strengthened in all the virtues and will continue to increase in them unless we turn back and break Divine Laws. If that happens, everything is lost, however far we may have climbed towards the crest of the mountain. It must not be understood, however, that all these things take place because once or twice God has granted a soul this favor; it must continue receiving them, for it is from their continuance that all our good proceeds.

When this state is something that really comes from God, there may be languor, both interior and exterior, *but there will be none in the soul*, which, when it finds itself near God, is moved with great joy. The experience does not last long, and although the soul may become absorbed again, it does not go so far as to overcome the body or to produce in it any exterior sensation. In this case, less prayer is recommended: sleep and eat well, until your physical strength comes back again.

This sort of life will be a mortification, *but it is here that God wishes to test your love for Him by seeing how you bear His absence*; after a while He may well be pleased to restore your strength; if He does not, your vocal prayer and obedience will bring you much benefit.

There is one earnest warning: exert the greatest care to keep from breaking Divine Laws. For here the soul is like a child beginning to suck the breast, and if it were taken from its mother, what can it be expected to do but die? That will be the lot of anyone to whom God has granted this favor if he gives up prayer; unless he does so for some very exceptional reason, or unless he returns to it quickly, he will go from bad to worse.

Do not leave Him Who in His great love is yearning to give Himself to you as a Friend, and to prove His friendship by His works. I earnestly warn such people not to break Divine Laws, *because negative spirits set much more store by one soul in this state than by a great number of souls to whom God does not grant these favors*.

These spirits may see nothing else in you except that God is showing you special love, but this is quite sufficient to make these spirits do their utmost to bring about your fall. The conflict, then, is sterner for such souls than for others, and if they are lost their fate is less remediable.

Sometimes God leaves souls to their own nature, and when that happens, all the poisonous things in the mansions of this castle come together to avenge themselves on them for the time during which they have not been able to have them in their power.

This lasts only for a short time – for a single day, or a little longer at most – and in the course of the ensuing turmoil, which as a rule is the result of some chance happening, it becomes clear what the soul is gaining from the good Companion Who is with it.

For the Lord gives it great determination, so that it will on no account turn aside from His service and from its own good resolutions. On the contrary, these resolutions seem to increase, and so the soul will not make the slightest move that may deflect it from its resolve.

This happens rarely, but Our Lord's Will is for the soul not to forget what it is, so that it may always be humble, so that it may better realize what a great favor it is receiving in gratitude and praise for Her.

Padma: (This is a terrible time, full of spirit attack and inner strife. It came just before a big opening caused by renewed desire whilst in a weak place within. It strengthened me in deeper ways, creating what is now an impenetrable foundation.)

Do not imagine that because these souls have such vehement desires and are so determined not to commit a single imper-fection for anything in the world, they do not in fact commit many imperfections. Not intentionally, it is true, for God will give such persons very special aid as to this, and they are not completely proof against them; yet the thought that they may commit some without knowing it will cause them no small agony. Let whichever of you feels surest of herself, fear the most.

These favors are given to us to strengthen our weakness. How little one should think about resting, and how little one should care about honors, and how far one ought to be from wishing to be esteemed in the very least, if the Lord makes His special abode in the soul.

For if the soul is much with Him, it will seldom think of itself; its whole thought will be concentrated upon finding ways to please Him and showing Him how it loves Him. This is the aim of prayer, the purpose of the Spiritual Marriage, of which are born good works and good works alone.

Such works are the sign of every genuine favor and of everything else that comes from God. It will profit me little if I am alone and deeply recollected, making acts of love to Our Lord, planning and promising to work wonders in His service, and then, as soon as I leave my retreat and some occasion presents itself, I do just the opposite.

Although after making these resolutions we may be too weak to carry them out, His Majesty will sometimes grant us grace to do so, even at great cost to ourselves, as often happens. *For when He sees a very timorous soul, He sends it, much against its own will, some very sore trial the bearing of which does it a great deal of good;* and later, when the soul becomes aware of this, it loses its fear and offers itself to Him the more readily. If she wishes to find help in prayer, she must learn to subdue her own will and in these little nooks of ours there will be many occasions when you can do this.

The foundation of the Castle is humility, and, if you have not true humility, God will not wish your soul to reach any great height: in fact, it is for your own good that it should not; if it did, you would fall to the ground.

Therefore if you wish to lay good foundations, each of you must try to be the least of all, and the servant of God, and your foundation will be so firmly laid that your Castle will not fall.

You must not build upon foundations of prayer and contemplation alone, for, unless you strive after the virtues and practice them, you will never grow to be more than dwarfs. God grant that nothing worse than this may happen, for *anyone who fails to go forward begins to go back, and love can never be content to stay for long where it is.*

The only repose that these souls enjoy is of an interior kind; an outward repose which they get less and less, and they have no wish to get more. What is the purpose, do you suppose, of these inspirations, these aspirations, and of these messages that are sent by the soul from its innermost center to the folk outside the Castle and Mansions? Is it to send them to sleep? No, no, no!

The soul, where it now is, is fighting harder to keep the faculties and senses and everything to do with the body from being idle, than it did when it suffered with them. It is quite certain that, with the strength it has gained, the soul comes to the help of all who are in the Castle.

However much it accomplishes, it is strong enough inwardly to attempt much more, and this causes strife within it, for nothing it can do seems to it of any importance. This is what we should strive to attain: *desire to engage in prayer, not for our enjoyment, but for the sake of acquiring strength* that fits us for service.

Negative spirits sometimes put ambitious desires into our hearts, so that, instead of setting our hand to the work that lies nearest to us, and thus serving God in ways within our power, we rest content with desiring the impossible.

Apart from praying for people, by which you can do a great deal for them, *do not try to help everybody*, but limit yourselves to your own companions and those assigned to you; your work will then be more effective because you have the greater obligation to do it.

By your doing things which you really can do, His Majesty will know that you would like to do many more, and thus He will reward you exactly as if you had won many souls for Him.

If they become still better, their praises will be more pleasing to the Lord, and their prayers of greater value to their neighbors. *God does not look so much at the magnitude of anything we do, as at the love with which we do it.* If we accomplish what we can, God will see to it that we become able to do more each day.

THE SEPARATION OF THE SENSUAL AND NATURAL LOVE FROM THE SOUL

There are two main dark 'nights' of the soul that occur in our journey towards God, and these 'nights' can happen over periods of time. Each 'night' can happen a long time after each other, depending upon the strength of the soul involved and what they can handle in these deep purifications and purgings.

All of this is according to the Will of God who gives these to us when He feels the time is right. These nights are deep cleansings of the soul, spirit and senses, the sensual addictions of which are rooted in the soul.

The first dark night is the completing of the separation from natural love attachments and sensuality from the soul. This is for 'beginners.' The second night is the actual cleansing of the human soul itself as it reaches towards Union with God.

At the Fourth Sphere transition, the journey you have taken before in the first Four Spheres changes, as now you are at the half way point; there becomes a clear differentiation and a new journey, a more mystical and inexplicable journey to God begins, a more God dependent journey. The soul matures and becomes more proficient.

In the first Four Spheres of our soul's journey, we are moved to spiritual practices and prayer by the consolation, satisfaction and pleasure we find in them, and this spurs us on, revealing many of our imperfections and errors. We need this pleasure, and the receiving of Divine Love in order to progress through the first Spheres to deepen our humility, faith and assurance in God and our own knowing and feeling of our pure soul.

But as we grow in the purity of the soul, these 'pleasures' become a hindrance of sorts, and God will take away the sweetness you receive in prayer at some point in the Third and Fourth Sphere transitions so you can grow more completely.

St John of the Cross likens it to a child: *'The soul, after it has been converted to service of God, is, as a rule, spiritually nurtured and caressed by God, like a tender child by its mother, who warms it by the heart of her bosom and nurtures it with sweet milk, soft and pleasant food, and carries it and caresses it in her arms.*

But as the child gets bigger, the mother gradually ceases caressing it, and hiding her tender love, puts bitter aloes upon her sweet breast, sets down the child from her arms and makes it walk upon its own two feet so that it may lose the habits of a child and betake itself to more important and substantial occupations.'

We are given tasters of the glory of Divine Love, and then it is taken away to deepen our own cleansing process. This cleansing starts with the pleasures our human nature takes in as spiritual things comes to the spirit and the senses.

When the spirit, the higher part, is pleased, it is moved to pleasure and delight in God; and the *sensual or natural love nature, which is the lower part, is moved to pleasure and delight of the senses, sensuality and natural love,* because it cannot possess or lay hold of anything else, and this is its nature. So it therefore grabs on to the sense of pleasure, natural love and sensual delight, which seems good and right at the time, but which is in fact the impure and lower part of the soul.

It is this sensual or more natural love part of the soul that gets refined, corrected and purged in the first dark night, *as it no longer receives Divine Love within it, as it has been used to doing,* but rather it is received into the Spirit itself. Before this, our sensual or natural love parts are receiving Divine Love, albeit impurely, and gradually through the journey of the first Four Spheres this is cleansed until no more soul progress can be made (for those on the Divine Love Path) until the natural love tendencies are dissolved and the yearning for God and Divine Love becomes dominant.

In this dissolution, a resurrection subsequently occurs where the love for Divine Love and Truth becomes immutably anchored in the soul, and all that does not serve this, and the souls associated with this, are put in their rightful place within yourself.

The delighting in the sensual, material, natural love happens because we are still in suffering, and part of the journey is being truthful about that in all ways; so when any consolation, natural love, temporal beauty or Grace is given to us, we may immediately inebriate and delight in the sensual nature and plunge into enjoying the error and consolation at the same time, until such a time as one can see the error of this and the roughness of our actions that are not of the pure spirit.

We are lured by the sweetness and pleasure we find in prayer (especially in the Second and Fourth Spheres) spiritual exercises and natural love, and look more for this than spiritual purity and discretion. *Seeking for this ultimately halts our progression at the Third-Fourth-Sphere transition,* and does not work anymore. God will take this away to ensure we have the possibility to purify our souls and come closer to Him.

However, this pleasure and sweetness in prayer and appreciation is important in the first three Spheres, as it gives us the strength to continue deeper and further, and enables us to lose our love of the things of the world and the attachment and clinging to natural love. It is the initial tastes and experiences of Divine Love that enable us to endure the deeper trials of the soul as it becomes purified from all things to do with natural love.

As St John shares: *'When they are going about their spiritual exercises with the greatest delight and pleasure, and when they believe the sun of Divine favor is shining brightly upon them, God turns all this light of theirs into darkness and shuts against them the door and the source of the sweet spiritual water they were tasting in God ... not only do they experience no sweetness or consolation in the spiritual things and good exercises wherein they were wont to find their delights and pleasures, but find bitterness within.'*

God now sees you have grown a little, so He sets you down from His Arms for a moment and teaches you to walk upon your own feet, to find more resolution and depth in your own pure soul, which you may feel to be strange, for everything seems to be going wrong with you.

Desire is now deprived of pleasure, whereas before it was the most pleasurable thing, and the yearning for God becomes purer, deeper and has its care centered upon the pure soul and God alone. The sensual natural love and the physical body become weak, as does the soul feel itself to be, but this is all to make the soul strong in its purity.

One can feel arid, desolate, cut off from the sensual aliveness and vitality one has become accustomed to, the beauties of natural love, and therefore become sad (for no discernible reason at all).

But this is part of the purifying and separating of these two parts of the soul. This is disconcerting at first, but if one has any true faith it is flowed with and one surrenders deeper into a purer yearning for God, that is not so humanly pleasurable, but arises from a deeper and as yet relatively untouched part of the pure soul.

One's fears can arise too, that everything is going wrong, that God has now abandoned you, and different kinds of spirit attack can occur to do with temptation and sexuality in what St John calls *the spirit of fornication.* God separates any sexual desire within you from being with anyone apart from your twin flame, as this too is a wound, and in fact one cannot really enjoy the act of making love with anyone who is not part of your soul family or twin flame from this time forward.

Being with your twin flame is the highest expression of human love, and a bridge between human love and Divine Love, and it therefore remains after the purging of the sensual state is complete as it is God created for our enjoyment in Truth. The fullness and eternal nature of human love is only possible between Twin Souls.

Until a soul tastes and lives this, they will not experience the fullest potential depth of human love and how God created the human soul. This may not be a popular concept. BUT, unless you experience it, you will not know this. God has created us to live this: He really loves us all so much to give us this. Yet even this desire too can be completely abandoned if one's twin is not present, or if one chooses a totally celibate path to God for some reason.

Here may arise the *temptation at the gates of heaven,* part of the Original Wounding and one of the more subtle ways in which negative spirits may hook into you. The temptation that can arise here is to keep some of the glory and honoring of God for yourself. The separate self's last stand of dominion is to glorify itself as it reaches the gates of heaven. It may want others to recognize it too as God, continuing the Original Wounding.

Christ said, 'If I honor myself, my honor is nothing. It is my Father who honors me.'

The soul tastes Divine Love and experiences it frequently through the soul's humility and desire. She experiences the Divine power and healing abilities that come through its vessel, and may want to be the Guru, the feted Master on her throne, bowed to and adored, instead of being a Friend of the Heart to those souls around her.

She may want these things out of power, out of subtle forms of control, pride, inferiority, the need to be loved, or as a substitute for some lack of love within herself and some need to still be independent and 'whole' away from God, which then negative spirits will be able to manipulate; it may just be the last vestiges of the separate self trying to reassert itself, clinging on to what it knows, afraid of the unknown, of losing its power, pleasure and bliss, scared to enter the aridity, scared to progress further and lose itself.

If there are any traces of pride, wounding, ownership of any kind on any dimension, and lack of humility, the road will be hard at this point. Or it may not. It maybe a temptation that for some will easily be seen and let go of in their humility to become At-One with God.

'Honor me, honor me!'
the self cries.
'Recognize me, recognize me!'

Love replies,
'Lose yourself. Become a shameless fool for love, willing to do anything

and everything, and find Me.'

This battle is subtle, and can easily be validated by negative and natural love spirits who wish to work through you, and other humans who are enamored of you. The way out is the honoring and giving of glory to God, which constantly humbles you, and feels different at different stages of the path. At this stage, it is joyful, liberating, humbling and brings gratitude.

Once you have been given a little bit of God's Grace and powers, you are closer and can think that on some subtle level you own these powers, gifts and graces. When you are just starting out on the path, it is easier, as God is more unknown, one has less experience and gifts, and one also has more shame, keeping them small. Once most of this shame is gone, then temptation takes on a different hue.

'He that has not been tempted, what does he know?' Ecc. 9-10

'And he that has not been proved, what are the things he recognizes?' Jer. 18

This temptation is a genetic message, and only through vigilance, humility, and choosing to constantly nail yourself on the cross of Divine Laws and truths, over and over again, can this genetic beast be subsumed into Divine Love. And it does, inevitably, surely and certainly.

As Christ shares, 'Whoever desires to save his life will lose it, but whoever loses his life (the separate self) for My sake (Divine Love and truth) will save it.'[47]

Yet one cruelly glorious truth remains: the separate self can never, ever, achieve union. The separate human soul HAS to die totally for the Divine soul and God to fully reveal, for it is only I, myself, that prevents Divine Love from changing me from the mortal to the immortal.

One wishes to be alone more and more in this state, and cannot relate as much to natural love souls, or do many actions either internally or externally. One is absorbed internally in emptiness and flatness, and hence one's sensual part, previously fed by the things of the world and people, lessens and now becomes purified, allowing the soul to be fed by an inner contemplation, which has nothing to do with actions or the external world.

This contemplation replaces meditation and practices; *contemplation is the 'secret, peaceful and loving infusion from God, which, if permitted, will enkindle the soul with the spirit of love.'*

This contemplation is silent, has nothing to do with the mind or thoughts, and takes one over completely as one allows it to. It can remain with you for many days, if not forever in varying degrees, and once fully received, changes you forever into a more still, soulful yet detached being, untouched by this world and its temptations or desires in a deeper way than before.

'Because my heart was enkindled (that is to say in love of contemplation) my reins also were changed. My desires for sensual affections changed, from the way of sense to the way of the spirit, and I was dissolved in nothing, annihilated, and I knew not. The soul finds itself annihilated in respect to all things above and below which used to please it, and it finds itself enamored (in this contemplation) without knowing how.'

This process, which changes one's soul forever, is a natural surrender for a soul desiring At-One-ment with God, a progression from the natural love pleasure one has been receiving, into something deeper, purer, more simple yet far more powerful in its light, and now more still, silent and detached from anything of this world. One's sole/soul responsibility now is for your soul going to God and this takes on even deeper significance as all else drops away.

The means and preparation for knowing and feeling more of the glory of God at this point in the journey are not the great pleasures, delights and receptions of Divine Love in its bliss; it is flatness, emptiness, desolation and detachment from the sensual nature, *a dark night of desire,* which can feel like being in a desert, and yet in this there arises a greater peace, inner silence and stillness. *True humility dawns.*

This purification is intense and bewildering at times. The impurities of the heart-soul, the hara and the womb undergo deep purifying and separation from you, making you feel abjectly humble and deeply unworthy at times in a different manner of unworthiness than ever experienced before.

The glimpses and graces of receiving the next octave of Divine Love purge you even further, as this Divine Love is so much purer, and so much more purely received into the higher part of the soul alone, without diversion into natural love tendencies or sensual attachment. Even during this time of being purged, God and His Spirits may occasionally come to you at times in great comfort and love, communicating softly and delicately in new and deeper ways, soothing your brow from time to time.

In yourself you find no satisfaction at this point, as you had done before. All you can do are small things to serve God, but you do your best. Great patience, detachment from the dream of the world and the lack of importance of it, the ending of all sensual, natural love influence: all these arise as God graces you with this refining, correcting and purging. In this Night there is nothing you can do save surrender, as even prayer has little strength anymore.

This is a *clearing up shop time*. One expands and sorts out one's own foundation by aligning one's soul more fully to Divine laws and truths in order to allow more Divine Love into the soul in the Fifth Sphere. It is important to keep desiring this Divine Love in the Fourth Sphere, even though you feel less of it than in the Third Sphere.

I remember many times making it strongly, abundantly, even vehemently clear to God and my guides that I wanted God and Divine Love, bellowing it out that I did not wish to stay here with such little Divine Love, even though God has arranged it this way, and I trust Him. My guides replied, 'We ALL know!' with a smile.

Sometimes it can feel like your soul is being bleached of all semblance of connection, attachment, expectation or demand to receiving human love in any way from anyone or anything.

This is not painful necessarily, just more humbling, and the separation becomes clearer as your natural love purifies. Whilst soul mate love is still desired somewhat as a human experience and human desire, it is less and less important.

This separation of natural and Divine Love is necessary because it allows a divine foundation for human love to be expressed and shared, which is our Divine Design, rather than a human or natural love foundation for human love to be shared.

This purification, separation and rebuilding of foundations in Divine Truth, how God has created us to be, allows human love to be freely given and received without demand, expectation, need, validation or substitutution on a fundamental, felt soul level (see *What is love* chapter) rather than a technique, practice or methodology (the natural love way).

In this process, you become more and more surrendered to what *God is doing to you*. You actually do less whilst in this bleaching, cleansing and separating in your soul of the natural love from the Divine Love. Your soul is more passive, and it is clearly felt that God is doing things to your soul.

This is quite different to the other Three Spheres, for the Fourth Sphere marks a whole new bandwidth or set of laws that come into manifestation. There are two journeys now: the way you have done things before the Fourth Sphere, and the way that things happen after the Fourth Sphere, which involves more surrender and trust, which by this time are naturally occurring attributes for you.

Humility is the most important quality here in the purifying stage. Desire is strong but more occasional, as opposed to the other Spheres. Truth becomes narrower and more subtle. Choice is present and refined within the general feelings of quality of clarity, humility and sobriety.

I personally felt more unworthy in these transitions than in any other Sphere, as well as more vehement in prayer in certain ways. But I became aware that God, in His Mercy, did not make it so hard for me as He had for others in the past, even though I am an intense kind of fellow.

It was especially hard to be cut off from the rich Divine Love that had been flowing into me as if from a Celestial tap at will, because of this separation of natural and Divine Love occurring within the alembic furnace of my soul.

I was attached to the sensual feelings of delight and natural love pleasures, yet my desire was strong enough, my choices clear enough, and the guidance received from Teresa and John humbling enough, to make the transition.

This process was less hard for me, and will be less hard for you, than it was for other souls in the past, because they have pioneered this for us today. Thank you so much for this noble offering Christ Yeshua, St John, Teresa of Avila, St Dionysus, St Francis, Rumi, Shams, Kabir, and all the many other souls who went through this fire of purification.

I have felt some small part of the sheer agonies of these noble souls who have gone through the total transformation from human soul to Divine Soul, and from what I have felt in my pains, doubts, dryness, inability to desire, pray and feel God after He had become my only Sustenance; they are incredible, humbling and awe-inspiring souls and pioneers for us all. Thank you.

This process for us today is accelerated because we have more access to bodywork and emotional healing ways and wisdom which can be completed in Divine Love. This makes it more graceful, and these tools are ways these other souls did not have access to in the past. Thank God for this too!

THE TRANSFORMING FIRE OF DIVINE LOVE
St John of the Cross

The purgative and loving knowledge, or Divine Light, has the same effect on a soul that fire has on a log of wood. The soul is purged and prepared for union with Divine Light just as wood is prepared for transformation in the fire. Fire, when applied to wood, first dehumidifies it, dispelling all moisture, making it give off any water it contains.

Then it gradually turns the wood black, makes it dark and ugly, and even causes it to emit a bad odor. By drying out the wood, the fire brings to light and expels all the ugly and dark accidents that are contrary to fire.

Finally, by heating and enkindling it from without, fire transforms the wood into itself, making it as beautiful as itself. Once transformed, the wood no longer has any activity or passivity of its own, except for its weight and its quantity that is denser than the fire.

It possesses the properties and performs the actions of fire: it is dry and it dries; it is hot and it gives off heat; it is brilliant and it illumines; it is also much lighter in weight than before. It is the fire that produces all these properties in the wood.

Similar is this Divine loving fire of contemplation. Before transforming the soul, it purges it of all contrary qualities. It produces blackness and darkness and brings to the forefront the soul's ugliness; *thus one seems worse than before and unsightly.*

This Divine purge stirs up all the foul and vicious humors of which the soul was never before aware; never did it realize there was so much darkness and so many errors in itself, since these humors were so deeply rooted.

And now that they may be expelled and annihilated, they are brought to light and seen clearly through the illumination of this dark light of Divine contemplation. Although the soul is no worse than before, either in itself or in its relationship with God, it feels clearly that it is so bad as to be unworthy before God.

The very loving light and wisdom into which the soul will be transformed is what in the beginning purges and prepares it, just as the fire that transforms the wood by incorporating it into itself is what first prepares it for this transformation.

The experience of these sufferings does not derive from this wisdom – but from the soul's own weakness and imperfection. Without this purging it cannot receive the Divine light, sweetness, and delight of wisdom, just as the log of wood until prepared cannot be transformed by the fire that is applied to it.

Our imperfections are the fuel that catches on fire, and once they are gone there is nothing left to burn. When the imperfections are gone, the soul's suffering terminates, and joy remains.

And as the soul is purged and purified by this fire of love, it is further enkindled in love, just as the wood becomes hotter as the fire prepares it. Individuals, however, do not always feel this enkindling of love, and sometimes God works less forcibly, giving one a rest, *so they may have the opportunity to observe and even rejoice over the work being achieved, for then these good effects are revealed.*

It is as though one were to stop work and take the iron out of the forge to observe what is being accomplished. Thus the soul is able to perceive the good it was unaware of while the work was proceeding. So too, when the flame stops acting upon the wood, there is a chance to see how much the wood has been enkindled by it.

After this alleviation the soul suffers again, more intensely and inwardly than before. After this manifestation, and after a more exterior purification of imperfections, *the fire of love returns to act more interiorly, that is* on the consumable matter of which the soul must be purified.

The suffering of the soul becomes more intimate, subtle and spiritual in proportion to the inwardness, subtlety, spirituality, and deep-rootedness of the imperfections that are being removed. As the fire penetrates more deeply into the wood, its action becomes stronger, preparing the innermost part in order to gain possession of it, for the soul to be able to possess more Divine Love.

When the purification is soon to return, even though the soul's joy is ample during these intervals (so much so that it sometimes seems, as we pointed out, that the bitterness will never recur), there is a feeling that some root remains. And this does not allow complete joy, *for it seems that the purification is threatening to assail the soul again.*

The more inward part still to be purged and illumined cannot be completely concealed by the portion already purified, just as there is a very perceptible difference between the inmost part of the wood still to be illumined and that which is already purged. When this purification returns more interiorly, it is no wonder that once again the soul thinks all its good has come to an end and its blessings are over. Placed in these more interior sufferings, it is blinded as to all exterior good.

Fourth Sphere Transition to Fifth Sphere

All pedestals that yourself and others have put you on, and all pedestals you have placed others on, now go. The only pedestal left is for God and his Impeccable Love and Truth that you now go to, first and foremost. God will show you this in many ways, gently pushing you towards your sovereign soul connection with Him, and to fully become His follower rather than anyone else's.

Your sovereign soul becomes more individualized, and therefore your soul manifests more fully. The trust in and of your own pure soul, and its relationship to God strengthens in a human way, whilst the faith in God grows even more. One cannot say that one has complete faith in God until one is At-One with Him.

Up until this point, one's faith is growing, bit by bit, no matter how large it may seem to you or others. And things have to die, be purified, and pass away to allow this, be it parts of you subtly holding on to certain patterns or people that have prevented a fuller loving of oneself to occur, or the purging of the soul as it separates from the more earthly, sensual aspect of the soul.

God becomes an inexorable magnet drawing you to Him. He gives you everything and it all becomes very simple, in that there are few formalities and prayer is spontaneous and ongoing. Deep desire and humility are the main Qualities here, for God does everything else at the right time for you, orchestrating it all. By this time you are totally open to everything occurring in trust and faith, and this is wise, as much of the time you do not really know what is going on; and that is ok – more trust arises as doubt fleetingly passes through and dissipates once again. You become God's plaything in a way – you just have to trust Him, which by this time you naturally do. Internal ups and downs and vacillations between humility and unworthiness are often experienced at this point.

We separate from everything we have ever known or even had internal reference points around. Much fades away, leaving you bereft, devoid, with nothing, as all else drops away because of His Will. One feels a void as one makes the steps to transition into the Fifth Sphere.

One is being attacked by negative spirits continuously and constantly, tempting, testing, seeing if you will act on their suggestions; this is because one soul who makes it into the Fifth Sphere is a great hindrance to the power and influence that these negative spirits hold over humanity. In this transitional phase, there are no trumpets or avalanches of Divine Love – just a more complete surrender on a deep soul level previously unfathomable and unimaginable.

To have felt and desired so much, to now feel and desire little, is disconcerting – *the only thing that can keep you going is faith in God*. Even trust in your sovereign soul, moved through earlier in this Sphere, is unimportant now – all that is left is faith in God.

You are helpless, existentially depressed and totally dependent on God for movement in your soul, as it becomes blacked out and blanked out, like a blackboard that is being wiped clean of most of its marks and impressions, or a mirror being polished.

One can feel quite useless at times at this stage, as the ways your soul has been used to operating and motivating itself or moving through life and emotional issues changes. Other responsibilities cease to exist.

This leaves a dry and arid emptiness which is not filled by anything, as God is waiting to see whether you are ready and worthy to come closer to Him. *Are you going to substitute His Love for anything else at this time?*

This is also a time for a multi-faceted assault by negative spirits, who can see that you are about to leave their influence, *and* influence many others in a positive way in both spirit form and physical form; so this is their last stand to tempt you to turn back and enjoy the relative pleasures of the lower Spheres.

Sometimes it is an assault; at other times it is subtle suggestions, enticements, urges and thoughts that it may be ok to repeat previous errors against love *now* as you are serving God, and it will help the other person etc.

'Difficult times do one of two things to us: they either break us or they force us to go back to the primal ground of our being. Adversity wakes us up. It reminds us not of who we think we are in our vanity, but who we are in our simplicity.

Adversity tells us the truth of how things stand. It never deceives, never inflates, and never lies. For there to be a new prosperity, we must first have a new adversity. There can be no prosperity without adversity that has been wisely transformed.'[48]

All these adversities sort out the wheat from the chaff within you on a deeply interior level so you can progress and become closer to Him. As you journey deeper into the Fourth Sphere many more spirits, both good and bad, come to you.

Some may masquerade as good; others will be plainly wounded. One has to remain stoic and undisturbed by such encounters, and especially by those who pretend to be good spirits.

This is a vital test of discernment, to see how much of God's Laws you

227

know by now, how much you feel of Divine Love, and how you can stay with God's Truth even when others are sharing differently. Of course, genuine Celestial spirits may also come to you, and again, you will be able to feel and discern the difference.

These Celestial or Divine Love Spirits will tend to come through the Spheres 7 and 5 and downgrade their energy to share with you. Seventh Sphere spirits may communicate to you by going into the Fifth Sphere so you may be able to handle their love.

In the Seventh Sphere there are no words as such, just wordless communion and soul feelings in light and love, and if they wish you to really receive something in the form of impressions and words, they will drop into the Fifth Sphere or lower to give this to you. Seventh Sphere spirits will generally not come to anyone who is not beyond the Fourth Sphere, in most cases.

In moving through the Fourth Sphere, you come truly on the straight and narrow path to God.

THE FIFTH SPHERE OF DIVINE LOVE

'*To Love is human. To feel Pain is human. Yet to still Love despite the pain is pure Angel.*'
Rumi

Love conquers all. When love meets fear, anger and hate head on, it melts it. I have experienced this numerous times. This action of love melts even the hardest of hearts and the most angry and hurt of souls completely, within five seconds at the most, dissolving the most aggressive, judgmental, irrational and abusive attacks directed towards you.

This love arises from an empty, surrendered self, which allows the power of grace and love to radiate and emanate unhindered to the other soul. This emanation stops anger, fear and hate dead in their tracks, usually with the angry person breaking down, crying and falling on their knees; not because of me, but because I am no longer there, and the power of love is felt flowing through my empty vehicle.

Everyone has this capacity if they lose their addiction to their old self, even if it is just for a moment. This is the wave or cascade of love at its height, its fullness, the same wave that flowed through Christ and many other souls, alive and dead. To surrender to this action means you stand with these souls, even just for a moment. And the truth is that all these souls dissolved in this wave; the power of love melts all things.

We all have opportunities every day to do this if we see these opportunities for what they are, rather than judging them/others, running away from them or *only* feeling the pain of them. Dissolve and voluntarily let go of all senses of your self, *even if it is just for one moment.* This aligns you immediately with what is

229

happening RIGHT NOW in the irresistibly attractive force of the empty space found in the heart of each and every one of your cells.

Each time you make a big movement into 'dying to yourself a little every day,' you enter love. What does this lead to? To live beyond forgiveness in a Love that is untouched by anything and anyone of this world. This is what you begin to taste in the Fifth Sphere.

By this time your soul is much purified, and you are closer to God and more surrendered to His doings for you. You are being guided by spirits closer to God, and will need little external assistance, which is why there is not much to say about the higher Spheres. You know and feel more Divine Truth and Love, becoming ever more humble, with this more easily accessible in every situation; you are living it more and more.

The simplest qualities of choice, desire for Divine Love and truth, and humility are the driving forces for your soul's progression here. Life becomes simpler for your soul's progression – it is now simply about receiving more and more Divine Love. *You feel a deeper peace, gratitude and divine joy* come and go. This joy has no reason for its being – it just IS, and it is not human; rather it comes from the divine and is felt as the most beautiful and wondrous gift from God.

There is a new lightness of being suffused with this quiet joy; Divine Love is caressing you gently. This joy is different from human joy. And whenever it is felt, the heart always feels impelled, naturally and spontaneously, to give gratitude, glory, honor, praise and thanks to God automatically. Love contains within itself its own obedience.

It is so delicate, so light, so pure and sweetly free, far removed from the grosser human or natural love joy. It has been stripped of this lower part of the soul and is the joy that is in a more direct relationship with God, directly incoming into the pure part of the soul.

In this joy is an incredible lightness of being, a freedom from being human in a way. And with this comes more and more gratitude, sometimes with joy and sometimes without, and these feelings are for no reason save God.

The Fifth Sphere offers great opportunities for Divine Love souls to obtain the Love of God, and is truly the most mystical Sphere so far on the journey. All that matters is God, and the world matters little save how you may serve others to come closer to God.

Any and all family, worldly, social and fleshly attractions dissolve, *as if they were never there*, and one is separated from the bubble-like consciousness of humanity; it becomes almost like living in a different world: *in the world but not of it.*

Because you are being given so much, there is much more for you to do to serve God, and by effect, to serve others. You are constantly being given new tasks in joy to do and bring self and others closer and more directly to God, and this you automatically and gratefully do.

All that is left is the desire for God, and to be with Him more and more. The sweetest feelings of heartbreak, true Aloneness, deeper humility and softness happen in ever-deeper Prayer and deeper, softer, purer yearning. All a soul wishes to do is pray, live in this gratitude, and serve others to realize this Love.

There is nothing more important and there are no other desires or passions left save to share with the twin flame and God in some way.

One wants God more of the time; the relationship with the Beloved blooms here. It becomes a thirst, a hunger, and an all-encompassing urge to Be with Him as much as you can. *This step is one of hunger, where the soul is nourished in love; for even as is its hunger, so is its abundance.*[49]

The Fifth Sphere is when the soul progresses to a new, purer and higher octave of Divine Love that was first experienced in the Third Sphere. This time, this Love has been purified of all sensual, mental and natural love inclinations. The silent, free of thought, wordless soul feeling language of prayerful communion with the Divine, first tasted in the Third Sphere, advances to another octave.

This is a Blessed relief and joy after the trials, spirit attacks, and dark night of the soul where the separation of natural love from Divine Love occurred in the Fourth Sphere. One becomes even more grateful to God for all that is being given to you, both interiorly within the soul and exteriorly in the world and your manifestations.

Just focus on God and all, absolutely all, will be given once you ask for it and it is in alignment with Divine Laws and Love. By this time, almost all you ask for will be in this alignment. You realize even more your total dependence on God, and become even more grateful and *enloved* by It.

Souls on the Divine Love Path no longer find common interests with natural love souls; they are not interested in their accomplishments, conversations or beliefs. They have a fundamentally different spiritual path and a fundamentally different soul, and this leads to different interests. Divine Love achieves the purification of natural love in the soul.

Souls in the Fifth Sphere have obtained a considerable amount of Divine Love in order to arrive here, and have a highly purified soul. They do not need much time to reach their definitive purification. Many of them hurry to progress into the Sixth Sphere of natural love, and almost all return soon to the Fifth, where they try to obtain more Divine Love in order to be able to enter directly into the Seventh Sphere of Divine Love and the beginnings of the New Birth of the Divine Soul.

Those following a Natural Love path do not spend much time in the Fifth Sphere, for the only thing they lack is absolute purity; in eradicating the last traces of error and false but not harmful beliefs, this last stage of purification does not take long for them. They then progress into the Sixth Sphere, the ultimate goal of their spiritual path. There is no reason for them to wait here, since there is more happiness for them to be had in the Sixth.

In the Fifth Sphere more of the substance of your soul starts to change. You are no longer separate from God as you had been before, but neither are you perfected as a human soul in harmony with Him. Your ancestral and parental healing virtually completes and all residues, emotions, patterns, clingings, needs and characteristics release fully from your soul in Truth.

It is like being on a ladder with one hand touching and feeling your True, unwounded Pure Soul, one hand reaching further out to God and Relating with Him, and one leg still trailing behind, feeling human.

Your soul feels and knows without any doubt that its structure and substance is changing (you will have had moments of this before this, but the Fifth Sphere is on a deeper level) and you are a big step closer to God. All other loves are let go of and surrendered. Divine Love becomes the immoveable center and focus of all you do, with sexual energy fully refined and sublimated.

All idea of ownership of anything, of any self, dies here. God freely gives all, and to claim that anything is our own is to stop the flow of Divine Love, and erect walls. More humility means more space, and more space means more Divine Love can flow in. Love has no shame, and the fool for love will do absolutely anything for more of this Divine Love, no matter what it takes. What else is there to do?

Nobody owns anything. The moment we think we do, we lose sight of Reality.

With the first assumption of ownership, the urge to divide, separate, enclose and be apart from others, we replicate the first choice of separation from God. Truth is free. Love is free. What the world will pay for is what it wants, which is generally an illusion.

Truth and love are free, always have been, always will be. They are priceless, therefore they are free; therefore they are worth giving everything for. This is true worth. This everything is your totality of desire, commitment and soul, and has nothing to do with money.

The assuming of ownership sets in motion a whole chain of events and emotions that not only affect your soul by cutting it off from the humility that is the ground of Divine Love and flow, but also affects others, ensuring they assume complimentary emotional states and wounds, ranging from scarcity, greed and lack, to murder, fear and envy. Ownership is death to the soul blooming into Divine Love.

The world will try to tempt you into ownership of everything and anything, with all kinds of rational, plausible and reasonable explanations, theorems, ideas, moral obligations and pseudo spiritual arguments. All of it is false. God created us all equal, and to follow, listen to, and try to adapt to others who have forgotten this innocence is to stain your own innate innocence with fear. Why adapt to a profoundly sick society?

To give up all ownership is incredibly joyful and freeing. It brings about such a sense of gratitude within your soul to God and all that He has Created for us all to enjoy in such love, equally available for all beings; this is the Way God has created everything. It is totally free for everyone.

This is totally liberating to feel, and ensures, through only the obedience that love can ignite and impart, your continuing heart's desire to give all the glory and honor to God even more, for it brings about even more joy, love and gratitude!

The Fifth Sphere is a Sphere of harmlessness, of a more divine affection. One loves without illusion. One loves and lives harmlessly.

In the Fifth Sphere we start to pray and act in spontaneous action:

What would God do in this moment?
How does God feel about this issue right here, right now?
What would Truth do now?

What would Christ do now?
What would God's Love do now?

What would an innocent child do now?

Sit and feel-pray these simple Truths:

I am Christ
I am love

God wants me
God loves me
God loves me as his own Child
God loves me as His son, God loves me as Her daughter

The Fifth Sphere is where the human soul refines itself further, feeling the irresistible urge and pull from God to become At-One with Him. He Calls you, unmistakably and profoundly. Union becomes certain in joy, in prayer. At times this is very palpable; at other times it seems distant, like a far away dream.

This brings about a peculiar pure sadness and longing in the heart, for God is showing you something, beckoning you forth, and then it is taken away again.

Yet, God becomes closer to you here than ever before. Any soul who is in this Sphere is a Divine Representative, and has tremendous support from Higher Spirits in all aspects of life. Greater responsibilities are added to you as your possession of Divine Love increases, for you are being groomed to become a Celestial Spirit and to Co-create with God, as an extension of God.

Christ likened this process to leaven or yeast. Leaven has the capacity to permeate an entire lump of dough until its presence exercises a strong but hidden influence upon the entire lump. What does a life look like when it has been thoroughly leavened by God? In the Fifth Sphere, we allow this leaven to more thoroughly permeate our life.

As a loaf of freshly baked bread is leavened, that is, a rising agent is added to it, an enlivening factor is added that makes it soften further and rise, becoming a finished and whole product. Such is the soul here. The leavening of the soul takes place in the Fifth Sphere; it is brought higher, made softer, and is readied for union or consumption into God in the Seventh Sphere and beyond.

'God is busy with the completion of your work, both outwardly and inwardly. He is fully occupied with you. Every human being is a work in progress that is slowly but inexorably moving towards perfection.

We are each an unfinished work of art waiting and striving to be completed. God deals with each of us separately because humanity is a fine art of skilled penmanship where every single dot is equally important for the entire picture.'[50]

As one deepens in the Fifth Sphere, one is touched by a higher Celestial Feeling Vision and yearning. Human joys, delights and even previous soulful pleasures seem small and insignificant by comparison with the Celestial Living Light and Love that one is starting to experience by the Grace of God.

A strange wistfulness and lighter, purer yearning that overcomes all human passions and even the highest and purest of human delights arises; one wishes to be in the Celestial Spheres, a Divine Soul, in pure light and the beauty that can only be *fully* experienced in this more 'formless' form.

The attraction of being human in any way starts to fade once you have this particular experience, what Teresa calls the first meeting with God on the way to becoming His bride. The greatest human experiences you can have or have had seem like nothing.

Beauty, purity and love, in humility, gratitude and desire, Is the essence of this pure feeling vision of living in the Celestial spirit world, which is incomparable to anything that can be lived on this earth in our fragile physical bodies.

The spirit world is where we experience beauty, love and gratitude in incomparable music and even more sublime silence more of the time in a refined, purer and glorious way. In the Higher Spheres of Divine Love, this reality is truly glorious and so incredibly beautiful, luminous and heartbreakingly joyful that nothing else compares to it in the human plane *at all*.

A soul becomes more enamored and attracted to the purest Divine Light, Grace, beauty and Love that you are starting to taste here, and once tasted, it is easy to not look back, for in Truth It is what your soul desires.

The building of the Celestial Kingdom, the building of a Civilization of God-merged Souls based on the Truths of Divine Love is occurring right now in the spirit world. These doors were not opened until 2000 years ago, and in these 2000 years many spirits have reached At-One-ment with God; there is now a Call from God for the completing of this Kingdom for certain human souls now here on Earth who feel this Call, and who choose it.

Consistently desire Divine Love every day, ask many times a day, restate your desire from your soul in many moments. This threads and strings together these pearlescent openings into one stream of love. Let this desire melt away all that stands in the way. Allow the love received to permeate your whole being and soul, every single part, hidden and known, secret and open. Be total.

Every occurrence that happens in your life, every little thing that happens to you is to allow love to bloom, to deepen your inner silence and expression, for God's Plan to unfold.

Let the sweet blooming of your soul in each of these moments, in the mystery of inner silence, reach out and touch its Source, letting it be known that here lies a yearning soul, willing, able and desirous to dissolve into what can never be told.

Even silence has a melody; an inner rhythm, a movement. Silent smiles glow in the dark. Silence wafts, serene and undulating, bearing wordless messages ensconced within itself that the mind can never know, yet which the soul is nourished by, knowing itself in the peace beyond understanding.

Listen to it and its inner spaces; experience its flavors and moods, its symphonies and spaces, its intimate enveloping in the deepest of smallest spaces and its vast expansion, its cocoon and its infinity, its warmth and wide open space, its nakedness and aloneness, its intimacy and sadness, its sweetness and desolation, its heartbreak and inspiration, its balm and its bane, its healing and its breaking of you.

Its love and its rich, inviting caress, its silent sinking and rest, its gateway to stillness and the eternal repose of the heart that joy knows itself. Things are present through their absence in the void.

See yourself as a single mote of dust, illuminated briefly by a sparkle of sunlight, swirling in the air, to then vanish forever. Illuminated for a moment, gloriously seen by God's Angels, now you can lose yourself in eternity.

Like the mirage that dissolves the closer you get to it, like the love you see flicker in the eyes of a stranger, like the passing breeze that reveals a view of an infinite ocean, like the waters that part with each of your movements, rippling and dissolving, so present one moment and so absent the next, like the dust of the earth that holds your impression one moment, to be blown away forever by the wind the next.

God's Hand touches you through your desire, and you enjoy a magic moment of eternity's sunrise. As It leaves, all changes within you; if you want more, it will come again when you are ready. And maybe you will be ready, and maybe you never will be. It is Grace. Enjoy it as it flies.[51]

Here, Love is a rare and precious thing, secret and inner, a beauty facing inwards into the center of the soul, the sanctum sanctorum or sacred secret center. It is nourished and nurtured in this silent, secret way, secret in that only the soul's silent mind, beyond thought, surrenders to this with God.

The preciousness of this blooming Love, and the wisdom to stay with this Gift and Blessing, nurturing it and remaining in its inner presence deep within your soul, precludes all other attractions.

In this space, much can be known if you desire. One feels touches of the rarefied and pure Love of the Seventh Sphere[52], being called and attracted to That by these extensions of God's Love towards you, and by your being pulled towards That.

This is why the attraction of being human starts to fade. The Higher forms of Divine Love, once given by God, leave everything else pale in comparison. And this is just the Fifth Sphere. There are seventeen more ... and it is desire for Divine Love, to be overtaken by God, which brings you further, deeper.

When Shams of Tabriz, the soul mate of Rumi, met Rumi, who became one of the greatest poets on love, there is a story about desire.

Shams said, 'Did not Mohammed say, "Forgive me God, I could not know Thee as I could have?" whilst Bistami, a famous Sufi mystic pronounced, "Glory be to me, I carry God inside my cloak." If one man feels so small in relation to God whilst another man claims to carry God inside, which of the two is greater?'

Rumi replied: 'God's Love is an endless ocean, and humans strive to get as much water as they can out of it. But at the end of the day, how much water we get depends on the size of our cups. Some people have barrels, some have buckets, whilst some others only have bowls.'

Bistami's container was relatively small, and his thirst was quenched after a mouthful. He was happy in the stage he was at. It was wonderful that he recognized the Divine, but even then there remains a distinction between God and Self. Unity is not achieved.

As for the Prophet, he was the Elect of God and had a much bigger cup to fill. This is why God asked him, 'have we not opened your heart?' His heart thus widened, his cup immense, it was thirst upon thirst for him.[53]

So ... what about you? Tell me, how big is your cup?
Do you have the heart to go further, till the very end?
Tell me, how big is your cup?

THE FIFTH MANSIONS

How shall I ever be able to tell you of the riches, treasures and delights which are found in the Fifth Mansions? No one can describe them, the understanding is unable to comprehend them and no comparisons will avail to explain them; earthly things are quite insufficient for this purpose. All our desires here are occupied in desiring to please God.

According to what you know yourself to have given to God, the favors He will grant you will be small or great.

Here we are asleep to the things of the world, and to ourselves. *There is less opportunity for negative spirits to enter*; a few little lizards, being very agile, can hide themselves all over the place, and although they do no harm – especially if we take no notice of them – they correspond to little thoughts which proceed from the imagination and are troublesome.

Agile though they are, however, the lizards cannot enter this Mansion, for neither imagination, memory nor understanding can be an obstacle to the blessings that are bestowed in it.

God is in such close contact with the essence of the soul that negative spirits will not dare to approach, for they cannot understand this secret thing, still less will they *understand a thing so secret that God will not even entrust our own thoughts with it.*

Oh, what a great blessing is this state in which accursed ones can do us no harm! Great are the gains that come to the soul with God working in it, and neither we ourselves nor anyone else hindering Him. What will He not give, He Who so much loves giving and can give all that He will?

If we are fond of vanities, negative spirits will send us into transports over them; but these are not like the transports of God, nor is there the same delight and satisfaction for the soul, or the same peace and joy. *That joy is greater than all the joys of Earth, and greater than all its delights and satisfactions;* these satisfactions and those of the Earth do not have any common origin; and are apprehended very differently too, as you will have learned by experience.

Anyone who does not believe that God can do much more than this, and that He is pleased to grant His creatures such favors, has closed the door fast against receiving them. Therefore, trust God more and more, and do not consider whether those to whom He communicates His favors are bad or good.

The soul is made completely foolish in order the better to impress upon it true wisdom. For as long as such a soul is in this state, it can neither see nor hear nor understand: the period is always short and seems to the soul even shorter than it really is. *God implants Himself in the interior of that soul in such a way that when it returns to itself, it cannot possibly doubt that God has been in it and it has been in God.*

So firmly does this Truth remain within it that, although for years God may never grant it that favor again, it can neither forget it nor doubt that it has received it (and this quite apart from the effects which remain within it). This certainty of the soul is very material, which can be put there only by God.

But we cannot enter by our own efforts; God must put us right into the center of our soul, and must enter there Himself; and, in order that He may better show us His wonders, it is His pleasure that our will, which has surrendered itself to Him, should have no part in this.

Nor does He desire the door of the faculties and senses, which are all asleep, to be opened to Him; He will come into the center of the soul *without using a door*, as He did when He came into His disciples. God's Will that the soul should have fruition of Him is in its very center, in the last Mansion.

Everything the soul sees on Earth leaves it dissatisfied, especially when God has again and again given it this wine which almost every time has brought it some new blessing. All that it can do for God seems to it slight by comparison with its desires. Ties of relationship, friendship or property no longer bind it. Everything wearies it, because it has proved that it can find no true rest in creatures or the world.

If anyone told me that after reaching this state he had enjoyed continual rest and joy, I should say that he had not reached it at all, but possibly had experienced some kind of consolation enhanced by physical weakness, and perhaps even by negative spirits, who give peace to the soul in order later to wage a far severer war upon it. Those who attain to this state have a very high degree of peace, for their trials are of such sublimity and come from so noble a source that, severe though they are, they bring peace and contentment.

The soul has now delivered itself into His hands and His Great Love has so completely subdued it that it neither knows nor desires anything save that God shall do with it what He Wills. *Never will God grant this favor save to the soul that He takes for His very own.*

His Will is that the soul shall be sealed with His seal. In reality, the soul in that state does no more than the wax when a seal is impressed upon it – the wax does not impress itself; it is only prepared for the impress: that is, it is soft, and it does not even soften itself so as to be prepared; it merely remains quiet and consenting. *See what God does to the soul in this state so that it may know itself to be His? He gives it something of His own.*

It is God's Will that so great a favor should not be given in vain, and that if the soul that receives it does not profit by it, others will do so. For as the soul possesses these aforementioned desires and virtues, it will always profit other souls as long as it leads a good life, and from its own heat new heat will be transmitted to them.

Even after losing this light, it may still desire others to profit and take pleasure in describing the favors given by God to those who love and serve Him, in which case the Lord will give the 'fallen' soul new light.

True union can be achieved with the favor of Our Lord if we endeavor to attain it by not following our own will but submitting it to whatever is the Will of God. Oh, how many of us who say we do this and think we want nothing else, and would die for this truth! This soul sees clearly that God knows what God does better than it knows itself what it desires.

Death comes more easily when one can see oneself living a new life, whereas our duty now is to continue living this present life, and yet to die of our own free will. This may be harder, but it is of the greatest value and the reward will be greater too if you gain the victory. But you must not doubt the possibility of this true Union with the Will of God; it is this that is the most genuine and the safest path.

But alas, so few of us are destined to attain it! There are always a few little worms, which do not reveal themselves until they have gnawed through our virtues. Such are self-esteem, censoriousness (even in small things) concerning our neighbors, lack of charity towards them, and failure to love them as we love ourselves.

You will often have heard that God betrothes Himself to souls spiritually. The spiritual joys and consolations given by the Lord are a thousand leagues removed from those experienced in marriage. It is all a union of love with Love, and its operations are entirely pure, and so delicate and gentle that there is no way of describing them; but the Lord can make the soul very deeply conscious of them.

It is like what happens in our earthly life when two people are about to be married. There is a discussion as to whether or no they are suited to each other, and are both in love; and then they meet again so that they may learn to appreciate each other better. So it is here.

The contract is already drawn up and the soul clearly understands the happiness of her lot and is determined to do the Will of her Spouse in every way in which she sees that she can give Him pleasure. His Majesty, Who will know quite well if this is the case, is pleased with the soul so He grants her this mercy, desiring that she shall get to know Him better, and that they shall meet together, and He shall unite her with Himself.

We can compare this kind of union to a short meeting because it is over in the very shortest time. All giving and taking have now come to an end and in a secret way the soul sees Who this Spouse is that she is to take. By means of the senses and faculties she could not understand in a thousand years what she understands in this way in the briefest space of time.

But the Spouse, being Who He is, leaves her after that one visit, worthier to join hands with Him; and the soul becomes so fired with love that for her part she does her utmost not to stop this Divine Marriage. If she is neglectful, however, and sets her affection on anything other than Himself, she loses everything, and that is a loss every bit as great as are the favors He has been granting her, which are far greater than it is possible to convey.

So, souls whom the Lord has brought to this point on your journey, I beseech you, for His sake, not to be negligent, but to withdraw from occasions of sin, for even in this state the soul is not strong enough to be able to run into them safely, as it will be after the Betrothal has been made (the Seventh Mansion).

For this communication has been no more than one (or two) short meetings, and negative spirits will take great pains about combating it and will try to hinder the Betrothal. Afterwards, when they see that the soul is completely surrendered to the Spouse, they will dare not do this, for they are afraid of such a soul and know by experience that if they attempt anything of the kind they will come out very much the loser and the soul will achieve a corresponding gain.

I have known people of a high degree of spirituality who have reached this state, and whom negative spirits have, with great subtlety and craft, won back. For this purpose they will marshal all the powers of hell, for if they win a single soul in this way they will win a whole multitude. If we consider what a large number of people God can draw to Himself through the agency of a single soul, one can see.

If the soul is so completely At-One with the Will of God how can it be deceived, since it never desires to follow its own will? By what avenues can negative spirits enter and lead you into such peril that your soul may be lost, when you are so completely withdrawn from the world and so often approach God? For you are enjoying the companionship of Angels, since you have no other desires than to serve and please Him in everything.

If this soul invariably followed the Will of God, it is clear that it would not be lost. But negative spirits come with artful wiles, and, *under the color of doing good, set about undermining it in trivial ways, and involving it in practices which are made out not to be wrong.* Little by little they darken your understanding and weaken your will, *until in one way and another you begin to withdraw from the Love of God and indulge in your own wishes.*

There is no enclosure so strictly guarded that these spirits cannot enter it, and no desert so solitary that they cannot visit it. God permits this so that He may observe the behavior of the soul which He wishes to set up as a light to others; for, if it is going to be a failure, it is better that it should be so at the outset, than when it can do many souls harm.

Continually ask God in your prayers to keep you in His Hand, and bear constantly in mind that if He leaves us we shall at once be down in the depths. But most of all, we must walk with special care and attention and watch what progress we make in the virtues, and discover if, in any way, we are either improving or going back, especially in our love for each other and in our desire to be thought of as ordinary.

When God brings a soul to such a point He does not let it go so quickly out of His Hand that these spirits can recapture it without much labor.

His Majesty is anxious for this soul not to be lost, and so He gives it a thousand interior warnings of many kinds, and thus it cannot fail to perceive the danger. We must strive all the time to advance, and, if we are not advancing, we must cherish serious misgivings, as negative spirits are undoubtedly anxious to exercise their influence upon us.

It is unthinkable that a soul, which has arrived so far, should cease to grow. A soul which has set out to be the bride of God Himself, and has already had converse with His Majesty and reached the point which has been described, must not lie down and go to sleep again.

Let us take special care to pray to God for others, and not be negligent. To pray for those who are in much error is the best kind of almsgiving. Imagine a man with his hands tied behind him, bound with a stout chain, fastened to a post and dying of hunger; not for lack of food, since he has beside him the most delicious things to eat, but because he cannot put them into his mouth, even though he is weary to death and knows he is on the point of dying, and not merely a death of the body, but one which is eternal.

Would it not be extremely cruel to stand looking at such a man and not give him this food to eat? And supposing you could loose his chains by means of your prayers? You see now what I mean.

For the love of God, I beg you always to remember such souls when you pray.

THE SECOND DARK NIGHT OF THE SOUL

When most parental, ancestral and individual soul healing ends, along with the Original Wounds[54] being directly encountered and moved through (although still not yet completed) another pathway to God accelerates, more focused on God. This is the mystic's pathway as nothing of this world can describe it, neither its structures or beliefs for it is not of this world or what is called 'being human.'

As the soul enters the second night, God now takes you in hand with His direct Way, different to what you have been doing thus far. Before this, we could not handle this Way, as we were like children. Now we are set on our feet and told to walk! All the key qualities of the first four Spheres – trust, truth, Divine Love and desire – all get remodeled in how they work, although the principles remain the same.

Your human love desires, passions, inspirations, methods, under-standings and affections have been largely extinguished; and in the process have been replaced by strength, softness, and *a deeply anchored living faith* that is a living, breathing part of you, as real as your fingers and toes, as vital as your mouth and heart, a living faith that is constantly nourished by, and in, the Divine.

This dark night is an inflowing from God into the soul in *contem-plation*, dissolving from the human soul its ignorance, imperfections and habits, both natural and spiritual. God secretly shares with the soul (beyond the mental) the perfecting Love without the soul doing anything; the soul is more passive here as there is little it can do.

The purer the light of the Divine, the more simple It is, the more sublime suffering the soul may undergo as it receives it. As John shares, '*As this Divine infused contemplation has many excellences, and as does the soul have many miseries, which are not yet purged, the two cannot co-exist in one subject – the soul – and it must of necessity suffer since it is the subject where these two contraries war against each other, working against each other.*'

This working against each other is the alchemy, the inner secret furnace incomprehensible to the mind, and is the beginning of the real dissolving of the human soul into a Divine Soul.

Souls that enter this Night have had many blessings from God and have received much Divine Love, relatively speaking, and have served Him well up to this point. This Dark Night is God Loving us through this pain, as the pain is what purifies the human soul, detaching it from its very creation and existence *as human itself.*

This is magnified by us feeling that God is no longer present for us as He once was. Our prayers may feel like they are not heard in the same way as before, and when one does pray, there is such little strength and sweetness in the prayer that the soul thinks God neither loves it nor hears it.

This is the most painful thing for a soul here to experience. This cuts right to the heart and soul – for God to have been there so abundantly, and now suddenly not. We still have a great love for God here – it just feels like we are being deprived of Him and left in our own miseries, and even in our loving of God we feel greater affliction, for it is not felt as much by us as we once did, and we feel we are not received either. This is very hard for a soul to bear.

This Dark Night humbles us and makes us sad, miserable but strangely not lonely. By this time, the soul will have conquered any feelings of human loneliness, yet it empties us of natural love affection, making of us a different creature that no longer feels love in the same way we have been used to.

God does these things so we may grow and become exalted with Him. Simple, pure and detached we become, and without this purging we are unable to feel the delicacy, the sublime, intimate sweetness of Divine Love and its communications.

The feelings, affections and understandings of Divine Love are different from natural love. The natural light must be purged for Divine Light to more fully enter and take its place.

As John shares, *'Because the soul is to attain possession of Divine knowledge, very generous and full of sweetness, which falls not within the common experience and natural knowledge of the soul, because it looks on them with eyes as different from those of the past as spirit is from sense and the Divine from the human.*

For this night is gradually drawing away the spirit from its ordinary and common experiences and bringing it nearer the Divine sense which is a stranger and alien to all human ways.

The soul goes about marveling at all the things it hears and sees, which seem to it strange and rare, though they were the same as it was used to experiencing before. The soul is now becoming alien and remote from common sense and knowledge, becoming annihilated in this respect, so it may be informed with the Divine ...'

All the old ways of feeling and processing wounds, whilst the principles remain the same, disappear, as one is dealing with something beyond any comprehension and is purely down to the Will of God. We simply cannot understand this with the mind but rest in the soul and in pure, dark faith in God, that He knows and loves us, even at this time.

Help me to have faith, such faith, as will cause me to realize that I am Your Child, and I am one with You in very substance, not in image only.

As there are no longer the usual suspects of family, childhood, parents and partner events to feel into, there are no reference points left at all. What to do? Here is where a deeper humility and an even deeper faith arises. Even deeper and inexplicable feelings of parts of the soul God has not touched until now arise, *from a totally internal reference point between your soul and God.*

The emotions are deeper in this sense, and twist more inside you, for having no reference point or discernible wound, it is harder to pray for help with it and know what it is about in order to heal it, as has been the case before.

Tears are blessed relief, but come rarely in this stage whereas before they were free flowing. 'Human' emotions, as you have known them, change, and you cannot process them like you have done before. This is a different path, a different dimension, and truly is a time for deep, dark faith, for the pure *soul's mind* to arise fully.

The inner peace that has been built up before this, whilst seeming and feeling real to the soul, has to be dissolved and let go of in order for a true tranquility to dawn based in Divine Love. This is the beginning of the peace that passes all understanding, but to arrive at this peace the previous peace we had felt, built on a temporary foundation (for we are not healed fully until we are At-One with God) has to be dismantled.

This too is disquieting in itself, as before this in the Fourth

Sphere little or nothing could faze you at all. This dismantling is arranged by God directly into your soul or triggered through your twin, which again is unnerving because by this time you will have been living in harmony for some time with him or her.

In essence this was not true peace beforehand, just the soul following its inclinations for it in a human way. This 'peace,' which seemed so true and loving beforehand, has to be purged from the soul, and abandoned by the soul in a state of disquiet. This is painful, disturbing, and involves some fundamental shifts within you on a core soul level, leading to doubts, misgivings, and not being sure of anything anymore, not knowing of anything that had served you thus far in your progression, as well as becoming more humble and, yes, unworthy in a sense. And this after having seemingly 'conquered' or come to terms with previous unworthiness!

God gives us this Dark Night in the ways and manners we can handle it depending on our soul; and it may also come and go, as it is not linear or limited in any way, and is dependent purely on God's Will and Knowing of what is best for us. Interspersed with moments of Divine Love and blessing is this Night.

As John shares, 'The spiritual suffering is intimate and penetrating because the love to be possessed by the soul will also be intimate and refined. The more intimate and highly finished the work must be, so the more intimate, careful and pure must the labor be.

In the state of perfection toward which it journeys by means of this purgative night, the soul must reach the possession and enjoyment of innumerable blessings of gifts and virtues in both its substance and its faculties, and it must first in a general way feel a withdrawal, deprivation, emptiness, and poverty regarding these blessings.'

A story from Shams of Tabriz, Rumi's Beloved:
A dervish says, 'I am burning up with this pain, I cannot stand it.'
God says, 'It is this for which I am holding on to you.'
And the dervish says: 'O Lord! I am burning up – what do you want of
this servant of yours?'
God replies: 'This burning of yours.'

It is like the story of the breaking of the pearl: the Lover asks his
Beloved,
'Why did you break the pearl?'
The Beloved answers, 'I broke the pearl so that you might ask me about
it.'

The secret wisdom of this is that the Sea of Compassion wants to rise
and overflow. And the cause of that is your yearning, weeping and
crying out. If the clouds of your anguish don't arise, The Sea of divine
mercy and knowledge doesn't surge forth. Does a mother nurse her
baby, tell me, unless from hunger the baby cries?

THE SIXTH SPHERE OF NATURAL LOVE

PURE HUMAN SOUL REALIZATION
NATURAL LOVE and MEDITATIONAL PERFECTION
SEXUAL HEALING COMPLETED IN ORIGINAL INNOCENCE
CHILDHOOD INNOCENCE REALIZED
MADE IN THE IMAGE OF GOD

'Except ye become as little children ye cannot enter the Kingdom of Heaven.'

The Sixth Sphere is a place of purity, where there are no more obstacles, no more wounds, simply peace and contentment. In this Sphere you become truly Human as God Created you to be originally, but not human as others may think 'human' to be. You become Soul Realized.

You become a master of suffering, a master of the art of transcendence. In everything you do, your main goal is to serve God, and if on a natural love path it will be to serve others to Realize the Self, which is what you have realized at this point of the journey.

The Sixth Sphere has fewer spirits in it than most other Spheres, and even fewer souls living within it alive on the Earth today, *and* even less Divine Love spirits residing within it as it is a natural love Sphere!

It is not hard to understand that this Sphere takes the longest to move through, and indeed one can spend many years in this Sphere thinking one has 'made' it and there is no further to evolve and grow vertically. This is true of the Self Realized or Satsang Teachers on the planet.

Feeling you are everything, nothing and nobody is fine for one who thinks the universe is all there is, but those on the Divine Love path are looking to merge in Union with the Creator of the creation: to go beyond that which has been created, which of course includes one's own human self.

Go to the Source of the Love which created all things, including me, you, every life form, star and planet in every universe, and to leave behind creation to Become like the Creator.

Along the way, embrace and live your full humanity, for as Rumi shares, *'You must marry your soul. That wedding is the way.'*

One can get stuck here, as there is little to desire, for one has everything a human can have, as we have been Designed to be. Both internally and externally, all is given and received, and we want for nothing. One lives in inner abundance, and, depending on your inclination, the external abundance can be there, although by this time the soul will be content with little externally.

The pile of dung in the road sitting next to the pile of gold is one and the same; the beauty is within you, the happiness is within you and the outside matters not; it all has the same value, a value given by your inner peace, clarity, and the simple fact that you have reached the end, or the beginning, of the journey of what it means to be human. But not Divine.

This is a simple state. The will is perfected, the heart is cleansed, the mind is still, at peace and in rest, and it is used as a tool with which to create and serve. Genius becomes exalted and the sharpened yet smooth, clear mind reaches its zenith in any creative avenue one is inclined to; one becomes a master in this.

Many souls say this is Mastery, to reach the Soul Realized state.

Yet, this is a quiet place, unobtrusive and invisible for those who wish to continue evolving. For others who wish to share this state, they can reach heights of fame and renown in both the human world and the spirit world. It is quiet in the sense that it is not glamorous, having the 'wow' factor that many associate with being 'enlightened.'

This is just a stage to rest in, to enjoy briefly, but not stay too long; for if one stays here too long they can lose the desire that moves them closer to God. This is the big danger here; to stop, lose the desire, even lose some humility through the enjoying and acquiring of status, and resting in the relative truths of this Sphere.

For most souls this Sphere is a Heaven on Earth. It is a 'perfect' life inside and out. The entropy, the 'drag' and Self satisfaction, the contentment of having little wounds or seeking or striving left (that is the state of this relative heaven), these things can claim you; and you will find it hard to move out of this Sphere and come closer to God, who is just a few steps away for those on the Divine Love Path.

Many 'great' souls, as your culture has put it, have become stuck here, whilst many more humble ones have passed on invisibly into the ever-loving arms of God. This is why this Sphere is quiet for those who love God, as they simply enjoy the rest and then move on, or even drop back into the Fifth Sphere again to possess more Divine Love so they can then move into the Seventh Sphere of Divine Love when God desires it.

In the Sixth Sphere, all 'human' desires become completed and satisfied. God has created us in a way of Love, so that this Love can be felt, expressed and shared *in every way* so we can enjoy the full bounty of God's Love for us, and give this honor, love and glory back to God in our gratitude and love for Him.

This is mutual love of a high order, an infinity loop of direct relationship with God borne in Love. We love each other, and God loves us so much He wants to give us everything.

There is a part of your soul that has never been in separation; when your soul was created by God in its pure state. It is in harmony with everything. And that part of you is here, in original innocence.

All reference points become internal when you feel the purity of your original soul. Your wounded self and your masks cannot be trusted, for the false wisdom generated from them are eminently untrustworthy, full as they are of erring voices, your conditioning, your projections, filters and judgments. None of that can be trusted, because it is this artificial self that is living in distrust, in opposition to your Pure Soul as God created it to be.

The Sixth Sphere is where you are now made in the Image of God. You have returned to Original Innocence, free of your sacred wounds. This Pathway is now complete. The loss of innocence is the loss of being able to love yourself. The return of innocence is the return of your ability to fully love yourself as God loves you.

You are a pure soul, no longer with any masks, wounds or errors, and are Soul Realized. You are living in peace and happiness, in a loving and joyful state. One has to remember though that this is the perfection of natural love – not Divine Love. You live without wounding, in a happiness that is beautiful but temporary; it is without the happiness of being with God.

This can be an innocent, playful time (the Dalai Lama is a good example of this) full of laughter, without any shame or guilt, sexually pure and innocent, open yet fluid. There is no shame left in sexuality AT ALL.[55] Before this there is, no matter what you may think or feel.

This is the Garden of Eden, where like children we roam in the bounty and beauty of nature, enjoying all her gifts in our naked, innocent peace. As St Thomas said, *'When you trample underfoot all shame and guilt within, then you enter the Kingdom of Heaven.'* This is as opposed to the Celestial Kingdom of God, where the human soul becomes the Divine Soul.

Just before we step into this Original Innocence fully, we feel the loss of a certain quality of our childhood innocence. We have all lost a part of our childhood essence. It hurts deeply to feel this loss in the core of our soul, a loss that is inexplicable, stemming back to the loss of innocence of the First Human Parents.

We feel this in our childlike nature, for we were briefly in this state before separating from our Twin; then the environment, our parents, and our own wounds manifested through us as we were born from our biological mother's womb.

Look at a picture of yourself as a child. Look into your eyes. This is what you were. Look and feel now at who you have become. What do you feel about the difference, or the similarities between the two? What feelings characterized your childhood?

To become reborn into this innocence is to become a pure soul, different to becoming a Divine Soul; but every point at which we stop along the journey through the Spheres of Love requires a felt redefinition of our destination.

'True and pure childhood is Eden, the place of vanished origins, lost

beginnings, all that haunts us that we try and find again. It is the cradle of our future flowering; the celebration of our innocence, our first love, first evil ... within each human soul.

Childhood is the mother and father of humanity. Within it lie our greatest secrets, our hopes, our redemption and the cures to our malaise. Childhood is our future, not just our past. All great things incline us towards a higher childhood.

Eden has been transmuted into a future destination, shaped by our hearts that yearn for a world where the unsuspected within us can live and unfold ... childhood is the missing key to our future.'[56]

As we travel along this Path, we feel, stumble upon and experientially discern the difference between innocence, naïveté, and Divine Love / Truth. Sometimes they can all be mixed up within us, and we have to sort out the wheat from the chaff from within our own soul's pure and hurt feelings. Innocence can only truly be within the soul when enough Divine Love is possessed by the soul. Innocence reaches its absolute purity when we are At-One with God.

We all get glimpses of innocence along our journey, and may often mistake it for naïveté. The difference between naïveté and innocence is that naïveté is a wishing for innocence coming from a wound, a suspected half-forgotten ideal and belief, without Divine Truth or Love in it.

One has to fully feel these long cherished hidden emotional beliefs, nostalgia, sentiments and inner losses that stem from our missing childhood and its innocent essence, that arise from a place of emotional loss. And we remember that this nostalgia, this sentimentality, this wishing to return to a paradise state with our parents in love is but a layer that points towards our true soul's yearning: to return to 'Eden,' the space where God created us in purity: the nostalgia and sentimentality, the wistful yearning is for this space of purity, with our true parent: God.

In this *felt* discernment and experience of the separation between innocence and naïveté, there are feelings of sadness and loss, a wishing to return to something intangible, mysterious, a quintessence one can never quite grasp with the mind.

One has to feel, release and leave behind the image and beliefs of the childish self, in order to obtain the substance of the childlike innocent Self of one's pure soul.

In India, this is known as *dwija* or the twice born soul. The twice born soul is a soul who has been born innocent, entered into their karmas and wounds, felt and released them fully, and emerged innocent or Soul Realized.

Childhood has a mystery, an elusive quality to it. Who would not like that essence back completely? This is what happens in God's mysterious way in the Sixth Sphere. But, this is still not the New Birth, the process which actualizes and is irrevocable in the Seventh Sphere.

In 'Eden' the very creation of free will for humans was brought into being, and with this onset of choice, the first act of violence occurred. Thus it is here that our free will can be brought back into its initial purity, with no prior experiences or preferences to color it.

Here we are a blank slate, emotionally clean, and with this comes the choice to remain here or progress until our own will and feelings are the same as God's. With the first act of violence *also comes the opportunity to become completely harmless*, which is what happens as one feels this pain and enters this Sphere.

New Man and New Woman spoke like children discovering light.[57]
'Lets dream again,' said New Man.
'Like we used to as kids.'
'Of Eden when it was new.'
'And after we have restored it.'
'With love.'
'And courage.'
'With patience.'
'And wisdom.'
'Let's play again,' said New Woman.
'As on the first day.'
'When we were the garden.'
'And the garden was us.'
'Let's be happy again,' said New Man.
'As on the first day.'

For many souls, it is enough to live in this state of happiness, no longer plagued by any human wounds, suffering, pain or fear. This is how God created us to be, and it is a glorious state to be in. All is smooth, clear, joyful, happy and all life works in harmony for you – everything is given to you and there is no more toil. Manifestation is relatively instant, as there is nothing blocking it.

The Sixth Sphere is where the clear, still mind (Buddha mind) merges with the perfection of natural love towards one's own self (self love) and all other humans, creatures and the Earth; *treat your neighbor as yourself.* One lives in this harmony and compassion, the state of Self- Realization.

It is not necessary to have great soul development in order to live in the Sixth Sphere, which is similar to the Fourth Sphere in quality, but taken to its absolute perfection and height; and similar to the Fourth, Divine Love souls will dip their toes in here for an experience of this state, refine whatever needs refining in their soul, experience whatever they need to experience, and move on relatively quickly.

This is because the frequency of the love and joy within the Sixth Sphere is actually 'rougher' and more human than the refined divine peace and joy of the Fifth Sphere. *'Love can never be content to stay for long where it is.'*[58]

This Sphere is one of great happiness and peace for natural love/meditational souls, as it is the highest they can attain in their progression, their pinnacle of spiritual development. The Buddha is the perfect example of this. It is the return to the Adamic state, or Adam Kadmon Body.

These souls enjoy themselves with advanced metaphysical and intellectual discussions, as their mental and meditational capacity has expanded enormously, along with spiritual development. This is a 'perfect' heaven, and these souls lack for nothing, unable to imagine anything better could exist.

The Sixth Sphere is a place for increasing knowledge, living a life in absolute harmony with God's laws of spirituality; a place where metaphysical science has reached its most spectacular, where the intelligence of its inhabitants is supreme, where absolute fraternity exists, *the brotherhood of man* such as people dream of on Earth. The Sixth Sphere is the Paradise which the Hebrews dream of and the Paradise that Christian churches teach of.[59]

But it is not At-One-ment with God; far from it. This is because it is still mind-orientated; any brotherhood or human community will always crumble at some point if it is not based on a greater Love and wisdom than that which humans can possess.

On the natural love path, the Sixth Sphere is the Sphere which Buddhists refer to as 'diamond mind,' the clear awareness of the pure and empty mind resting in the pristine spaciousness of the void, the zero point energy field, with its intrinsic connection and harmony with all existence. Self Realization and the void, or emptiness, are the attributes of the mind here that have reached their zenith of perfection.

The mind can go no further apart from to rest in this spaciousness and teach others about it, and the silence and purity it contains. This is absorption in Self, and states of Samadhi, drunken meditational bliss whilst absorbed in this state, are common for these souls.

The fullness of Divine Love lies beyond the void. To enter the Sixth Sphere whilst on a Divine Love Path, and to enter the Sixth Sphere whilst on a natural love path are two different things. If one enters this Sphere whilst on the Divine Path to God, which lies beyond this Sphere, one enters with love, desire for God, and shortly thereafter moves out of this Sphere to become a Divine Soul.

Those on a natural love path will have a clear mind and peace, but not have the Divine Love, and will still be a human soul. The souls on the Divine Love path will continue onwards; natural love souls will stop.

The Sixth Sphere is the furthest you can progress with your mind. You cannot progress beyond the Sixth Sphere without releasing all vestiges of the mind. Mental or meditational 'mindfulness' or witnessing/subjugation of thoughts and denial/banishment of negative feelings is the opposite of how the soul operates.

The soul operates through feelings as the cause of thoughts; in the natural love path, thoughts are seen as the creator of reality and the precursor of feelings, and this power is worked with to attain different states of consciousness.

The soul works through feelings, and any suppressed feelings then manifest thoughts secondly as an effect, as a reaction. Doing meditational practices to stop the mind and its chatter are treating the effects of the soul's unfelt feelings, and dealing with these as the cause, a basic error.

The mind is incapable of understanding your own soul, incapable of understanding the Soul of God, and is incapable of feeling that which God feels; it is only the soul that can do this. The mind will never help you to be At-One with God (although certain understandings can help along the way in the lower Spheres) and the mind will *always* interfere and create obstacles in becoming closer to your soul mate and more intimate soulful relations.

We may prefer mental or meditational dominance to avoid our emotional processing, to get away from the pain of our own emotions. We need to feel the pain of our emotions because they do not exist in the mind; the pain of our emotions is in the soul.

If we cannot release it, we will never be free of it. Conversely, the most pleasurable feelings are realized through the soul, and if we are mentally dominated even to a small degree we will not be able to realize the joy and deepest happiness that comes from the soul's relationship to God.

Your physical body is connected to the brain, and the spirit body with the mind. The soul has a 'mind' of its own, a 'Christ Mind'; its way of 'thinking' is feeling. When you are in your soul you 'think' by feeling into your soul. Just as we do not need the physical body in order to exist as a soul, so we do not need the mind as a part of the spirit body in the higher Spheres.

We have to develop a soul or feeling dominance rather than a meditational or thought dominance. The mind becomes the servant of the soul, and eventually dissipates altogether once you enter the Seventh Sphere. Yet, the soul is still logical. The soul is connected to God's Soul, and can channel feelings, the Mind of God or the Soul of God into our own soul, and can 'understand' everything in that space.[60] This is the major difference between the Divine Love Path and the natural love path made popular by new age techniques, psychology and Buddhism amongst others.

Of course, those in the Sixth Sphere can always move on and can potentially receive greater soul development, for Divine Love is free and waiting for all souls; but many in the Sixth Sphere seldom become dissatisfied enough with their condition of peace and happiness to desire or seek for a greater one; in fact, the majority of them will not believe that there is any greater happiness that they can attain, and a certain satisfaction possesses them.

After some of these spirits have been here for a long time, they start to realize the limitation of their happiness. They frequently make their first start by recalling their childhood days, when they were taught and believed that God loved them, and that His Love was the greatest thing in all the world.

THE CREATION OF THE SOUL

'The Truth is the mirror of the servant, and the servant is the mirror of the Truth.'

In the beginning of the creation of humans, God conferred upon our first parents pure natural love, a paradise, AND the potential of obtaining Divine Love, which COULD make us part of God. *'It does not make us a god, or the equal of God, but allows us to receive the substance of God's Great Love and so not remain the mere image.'*

We are not Divine because we are created in the image of God. Nothing that is an image is ever a part of the substance of which it is the image. Is a photo of a mountain the mountain itself? Is a photo of your loved one the loved one herself?

An image cannot ever have the qualities of the substance. The image has a likely appearance, and as a substitute may serve the purpose of the real until something arises that *'demands the production of the real,'* and then the image no longer serves the purpose.

The real here is the Divine Love of God, the most blissful of all the feelings a soul can ever experience, and to feel this, become a part of it and for it to be actually possessed by you so it never leaves, requires that the image of your soul and the substance of your soul are the same as God. In the Sixth Sphere, we merely contain within ourselves a reflection of the divine qualities and characteristics.

Our separation from our Creator is the origin of suffering and the basis of all anxiety. The origin of every soul is this paradise. The person who has reached this perfection has no original sin left, because the center of the human soul is pure and perfect.

Behind Creation is God's desire to be Known, which is partially fulfilled through this perfected human being. This perfected human being is reflective of the divine light, the reflection of God's nature in a purer form, and begins the fulfillment of God's desire to be known. Sufis feel that only those who have achieved this are normal, how we are meant to be, and everyone else is abnormal and ill, suffering from the sickness of the heart that originated with separation from the Creator.

The soul *alone* shows us where we are at on our journey. It is the discerner that shows us our moral and spiritual condition. Within your soul reside the love, affections, passions, inspirations, yearnings, desires, aspirations, feelings, and possibilities of receiving and possessing those things that will either elevate you or lower you into darkness and suffering.

The soul alone is the source of your suffering and elevation. The soul is subject to your will, and is influenced by the power of the will, either for good or evil. It may be dormant and stagnate, or it may be active and progress.

The human soul is a creation of God and not a part of God. Before its creation, it had no existence. It has not existed from the beginning of time and eternity, like many speak about, and *'there was a time when the human soul had no existence at all.'* It is neither a spark of the Divine nor Divine.

However, it does have the capacity to desire and wish to know its Creator more, for deep within it knows that it has been created and naturally has a question about this. Yet it can only aspire to live such Truths through desiring and yearning for Divine Love over time, and by this Divine Love flowing into its soul, transforming its very substance.

Seeing God in everything is impossible, as He does not exist in those things that have not yet desired and do not possess His Divine Love and substance. What we can see is a natural and pure love, this Self shining in others and us.

Even in the Sixth Sphere you are a human soul and even when you are a perfected human soul, you are still human. This is how God created the human soul in the beginning before the onset of the original wounds and your own unique soul wounds. So when you make the next step beyond this into At-One-ment, the very substance and fabric of your soul will completely change.

You will not be the soul you once thought you were. Your soul, even as healed and perfected as it is in the Sixth Sphere, will transform into a Divine Soul, a Celestial Spirit, a Divine Angel. So not only will it be a healed soul, step 1, but also the substance of your soul will change, as you become a Divine Soul with a substance made of Divine Love alone.

When you become a Divine Soul you cease being human; you have gone to the complete next level and octave of evolution. This is the evolutionary leap that many talk about, and it is only possible through Divine Love and the Will of God. The human being is just a stepping stone, a temporary stage, a station along the road of evolution, into At-One-ment with God.

As Muhammad said, *'There is another universe; run there.'*

THE BEATITUDES

The Beatitudes of Christ Yeshua mark out the journey through the Spheres, and the later Beatitudes in particular mark out the journey of integration into love's truth through the Fifth and Sixth Spheres.

The 8th Beatitude of Yeshua:

'Blessed are they who are persecuted for truth's sake; theirs is the Kingdom of heaven.'

When you are judged, chastized or banished because of your path and the values Divine Love and Divine Truth bring, when you leave all that does not support this flowering, when you are scorned for following this against the values and norms of this world, know that your new home is the flow of Divine Love and Truth, not a home of this world.

The Kingdom of Heaven awaits in the Sixth Sphere. But first, one has to go through the blessings of persecution, healing whatever charges and pains lie within you, resulting in neutrality, peace, presence, compassion and wise, skillful understanding that can give and help the other in pain, if they are ready for it.

Persecution and judgment is the very energy of duality itself, and it is by staying in peace that one is refined and forged into more love, along the way healing all that is not love within you.

Those who judge and condemn you are your Blessing, for they teach you how to love.

The 9th Beatitude of Yeshua:

'Blessed are you when men revile you, and say all manner of evil and judgment against you falsely for my sake.'

Others will project and attack you with negative words, thoughts, emotions and projections because they dare not look within themselves for healing, and they will separate from you because your path and values are not theirs. 'For my sake' is for the sake of love's truth, beyond mortal and conditioned ideas of what love is, what it should be, and what it is not.

You are blessed to use this opportunity to deepen into Presence and peace, when there is no reaction, healing or charge left in you; you will be blessed when you choose to leave those who revile you to their own reflections and healings within themselves.

God forgives the most – those who love the most.

The 10th and Final Beatitude of Yeshua:

'Rejoice and be glad; great is your reward in heaven. They persecuted the prophets That came before you.'

Choose to not respond according to what is perceived through the filters of mind, programming and the wound: fear, denial of pain, lack of self-honesty and humility, that all result in a negative charge; instead, choose to expand into Divine Flow from within the luminous seed of your own soul center. Ask to receive Divine Love instead.

Bathe yourself in this Divine Love and Divine Light, stay in quiet, centered Presence, the neutrality of the open heart, and enjoy the delight, humility and joy in receiving Divine Love; move forward in this, the one and only true Power, praying for those who attempt to judge and persecute, giving to those in fear. Conceive a special place in your heart for these souls who are your great helpers along the pathway to Union.

Heaven and Paradise is a state and condition within the pure human soul, AND a place/dimension *as well*. A prophet is one who speaks truth because he or she is plugged into the center of their pure soul made from love and speaks from it without fear, and without need for approval, acceptance or love from others.

The persecution attempted by others is an opportunity to deepen your own connection to love's truth. Demonstrate you do not need to get 'hooked' by the choices of others, who live from fear and their unfelt, unhealed wounds.

Now it is time to get radical: wait for no one to be what you Truly are. Find your real validation and honor in living by Truth, not in the appearances and relative 'truths' of this world. There are actually very few people who do truly love you; many profess to, and know not what love is.

THE SIXTH MANSIONS

The soul, which has had sight of Him in the Fifth Mansion, is so deeply impressed upon by this that its whole desire is to enjoy it once more. The soul is now completely determined to take no other spouse; but the Spouse disregards its yearnings for the conclusion of the Betrothal, desiring that the soul should become deeper, and that this greatest of all Blessings should be won by the soul at some cost to itself.

And although everything is of but slight importance by comparison with the greatness of this gain, if the soul is to bear its trials, it has no less need of the sign and token of this gain which it now holds.

In the Sixth Sphere, an outcry is made by people with whom such a person is acquainted, and even by those with whom she is not acquainted: 'How holy she's getting!' they exclaim, or 'She's only going to these extremes to deceive the world and to make other people look sinful.'

Then people whom she had thought her friends abandon her, and it is they who say the worst things of all and express the deepest regret that she is 'going to perdition' and 'obviously deluded,' that 'this is the devil's work,' that 'she's going the way of So-and-so, who ruined their own lives and dragged good people down with them.'

And they actually go to her friends, guides and confessors and tell them so, illustrating what they say by stories of some who ruined their lives in this way: and they scoff at the poor creature and talk about her like this, in times without number.

Other people warn each other to be careful not to have anything to do with persons like oneself. There are also those who speak well of one. But how few there are who believe the good things they say by comparison with the many who dislike us!

The soul is fortified rather than daunted by censure, for experience has shown how great are the benefits it can bring, and it seems to the soul that His Majesty is permitting this for its great advantage. Being quite clear about this, it conceives a special and most tender love for them and thinks of them as truer friends and greater benefactors than those who speak well of it.

The Lord is also in the habit of sending grievous infirmities. This is a great trial, especially if the pains are severe, for they affect the soul outwardly and inwardly. Still, at the very worst, they last no longer than other bad illnesses do. For, after all, *God gives us no more than we can bear, and He gives patience first.*

There are many things which assault the soul with an interior oppression, keenly felt. In this tempest, there is no help but to wait upon the mercy of God, Who, suddenly and at the most unlooked-for hour, lifts the whole of this burden from the soul, so that it seems as if it had never been clouded over, but is now full of sunshine and far happier than it was before. It knows very well that it did not itself do any fighting, for it saw that all the weapons of hostility and ego with which it could defend itself were in the hands of its 'enemy.'

Great are the trials which the soul will suffer, within and without, before it enters the Seventh Mansion. Until we reach the Seventh Mansion nothing can be taken for granted, for it is only in the Seventh Mansion that the soul is almost continuously near His Majesty, and this nearness brings her fortitude.

In the Sixth Sphere, your identity has fully and permanently shifted to the pure center of the soul that has never entered separation. And the last steps, through Divine Will, can be given by Him in the Seventh Sphere.

THE SEVENTH SPHERE OF DIVINE LOVE

'You, all-accomplishing Word of the Father
are the light of primordial daybreak over the Spheres.
Your power like a wheel around the world,
whose circling never began,
and never slides to an end.'[61]

As we move through the Spheres, there is less and less that can be said about them, as there is less and less mind, less and less human wounding and more and more simplicity, inexpressible Love and Divine feelings that no human can ever really express.

The Seventh Sphere is the one that divides the souls who have meditational, energetic, intellectual or moral qualities developed to the highest degree of excellence, from those who have their souls developed by the Divine Love of God.

A soul who does not have the Divine Love cannot enter and become an inhabitant of the Seventh Sphere. The souls here have received Divine Love to an extent a little short of that which enables them to enter the first Celestial Sphere to make them At-One with God and immortal.[62]

This Sphere is only populated by Divine Love spirits. It marks a series of changes that leaves them totally different from any other spirits. The first change is that the soul completely manifests its mind, one totally different to the material mind that other spirits utilize. The material mind of the spirit body entirely withers away, leaving the spirit using the mind of the soul – the Divine mind of our Indwelling Spirit.

The Seventh Sphere is where you give up the mind's dominance of your life completely and everything flows from the pure soul.

The disappearance of the material mind and the absolute ascendancy of the soul's mind occurs. One needs a lot of God's Love, of His Substance, in one's soul to achieve this goal.

This process may be achieved in a relatively short time, but many stay longer in this wonderful paradise, enjoying and experiencing, taking their time to explore. They gain enormous knowledge without study. Knowledge simply comes to them.

The experience of this is totally led by God. There is nothing you can do here, you cannot even pray. God takes your human soul, and gently yet profoundly dissipates it into infinity. He dissolves it in the most tender, gentle opening, softly stretching the human soul to dissipate it into the immortal and infinite.

This is not personal at all, yet deeply and inexplicably intimate, as within God there is no human emotion or desire. One cannot relate, and will not relate to God in a human way here at all. This too dissolves.

For now you are in transition between being what you have been created as, human, to what you are now becoming, divine. This state is a constant contemplating and interior awakening, nothing that can be expressed or understood by most humans unless they too are near this state. You become different in actual soul substance to other humans – a different species in a sense.

One feels distinct but not separate to others, as all is held in an all-encompassing glow of gentle softness and peace. 'You' taste what it feels like to be Uncreated and formless in the substance of your soul and see the structure of the human soul as the created and temporary thing.

The human soul weighs 21 grams. The divine soul has no mass at all, and it is the mass of the human created soul that dissipates here, leaving you. In this process, a deep interior yet gentle sadness arises in the core of your soul. Simply sit with it and surrender.

This is all one can do here: surrender and be taken by God's wafting fragrance, pulled by Him into the gentle nothingness of the soul's dissolving, and into the golden infinity of Divinity.

This is an inexplicable movement that simply just happens – of God's Will. One day you will be sitting down, and it just starts. Everything else stops. Choose to stop everything else for this is the most important moment of your existence.

Anything that is not actually holding the substance of Divine Love, which is everything in creation, is seen as empty. The only value it holds is the opportunity for souls, created in pure love, to Realize they too can partake in the Real. The Real is Divine Love; anything else becomes unreal. Yet this is all held in a soft and tender love, without separation.

So, you become ready for the transition to the Celestial Heavens, which lie above the Seventh Sphere, and fuse with your Indwelling Spirit, which has accompanied you since your earliest years. You become a totally spiritual being, as opposed to a semi-material being.

'Give birth to the Beloved in me, and let this lover die.'
Rumi

When you are connected from your soul to God, or At-One with God, you are individual. Your individuality is more powerful in this state than in any other state, because you become more individual, not less; you become more of yourself, not less of yourself. Your soul becomes more of an individual *At-One with* God's feelings, in agreement with God's feelings, having the same feelings as God has in all issues, with all people.

If you have a feeling that 'something' is living through you, then it is not God, because God does not live through anyone. If you feel 'it' is talking to you then it is not God; it is a spirit of some kind, because God does not talk to anyone; God transmits Feeling to feeling, Soul to soul directly, without words or thoughts.

In the Seventh Sphere, God takes you as His bride, Her bride-groom. This is undeniable. This Divine Marriage transforms you from actually possessing a human soul. We change through God's Will and Love into becoming the Divine.

THE SEVENTH MANSIONS

'The dance of the people of God is subtle and light. They walk like a leaf on water. On the inside, they are like a mountain, they are weighty like a hundred thousand mountains, but on the outside they are as light as straw.'
Shams of Tabriz

When God is pleased to have mercy and grace upon the soul, which He has now taken spiritually to be His Bride, He brings her into the Seventh Mansion, just before consummating the Spiritual Marriage. *For He must have an abiding-place in the soul, just as He has one in Heaven, where His Majesty alone dwells: so let us call this a second Heaven.*

Within each soul there is a mansion fit for God. Now, when His Majesty is pleased to grant the soul the aforementioned favor of this Divine Marriage, He first of all brings it into His own Mansion.

His Majesty is pleased that it should not be as on other occasions, when He has granted it raptures, in which it is united with Him, although the soul does not feel called to enter into its own center, as here in this Mansion, but is affected only in its own higher part.

Actually it matters little what happens: whatever it does, the Lord unites it with Himself, *but He makes it blind and dumb, and so prevents it from having any sense of how or in what way that favor comes which it is enjoying;* the great delight of which the soul is then conscious is the realization of its nearness to God. But when He unites it with Him, it understands nothing; the faculties are all lost.

In this Mansion everything is different. Our good God now removes the scales from the eyes of the soul so that it may see and understand something of the favor which He is granting it, although He is doing this in a strange manner, birthing the Divine Child in the most interior, secret place of the soul and in the greatest depths of Divine companionship.

This may lead you to think that such a person will not remain in possession of her senses but will be so completely absorbed that she will be able to fix her mind upon nothing. *But no: in all that belongs to the service of God she is more alert than before; and, when not otherwise occupied, she rests in that happy companionship.*

Unless her soul fails God, He will never fail to give her the most certain assurance of His Presence. *She has great confidence that God will not leave her, and that, having granted her this favor, He will not allow her to lose it.* For this belief the soul has good reason, though all the time she is walking more carefully than ever, so that she may displease Him in nothing.

This Presence is not of course always realized so fully and clearly, as it is when it first comes, or on other occasions when God grants the soul this consolation; *if it were, it would be impossible for the soul to think of anything else, or even to live among men.* But although the light that accompanies it may not be so clear, the soul is always aware that it is experiencing this Companionship.

We might compare the soul to a person who is with others in a very bright room; and then the shutters are closed so that the people are all in darkness. The light by which they can be seen has been taken away, and, until it comes back, we shall be unable to see them, yet we are none the less aware that they are there.

It may be asked if, when the light returns, and this person looks for them again, she will be able to see them. To do this is not in her power; *it depends on when Our Lord is pleased that the shutters of the understanding shall be opened.*

It seems that God, by means of this wonderful Companionship, is desirous of preparing the soul for yet more. For clearly she will be greatly assisted to go onward in perfection. The essential part of her soul never moves from this dwelling-place, although exterior comings and goings occur, *giving the appearance of a division.*

It is possible to make observations concerning interior matters and in this way we know there is some kind of definite difference between the soul and the spirit, although they are both one.

So subtle is the division perceptible between them that sometimes the operation of one seems as different from that of the other as are the respective joys that the Lord is pleased to give them. The soul is a different thing from the faculties (the mind); they are not one and the same.

The difference between spiritual union and spiritual marriage

When granting this favor for the first time, His Majesty is pleased to reveal Himself to the soul, so that it may clearly understand what is taking place and not be ignorant of the fact that it is receiving so sovereign a gift. The experience will come in different ways to different people.

To one person, the Lord revealed Himself one day when she had just received Communion, in great splendor, beauty and majesty, and told her *that it was time she took upon her His affairs as if they were her own and that He would take her affairs upon Himself.*

This vision came with great force, and because the words which He spoke to her came to *the interior of her soul, where He revealed*

Himself to her, where she had never seen any visions but this.

There is the greatest difference between all the other visions we have mentioned and those belonging to this Mansion, and there is the same difference between the Spiritual Betrothal and the Spiritual Marriage as there is between two betrothed persons, *two who are united so that they cannot be separated anymore.*

The Betrothal has no more to do with the body than if the soul were not in the body, and were nothing but spirit. *Between the Spiritual Marriage and the body there is even less connection, for this secret union takes place in the deepest center of the soul.* The Lord appears in the center of the soul, and this instantaneous communication of God to the soul is so great a secret and so sublime a favor, and such delight is felt by the soul, that the Lord is pleased to manifest to the soul at that moment the glory that is in Heaven, in a more sublime manner than is possible through any vision or spiritual consolation.

The spirit of this soul is made one with God, and He is pleased to reveal the love He has by showing to certain persons an extent of that Love. *He is pleased to unite Himself with His creature in such a way that they have become like two who cannot be separated from one another. He will not separate Himself from her.*

Spiritual Betrothal is different: here, two persons are frequently separated, as is the case with union, for by union is meant the joining of two things into one, each of the two can be separated and remain a thing by itself. This favor of the Lord passes quickly and afterwards the soul is deprived of that companionship. In this other favor of the Lord it is not so: the soul remains all the time in that center with its God.

We might say that union is as if the ends of two wax candles were joined so that the light they give is one: the wicks, the wax and the light are all one, yet afterwards the one candle can be perfectly well separated from the other and the candles become two again, or the wick may be withdrawn from the wax.

But here it is like rain falling from the heavens into a river or a spring; there is nothing but water there and it is impossible to divide or separate the water belonging to the river from that which fell from the heavens. Or it is as if a tiny streamlet enters the sea, from which it will find no way of separating itself, or as if in a room there were two large windows through which the light streamed in: it enters in different places but it all becomes one.

St. Paul says: 'He who is joined to God becomes one spirit with Him.' He is referring to this sovereign Marriage, which presupposes the entrance of His Majesty into the soul by union. It is here that the little butterfly of the soul dies, and with the greatest joy, because God is now its life.

With the passage of time this becomes more evident through its effects; for the soul clearly understands, by certain secret aspirations, that it is endowed with life by God.

For from those Divine breasts, where it seems that God is ever sustaining the soul, flow streams of milk, *which solace all who dwell in the Castle*; it seems that it is the Lord's Will for them to enjoy all that the soul enjoys, so that, from time to time, there should flow from this mighty river, in which this tiny little spring is swallowed up, a stream of this water, to sustain those who in bodily matters have to serve the Bridegroom and the bride. A person suddenly plunged into such water would become aware of it, and, however unobservant he might be, could not fail to become so.

For just as a great stream of water could never fall on us without having an origin somewhere, it becomes evident that there is someone in the interior of the soul who sends forth these arrows and thus gives life to this life, and that there is a sun whence this great light proceeds, which is transmitted to the faculties in the interior part of the soul. *The soul neither moves from that center nor loses its peace.*

We ourselves fail by not preparing ourselves and departing from all that can shut out this light; we do not see ourselves in this mirror into which we are gazing and in which our image is engraved. *When we empty ourselves of all that is animal and rid ourselves of it for the love of God, that same Lord will fill our souls with Himself.*

These are those who are prepared to put away from them everything corporeal and to leave the soul in a state of pure spirituality, so that it might be joined with Uncreated Spirit in this Celestial Union.

When God brings the soul into this Mansion of His, it seems, on entering, to be subject to none of the usual movements of the faculties and the imagination which injure it and take away its peace. It may seem that when the soul reaches the state in which God grants it this favor, it is sure of its salvation and free from the risk of backsliding.

But *the soul only seems to be in safety for so long as God holds it by the hand.* Even if this state has lasted for years, it does not consider itself safe, but refrains more carefully from committing the smallest offense against God.

Its real penance comes when God takes away its health and strength so that it can no longer perform any works. This is a great distress. This is due to the nature of the ground in which the soul is planted, for a tree planted by the streams of water is fresher and gives more fruit, so how can we marvel at the desires of this soul, since its spirit is made one with the celestial water of which we have been speaking?

It must not be thought that the faculties, senses and passions are always in a state of peace, though the soul itself is. In the other Mansions there are always times of conflict, trial and weariness, but they are not of such a kind as to rob the soul of its peace and stability, at least, not as a rule.

To draw a comparison to this: A king is living in His palace. Many wars are waged in his kingdom and many other distressing things happen there, but he remains where he is despite them all.

So it is here: although in the other Mansions there are many disturbances and poisonous creatures, and the noise of all this can be heard, nobody enters this Mansion and forces the soul to leave it; and, although the things which the soul hears may cause it some distress, they are not of a kind to disturb it or to take away its peace, for the passions are already vanquished, and thus are afraid to enter there because to do so would only exhaust them further. Our whole body may be in pain, yet if our head is sound the fact that the body is in pain will not cause it to ache as well.

These comparisons make me smile and I do not like them at all, but I know no others. Think what you will; what I have said is the truth.

This little butterfly of the soul has now died, full of joy at having found rest, and within her lives Christ. Let us see what her new life is like, and how different it is from her earlier one, for it is by the effects which result from this prayer that we shall know if what has been said is true.

First, there is a self-forgetfulness which is so complete that it really seems as though the human soul no longer existed. She has neither knowledge nor remembrance that there is either heaven or life or honor for her, so entirely is she employed in seeking the honor of God.

It appears that the words that His Majesty addressed to her have produced their effect: namely, that she must take care of His business and He will take care of hers. She seems no longer to exist, and has no desire to exist, save when she realizes that she can do something to advance the glory and honor of God, for which she would gladly lay down her life.

Do not understand by this that she neglects to eat and sleep or to do anything which is made incumbent upon her by her profession. We are talking of interior matters: as regards exterior ones there is little to be said.

Anything that she is capable of doing and knows to be of service to Our Lord she would not fail to do for any reason upon Earth. So extreme is her longing for the Will of God to be done in her that whatever His Majesty does she considers to be for the best.

These souls bear no enmity to those who ill-treat them, or desire to do so. Indeed they conceive a special love for them, so that, if they see them in some trouble, they would do anything possible to relieve them; they love to commend them to God, and they would rejoice at not being given some of the honors which His Majesty bestows upon them if their enemies might have them instead and thus be prevented from offending Our Lord. What surprises me most is this. You have already seen what trials and afflictions these souls have suffered because of their desire to die, be reborn, and thus to enjoy Divine Love.

They have now an equally strong desire to serve Him, and to sing His praise, and to help some soul if they can. So *what they desire now is not merely not to die but to live for a great many years and become the means whereby the Lord is praised, even in the smallest thing.*

Their conception of glory is of being able in some way to help the Crucified, especially when they see how often people offend Him and how few there are who really care about His honor and are detached from everything else.

True, they sometimes forget this, turning with tender longing to the thought of enjoying God and desiring to escape from this exile, especially when they see how little they are doing to serve Him.

But then they turn back and look within themselves and remember that they have Him with them continually, then they are content with this and offer His Majesty their will to live as the most costly oblation they can give Him.

The desires of these souls are no longer for consolations or favors, for they have with them the Lord Himself Who now lives in them. These souls have a marked detachment from everything and a desire to be either alone or busy with something that is to some soul's advantage. They have no aridities or interior trials but a remembrance of Our Lord and a tender love for Him, so that they would like never to be doing anything but giving Him praise.

When the soul is negligent, the Lord Himself awakens it in the way that has been described, so it sees quite clearly that this impulse proceeds from the interior of the soul. It is now felt very gently, but it proceeds neither from thought nor from memory, nor does the soul have any part in it.

This is so usual and occurs so frequently that it has been observed with special care: just as the flames of a fire, however great, never travel downwards, but always upwards, so here it is evident that this interior movement proceeds from the center of the soul and awakens the faculties.

Our realization of God's special care for us in His communing with us, and of the way He keeps desiring us to dwell with Him (for He seems to be doing nothing less), is sufficient that all trials would be well endured if they led to the enjoyment of these gentle yet penetrating touches of His Love. When the soul reaches this Prayer of Union, the Lord begins to exercise this care over us if we do not neglect the keeping of His commandments.

When this experience comes to you, remember that it belongs to this innermost Mansion, where God now dwells in our souls, and give Him fervent praise, for *it is He who sends it to you, like a message, or a letter, written very lovingly and in such a way that He would have you alone be able to understand what He has written* and what He is asking of you in it. *On no account must you fail to answer His Majesty, even if you are busy with exterior affairs and engaged in conversation.*

It may often happen that Our Lord will be pleased to bestow this secret favor upon you in public; and as your reply may need be an interior one, it will be easy for you to make an act of love or exclaim like Saint Paul: 'Lord, what wilt Thou have me to do?'

Then He will show you many ways of pleasing Him. For now is the accepted time: *He seems indeed to be listening to us and this delicate touch almost always prepares the soul to be able to do, with a resolute will, what He has commanded it.*

The soul is almost always in tranquillity, and is not afraid that evil spirits may counterfeit this sublime favor, but retains the unwavering certainty that it comes from God.

For the senses and faculties have no part in this: God has revealed Himself to the soul and taken it with Him into a place where evil spirits will not enter, because the Lord will not allow them to do so; and *all the favors which the Lord grants the soul here come quite independently of the acts of the soul itself,* apart from that of its having committed itself wholly to God.

So tranquilly and noiselessly does the Lord teach the soul in this state and do it good that I am reminded of the building of Solomon's temple, during which no noise could be heard; just so, in this temple of God, in this Mansion of His, *He and the soul alone have fruition of each other in the deepest silence.*

There is no reason now for the understanding to stir, or to seek out anything, for the Lord Who created the soul is now pleased to calm it and would have it look, as it were, through a little chink, at what is passing. Now and then it loses sight of it and is unable to see anything; but this is only for a very brief time.

On reaching this state, the soul has no more raptures, transports and flights of the spirit. These raptures happen rarely, hardly ever in public as they often did before. Nor have they any connection with great occasions of devotion, as they did before; if we see a devotional image or hear a sermon, it is almost as if we had heard nothing, and it is the same with music. His Divine Truth surpasses all that we can imagine here on Earth.

THE EIGHTH SPHERE: THE DIVINE SOUL

'When Christ said, "I and my Father are one," he did not refer to the At-One-ment between the mere image and the Substance, but to the At-One-ment which remakes the soul, giving to us the very Substance of the Father.'[63]

'I Am in the Father, and the Father in me.'
'I Am in my Father, and you in me, and I in you.'

God comes to dwell in the very center of the transformed soul forever.

Only Divine Love can bring one to the New Birth, where the very substance of the human soul changes forever into a Divine Soul or Divine Angel. God is overflowing in Love and desires this for us too.

God is not wounded. God's Relationship to the human soul is that of Creator to the created, whereas the relationship of God towards the Divine Soul that has received the New Birth is of Co-Creator.

As Divine Love takes possession of the soul, the soul becomes the same substance as the Great Soul of God. There is nothing left hidden from the Soul at this point because it has been completely assimilated. This does not mean you house all the attributes of God, although Divine Love is the Primary Quality that all Celestial Spirits share; rather there is a perfect manifestation of a *single attribute* or name or God.

As Rumi shares:

'Once again, I shall die as Man

To soar with Angels blest;
But even from Angel-hood I must pass on:
All except God doth perish.
When I have sacrificed my Angel-soul
I shall become what no mind ever conceived.'

In the Eighth Sphere and beyond, the Divine transfigured Soul you now are, becomes a Co-Creator with God, an extension of God. Because you are At-One with God's Feelings and Divine Laws, and are flowing fully in Divine Love, for that is the very substance and quality of your Soul, you instantly feel and know what there is to Co-Create in God's Plan of Love.

This is not our human way of co-creating. In this Way, now one can create on a multi-universal scale, and enjoy the freedom, joy and Love that comes with having universes as your playground.

For example, one can Create Grids for entire planets to help an entire species of billions of life forms get closer to God. God Himself does not do this Work personally – Celestial Spirits that are At-One with God do it, but they too realize they are not the True Creator.

This is what happened with our planet, Gaia. A group of Higher Spirits created the Unity or God Grids of this planet to allow human souls to reach a perfected state in the Sixth Sphere. But these Grids serve a greater purpose: the ability to receive more Divine Love and to become At-One with God.

Waves of Divine Love cycle around our Universe at specific time periods, coming from the Creator, and reaching Earth at specific times. These Grids of God's Blueprint of Love and Harmony for all Creation were created to serve as antennae or lightning rods, conductors and transducers of these Incoming Waves of Divine

Love. These Waves are incoming NOW in 2012 and accelerating to a peak within the next ten years.

The true purpose of the Grids are as conductors for Divine Love to flow into us, and the more we harmonize with them, and live the Living Earth Blueprint that they hold (as created by God for us to live in harmony with Him and all Life) the more Divine Love we will be able to receive through our desire for it and our consistent choices to live by Divine Laws. The times we are living in are the fastest time to accelerate into God Consciousness or Divine Love.

There are specific ways to harmonize with these Grids, which create a highway of Living Light from these Waves, through the Grids, into our souls. These Ways come from the Celestial Spirits who created the Grids, yet they have made it known that few humans are utilizing these Ways because of their unwillingness to feel the emotions and wounds of their souls.

To access these Ways is not a channeled or informational phenomenon; it is accessed through the true state of your own soul condition, which allows direct access to these Ways once your soul is clear enough to live in the frequency of Love.

The two Poles of this Unity Grid are held, at the present moment, between Egypt as the Perfected Masculine, and Moorea as the Perfected Feminine (Sixth Sphere). This will change in time, for just as the magnetic physical poles of the Earth will shift, so will these energetic Grid Poles; but for now these are the Poles which we can align ourselves with and which will greatly accelerate our souls' growth in Love if we utilize them in union with Divine Love.

The Divine Love Prayer is the Blueprint for the FULL reception of the Incoming Waves of Divine Love into our souls. It is the octave beyond the Unity Grids, with the Unity grids acting as lightning rods or conductors for this love into our souls.

This Prayer is the Blueprint, the Immaculate Template of God's desire for us, and for the transformation of the soul into the Divine. So, one can access a Sixth Sphere Unity Grid Consciousness through these Grids, AND receive vaster amounts of Divine Love by tuning into this higher aspect of the God Grids.

The Divine Ladder

When you obtain enough Divine Love in your soul you leave the Seventh Sphere, which is much connected to the First Celestial Sphere, to then progress into the second Celestial Sphere, and on to the third Celestial. Above the third Celestial Sphere there are un-numbered' Spheres in the Celestial Heavens, each more magnificent than the rest. Words simply cannot describe these Spheres.

Within all the Spheres lies a Divine Ladder. This is a Ladder that Celestial Spirits At-One with God or Souls in the Seventh and Fifth Spheres use to groom potential human souls into becoming Divine Souls, and *taking their place*. All these souls and spirits are serving the soul progression of innumerable souls in God's Universe, serving others to get closer to God.

They are in Love, gratitude and joy with their roles, yet their progression closer to God is tempered by certain services they perform for souls less developed than themselves. They stay in certain positions within the Father's Hierarchy and in certain Spheres in order to perform certain Works. For them to move further onwards into deeper Communion with God, they find other souls who will then take on their roles, functions and purpose.

For example, a Seventh Sphere Spirit will stay there until a Fifth or Sixth Sphere soul ascends and takes over their role, or completes a task that is their responsibility, thus freeing them to become At-One with God.

Similarly, a Spirit At-One with God will desire to move to the next Celestial Sphere of Divine Love and Truth, but out of love and choice will not do this until another soul takes its role and function, and the work and responsibility is fulfilled.

These souls see the light, desire, willingness and humility of the souls less developed than they are, and assist them to become closer to God, as this is the most self-loving action for them, as it fulfills their desire, also because it is the most loving action for the true desire of the soul being assisted, and for God, who desires *all souls* to become closer and closer to Him. *It is a win-win-win situation.*

The souls who have this deep desire, humility, willingness and totality of giving everything in all ways to their quest (as well as various other secondary attributes) to become At-One with God will be easily recognized by Higher Spirits closer to God, and they will be greatly assisted in many ways to come to *their station*. Not all souls have these attributes which enable them to be more greatly helped, but nonetheless all souls are helped by different degrees.

It greatly helps to be part of a very focused and dedicated group of souls who are doing this Work with a capable guide who is living in the Higher Spheres in order to access this Ladder. The light and desire in action of such a group is far stronger than *any* single individual, and far more assistance and Divine Love is given to such a group, both individually and collectively as a Group Field, allowing even more Divine Love to flow in!

This greater assistance is being given in part to complete the *Celestial Kingdom*, a Kingdom of Souls At-One with God. The doors to this Celestial Kingdom are open at the moment for any soul, but will soon close once enough souls have completed the transformation from human soul to Divine Soul.

No one knows when these doors will close, but it will be sometime in the twenty-first century. Once these doors close, no more souls will be allowed into the Celestial Kingdom in this cycle of time and history, and the greatest progression human souls can then make will be into the Sixth Sphere of pure, natural love.

Many Celestial Spirits call this closing of the doors a *'Second death'* as the glory and fullness of God and Divine Love will no longer be fully available for mortals.

The

POWER

of PRAYER

Prayer is how the soul communicates with God through pure feeling. Pure feelings, yearnings, deep desire and fervent aspirations are the language of the soul reaching out to God. This sincerity will *always* be received by God, as it is the language of love that He has created for us to be with Him as our Beloved.

Prayers are answered when they are selflessly prayed, for no reason other than the heart's deep yearning. Prayers are most deeply felt when they are no longer words or thoughts, but soul emanations, communicated through desire and love from your soul to God's Great Soul.

Prayers shape the soul, crafting and refining her more into Essence. In the sublime depths, ecstasies and heartbreaking moments of genuine prayer, the soul prays wordlessly; the mind knows not, speaks not. Prayer becomes secret and silent, hidden from the minds of all.

Prayer is the presence of the gratitude we feel and the closeness we desire for God, just for the sake of it. This is when the soul is closer to its secret center.

Whilst we may start praying with words and wishes, with intentions and thoughts, and this is good and well, prayers are answered more fully when they are no longer intentions, but rather giving all of yourself without reservation to God, and asking from God what God desires to give us most: Divine Love.

This is what touches Him most, for this is the purpose of our creation, and God's Greatest desire for us all. This is the most powerful Prayer, and the one He is waiting for from your earnest soul. *Beloved Father, Mother God, help me receive Your Divine Love.*

God is willing and ready to help us in our suffering and

distresses, and has given us the ways and means in which He can help us, along with the absolute certainty of this help being given *if* asked for sincerely, and if we are humble enough to accept the truths shown to us.

Only you yourself can prevent God from answering your prayers. By your own choices and actions, you place yourself in such a soul condition that God would have to violate His own Laws to respond to insincere, false and self-serving prayers, which He will not do. This is your work, to discover, excavate and feel the sources of your own errors that keep a wall between you and Divine Love entering your soul, and the happiness that awaits you.

Precise prayer is when you direct your desire to God to feel specific emotions, specific parts of your soul and spirit body, and specific prayers to strengthen your soul. When you direct your desire to God to feel the precise soul wounds you have, you ask to feel the emotions you have never dared to feel.

Prayers are answered if they come from this humility and soul recognition that you have done harm to yourself and others, and totally desire to feel and release this, no matter what the consequences are to your current life, job, status and relationships.

Prayers are answered when you desire to follow Divine Laws and search out what these Laws of Love are. Prayers are answered more when you make the effort in all areas of your life to seek out your unfelt emotions and patterns of thinking deep within you and apply Divine Truths honestly and unashamedly to every single part, facet and aspect of your existence *without exclusion* and *without exception*.

When you feel this pain, then God, through His Divine Love, can come in, because *you are removing the wall you have created to block Him by refusing to feel.* Divine Love comes in through your humility and through His Feeling that you have now learned a lesson of love, and become more of a self-responsible soul.

This is how God loves us: He gives us what we need rather than what we erroneously desire borne out of the false wisdom of our wounds, needs and earthly appetites; choices that are out of harmony with love, even if we think they are harmonious with love. Changing the very nature of the primordial power of desire itself into pure desire for God is how prayer works best.

'I must tell you that when the soul of a mortal prays in earnestness and with true longings, all the powers of all the spirits in the spiritual or Celestial Heavens cannot prevent that Love from responding to the prayers, and from making the longing soul free and at one, to a degree, with the Father. The sentences of spirits and angels cannot exist contrary to that Love's demands.

And this being so, mortals can readily understand that all the powers of the hells and the evil ones cannot prevail against that Love. And thus further will you understand that the true prayers of a longing soul are more powerful, and will bring the response from the Father, than all the powers of angels, spirits and devils combined.

Thus you may comprehend what an important creature is one poor mite of a mortal when in truth and earnestness he comes to the Father, seeking His Love.'[64]

Divine Love is infinitely vast, infinitely full, all encompassing and beyond any mortal understanding. So endless and infinite is It, that It can fill every single soul in all universes completely, and still keep going and create an infinite number of souls and an infinite number of other universes AND fill all those souls it has just created with Divine Love too.

And it can keep going, and going, and going, ad infinitum. And It has done, It is, and will ever do so.

There is no scarcity, no lack in how we are loved perfectly. Ask and you shall receive.

GROUP PRAYER

When a group of sincere souls pray together, profound openings and receiving of Divine Love becomes hugely amplified. I have observed hundreds of times that most members of the group rise up to three Spheres beyond where they normally exist! As Christ shares, *'Where more than one is gathered in my name, there so shall I be.'*

A recent group that engaged in Group Prayer to receive Divine Love reported feelings of:

'Profound gratitude, love, honesty, ecstasy, feeling so small and the feeling of being loved so much, humility, dissolving of pride and shame, connection, the need to give myself to God, healings from God, dissolving of self-reliance, warmth and softness of love and pain, nourishment, intense pressure in the head, worthlessness and magnificent peace at the same time, forgiveness, embrace, expansion, vastness, pure, powerful presence, love, a hot and expanded heart, whole body burning, so blessed and graceful, for the first time not feeling unworthiness, realizing how finite I am and yet can receive so much.'

As TA shares, 'When I connect to this space it is painful, like a new opening, so loving, so pure, so exquisitely tender. There's this sense that I am received and I can receive so much more. I am in so much gratitude ... in this place I have complete faith ... a deeper trust.'

Pray to receive Divine Love, *and* also pray to feel more of the wounds and unfelt emotions within you that stop you from living in this space. *Do both: it is beautiful and devastating.*

God cannot help but come to you from this pure place of desire. He has to come to you, because that is the way He has created the universe. So you can all do this. It is the most natural, most simple, most fundamental part of your soul. Through that purity of your soul and desire, God Himself will come to you. Just remember that.

As John shares from 'The Book of Truths : ''Of all the important things on earth for humans who are seeking salvation, happiness and development of soul, prayer is the most important - for prayer brings from the Father not just love and blessings, but the condition of mind and intent that will cause men to do ... great works.

Prayer is the cause of the power being given to humans that will enable them to do all the great works which will bring reward to the doer, and happiness and benefit to the one who receives the works.

So you see, the results can never be as great as the cause, for the cause, in this instance, not only gives to humans this ability to work, but also to love and to develop their soul and to inspire them with all good and true thoughts.

Works are desirable, and in some cases necessary, but prayer is absolutely indispensable. So let you and your friend understand and never doubt that without prayer the works of humans would be unavailing to accomplish the great good which even now humans performs for their brothers.

Pray, and works will follow. Work, and you may do good, but the soul does not benefit, for God is a God that answers prayer through the ministrations of His angels and through the influence of His Holy Spirit which works on the interior or real part of humans. ''

THE DIVINE LOVE PRAYER

'My Grace is sufficient for you, for my power is made perfect in weakness.'
2 Cor. 12:9

It is from love that all languages originate, as a Divine impulse to connect all living beings in all ways, but most especially to connect our soul to the Great Soul of God. Our connection to God is deeply, intimately personal, and the deeper we take this, the more God can reveal to and through us.[65]

Expression is the medium for transparency. Without expression there is little intimacy, and transparency is vulnerability, love's naked openness. Transparency is the pathway for love. Deeper expression allows your self to be known. Becoming known means there are no more secrets, emotions to hide behind or retreat under. In the revealing lies the softness, the gentling. All that is rigid melts and opens.

Expressing intimacy, with yourself, with God, and with another allows you to know yourself completely. Knowing yourself means you begin to realize a fuller potential, for God gives the most to those who have a high degree of self-knowledge.

Be intimate today; share your deepest secrets and unsaid feelings with God. You may be pleasantly surprised. This entails an ever-deepening and keenly felt human vulnerability, which is true strength and courage. This sublimely transforms into an ever-increasing reliance on God, *as you consciously allow yourself to be known*, allowing love into every nook and cranny, willingly, humbly and gratefully.

The Arms of God are a safe harbor for all emotions to be felt, processed and healed. All emotions, whatever they are, can be felt here once prayed about, which leads us into a state of love, not fear.

'Do the thing you fear the most, and the death of fear is certain.'
Mark Twain

'When you pray for and receive Divine Love, the Power of this Love in your soul goes to work on your encrustments, your armourings, your core wounds, and pays your debt of compensation.

When a person prays for Mercy and forgiveness for past sins and errors, this prayer will bring Divine Love into the soul, and this Love will do the work of forgiveness.[66]

When a person prays and is totally willing to feel the harm (karma) they have done, and prays for Divine Love to enter their soul, this genuine repenting will help the work of forgiveness.

There is a vast difference between spiritual development in becoming transformed by Divine Love, and gradual purification of the soul through renouncing sin and doing good deeds to "make up" for your karma. The former accomplishes the latter and then commences the transformation totally.'

The Aramaic Divine Love Prayer

Ah-bwoon d'bwa-shmaya
Neeta – qahdasha – schmach
Tay-tay mal-koo'-tha
Nehwey tzevyanach aykanna d'bwashmaya aph b'arha
How-lahn lachma d'soonkahnan yow-manna
Wash wo-klan how-bane eye-kanna dahp hahnan shwa-ken el'high-ya-bane

Oo-lah tah-lahn el-nees-yo-nah ella pah-sahn min beesha
Metahl dih-lah-kee mal-kootha,
oo-high-la, oo-teesh-bohk-tah.
La-alahm, ah-meen.
Ah-mayn

The Modern Divine Love Prayer

My Beloved Father God, my Beloved Mother God, Creator of my soul, Creator of all souls, Creator of Heaven and Earth; I feel You are all holy, loving and merciful. I Am Your Child, under Your care. We are the greatest of Your creations, the most wonderful of all your Handiworks; I Am the object of Your Great Soul's Love and tenderest Care.

I feel Your Will is that I become At-One with You, partaking in Your Great Love which You freely give to me through Your burning desire that I become, in Truth, Your Divine Child, not through harming myself, my Twin, or any other beings.

Beloved Father-Mother God, please open my soul to receive Your Divine Love. Please send Your Holy Spirit to bring into my soul Your Love in such great abundance so that my soul is transformed into the very essence and substance of Yourself. Beloved God, please help me receive more of Your Divine Love. I love You.

Beloved Father God, please help me have faith, such faith, as will cause me to realize that I Am Your Divine Angel and You are my Father, Bestower of every good and perfect gift. Beloved Mother God, please help me be humble, so humble, so as to release all the pain and error from my soul, that stops me from becoming At One with You.

Beloved God, Your Majesty, please keep me in the shadow of Your Divine Love and Infinite Truth Light every moment of this day and night. Help me overcome all temptations of the flesh, and the influence and powers of wounded spirits, who try to distract my thoughts, attention and desires away from love and truth, to the distractions and allurements of this world.

Thank You, thank You for Your Love, even just for the possibility of receiving it. You are my Loving Father, my Loving Mother. You smile upon me in all my weaknesses, always ready to help me and take me into Your Arms of Love.

I pray this with earnest longings from my soul. I trust in You Beloved Father-Mother God, I trust in Your Love. Your Majesty, Beloved God, I give You all the glory, honor and love that my pure soul can give You. I Love You.

By Christ Yeshua
Channeled by James Padgett
Modernized by Padma Aon

NOTES ON THE DIVINE LOVE PRAYER

The whole Divine Love Path is in this Prayer. Pure humility, desire and heartbreaking yearning for God, the Remembrance and Inspiration of the Divine Truth of who we actually are, pure gratitude, immense joy and celebration, and of course the receiving of vast quantities of pure Divine Love.

The Divine Love Prayer is the Blueprint and Immaculate Template for the FULL reception of Divine Love into our souls. This Prayer is the Blueprint of God's Holy Desire for us.

Our Father is the Creator of all things: the Sun, the heavens, the stars, the infinity of God's creation. Our Mother is the form and substance of all things, and for us she is the Earth, form, and nature. Once we feel this, we are left in joyful awe and celebratory wonder at the sheer magnificence and beauty of creation, and our Creator. This is innocence!

God loves us totally, completely, perfectly and unconditionally, without any wounds or agenda, in a way no human soul ever can, or will. God allows us to do whatever we choose, and through Mercy can help us to heal all the errors that we make in our lives against Divine Love and Truth, which are the deepest truths of our soul essence.

We are the ultimate creation, for we are created directly in the image of God. We have been tended to for millennia to step into this fully, so we have the means and the choice to become At-One with God, to become part of the substance of God as well as the image.

There is no greater feeling in existence than feeling, in deep gratitude and absolute joyful, humble certainty, that you are

God's Child. No other relationship touches this love. All other needs can dissolve when touched by this Love. Simply to feel this is enough.

We are not what the human condition and false teachers say we are. The plethora of new age teachings denigrating or ignoring God and exalting the false self under spiritual pretenses, and even of Divinizing the self, all lead people away from Divine Love, our birthright.

Humility gets thrown away, as the mind and ego, blinded by its own light, oblivious to its own buried feelings, takes center stage. It is this falsehood that many labor under, equating human love with Divine Love. They are two totally different qualities, but because Divine Love has been forgotten in favor of human love, human love has become the new god, and is understood by most to be the only 'love.'

Divine Will orchestrates everything in our lives so we may have the opportunity to step closer to God IF we ask for it and sincerely desire this. There is no forcing, just gentle openings and doorways of opportunity that we can step into, each and every day. Some we may take; some we may miss. The more we receive Divine Love, and choose to live by Divine Truths through our actions every day, the more we recognize these doorways and have the conscious choice of whether or not to step through them.

Do I have a burning desire to know God?
Do I have a burning desire to give God my love?
Do I feel that God desires my love?

Do I have a burning desire to be known by God?
Do I have a burning desire to receive love from God?
Do I feel that God desires to give Her Love to me?

Does God have a burning desire to know me?
Does God have a burning desire to be known by me?
Does God have a burning desire to receive my love?
Do I feel God has the ability to feel my love for Her?

Do I desire Love to be active in my life with all people?
Do I have a desire to change by receiving Divine Love?
Do I desire to have God's Perspective in Love?[67]

Now answer these questions honestly, and watch over the weeks and months how your soul will grow, how it will change.

Killing and eating animals and harm and anger directed to any being for any reason is not Love's Wish or action. Killing or harming other humans in any way is not Love's Wish or action. For you *to not* do these things means you are aligning to Love's Wishes.

By eating dead and slaughtered flesh, murdered in a state of abject fear, adrenal toxicity, pain and loneliness, we lower our vibration to absorb these negative emotions. We choose fear, pain and death instead of love, freedom and life. How would you like to be killed in a slaughterhouse?

As Gandhi shares, '*The killing or inflicting injury to any living being amounts to the killing or inflicting of injury to one's own self. Similarly, the compassion towards other living beings amounts to the compassion for one's own self (and similarly compassion for one's own self leads to more compassion for others). Hence, those who aspire to their own good renounce all violence.*'

Divine Love is the most transformative energy in the universe. What could take many years to heal can be done in weeks if you go directly to the cause rather than spend years dealing with the psychological effects, piece by piece. Through Mercy and Grace, through our own humility and recognition of our own flaws, we can pray to feel our wounds so Grace may come in and assist us.

The Holy Spirit is the part of God's Spirit that manifests His presence, Comfort and care in conveying to our souls His Divine Love. This Love is the highest, the greatest, the most holy of His possessions, and can be conveyed to us only through the Holy Spirit.

The Holy Spirit is the part of God's Spirit which transforms our souls into the Substance of the Soul of God. The Presence of the Holy Spirit is not to affect things of inanimate nature, for it is solely concerned with the relationship of God's Soul to our soul. It brings Divine Love into your soul to transform you into the Substance and Qualities of God.

The Holy Spirit has nothing to do with great mental or physical achievements; the scientist, inventor, artist or philosopher who does things without knowing where it comes from is not possessed by the Holy Spirit. Its great goal is the transforming of the soul into the Substance of God's Love; Its mission is bringing us into harmony with God, so our souls become part of God's substance, not just in image.[68]

As Christ shares, 'Except a man be born again he cannot enter into the Kingdom of God, and such attainment is possible only by the working of the Holy Spirit.'

We are made from body, soul and spirit, of which soul is the main and essential power. The *spirit is the active energy of the soul*, the instrument through which soul manifests itself. The spirit is inseparable from the soul, and has no other function *apart from to manifest the potentialities of the soul in action*. As the soul was created in the image of God, and as spirit is the active energy of the soul, so the Holy Spirit is the active energy of the Great Soul of God.

God is Spirit, but spirit is not God, only one of His instruments used to work with *our* spirits. To worship, yearn for and desire the instrument is an error, for only God alone is to be worshiped. Do not worship holy personages or any human, or the Holy Spirit; give all the glory, honor and love to God.

Faith arises from direct experience of Divine Love. As our experiences of Divine Love deepen, we become closer to God and actually begin to hold or possess more Divine Love within our very souls.

This occurs through a 'stepping down' process, where this Love is weakened many thousands of times so we can safely receive it through His Spirits into our souls. If this 'stepping down' process did not occur, our souls would implode. We cannot handle too much Reality in these fleshly bodies, and so we are given this infinite love drop by drop until our finite souls become infinite and Divine.

Faith is not believing in what others or scripture says. It is about testing it out within the laboratory of your own soul. Try it and see what happens, but try it with a genuine, heartfelt desire and openness.

Then you are doing yourself justice. Faith grows through direct experience until you no longer believe, but feel. As you feel and therefore Know, the experience of receiving Divine Love becomes more regular. And so faith deepens ...

'Belief may arise from a conviction of the mind, but faith never can. Its

place of being is in the soul. And no one can possess it unless the soul is awakened by the inflowing of this Love. So, when we pray to God to increase our faith, it is a prayer for the increase of Love. Faith is based on the possession of this Love.'⁶⁹

Faith becomes more real when the aspirations, desires and longings of your innermost, secret soul become a palpable, living and breathing existence within you and outside you, reflected in where you are, how you live, and who is with you and around you; it becomes certain because you are receiving so much Divine Love, that no doubt, confusion or question arises as to its reality.

Faith comes with the receiving and experiencing of Divine Love, and allows an ever-deepening transformation and trust to rule your life. It is a quality of the soul and the soul alone: it exists in and of the soul; the mind can be subject to it and carry out its wishes, but it is only the soul that can feel, receive and deepen into it.

The more Divine Love you receive, the more faith you will have. This faith enables your soul to see God in all Her Beauty and Love. Thus, faith is a progressive quality or essence of the soul, and is not dependent on anything else except Divine Love and feeling/seeing this in action in your life. It is not blind or bound to a mental understanding and is very wise in this sense, for it does not depend on other people, teachers, or teachings.

'Faith is based on the possession of this Love, and without it there can be no faith, because it is impossible for the soul to exercise its function when Love is absent from it.'⁷⁰

'If you want to strengthen your faith, you will need to soften inside. For your faith to be rock solid, your heart needs to be soft as a feather. Some of us get hardened and embittered by the losses and hardships in life,

whilst others become milder, more compassionate, more ensouled and closer to God. In this world, it is not similarities or regularities that take us a step forward, but blunt opposites.

All the opposites of the universe are present within each and every one of us. Therefore the believer needs to meet the unbeliever residing within. And the non-believer should get to know the silent faithful in him. Until the day when one reaches the state of the perfect human, faith is a gradual process and one that necessitates its seeming opposite: disbelief.'[71]

We doubt God because Her message on Earth has been distorted and because God does not force or control us to do, feel or think anything, unlike the control mechanisms on Earth today.

God is not an absent Mother or Father – He is always here waiting for us to recognize our own mistakes and ask for Divine Love, which She totally desires to give us. Through faith and yearning prayer, all can be given to us, tangibly and totally. Try it and see.

Try not to be misled and governed by your own pains created by misunderstandings of how God's Divine Laws and Love operate, or by hardships you have felt in your life; try looking at these events in a different light as your own learning curve and your own emotions.

'How we see God is how we see ourselves. If God is seen as to be feared, or as having abandoned us, then it is these very same emotions that live within us.'[72]

Try not to be sucked in by religious bigotry and childhood memories of God which were foisted upon you in Sunday School classes by preachers driven by their own fears and judgments.

This foisting has been deliberate, in order to lead you away from Divine Love, to give God a bad name, to make you self-reliant, feasting on a table of philosophical scraps and new age theorems couched in the language of spirituality but lacking any real substance.

'Keep me in the shadow of Your Divine Love and Infinite Truth and Light every hour and moment of this day. Help me to overcome all temptations of the flesh and the influences and powers of negative and wounded spirits.'

There is choice ever present in the universe, and some beings, even though they may *intellectually* know better, choose to do negative, or harmful things. Negative spirits may know of love and truth but choose to go against it, trying to bring as many souls with them into their own state *because they believe this is the truth.* Negativity is the absence of love.

These spirits deserve our greatest compassion and help, as they have turned against love, but really need to feel a touch of love to help them move through their own pains. Negative spirits are the most wounded of all souls, because they have the greatest unresolved and unfelt pain. They play their part in testing, tempting and refining souls who attempt to grow and progress into more Divine Love, for *the souls who aspire towards God receive the most negative spirit attack,* much more so than those souls on new age or meditational paths. *This is a tangible phenomena, not an idea or illusion.*

There are three main types of this distortion:[73]

Negative and invisible spirits, known classically as the 'devil.' DNA and sexual manipulation, misinformation and distortion. 'The world': most of the governments of the world, the secret government that runs and ruins the world, the spirit networks of wounded sisterhoods and wounded brotherhoods united in fear by their wounds from the opposite sex, and their Spirit Hierarchies who stand in opposition to the Brotherhood of Light Spirit Hierarchies, *all of whom exist both in spirit and physical form.*

The voices and feelings of negative spirits can be heard within you as they align to the holes and wounds that you have. They have the same wounds as you, and therefore resonate with and amplify the frequency of your wound, bringing it to the forefront of your attention, fast.

This is both uncomfortable and a blessing, as it forces you to look at the wounds within you that are causing the spirits to be attracted to you. The voices of these spirits can be subtle urgings, fearful feelings, emotional blackmail, or full-blown murderous thoughts that may seem totally bizarre and alien to you.

Pleasures and allurements are substitutes for our pure desire for Divine Love and our highest potential. These spirits feed off the way you substitute love for more mundane things, addictions, denials, busyness and other distractions in your life.

Some of these pleasures and allurements are our own addictions, denials and ignorance, and some are foisted upon us by the tools of media control and disinformation, and through deliberate government control and repression. Additionally, over thousands of years, society has been indoctrinated to pass down, from generation to generation, false 'laws' and information so they become part of our commonly accepted status quo or *zeitgeist* today.

Part of this is due to the infiltration of almost all spiritual movements and religions by ignorant but well-meaning people *and* agents of the secret government, negative spirits and Annunaki. It is wise to be aware of these forces, as they touch everyone's lives, whether you believe in them or not.

The many distractions offered by this world and its 'authorities' are varied and numerous, and most of them are validated and held up as 'normal' and approved-of activities which help us fit in to society and fulfill our need to be loved. We are highly encouraged to fit in to society and its false laws from birth by our parents, and most of this leads us away from truth and the love that arises from truth.

These spirits work to keep humans separate from Divine Love and divine sexuality. Sex without human love and Divine Love is a huge influence that keeps us away from the true nature of our soul and God. Sex with true, soul-flowing, soul-inspired human love and the asking for and receiving of God's Love is a huge influence, that when merged together is the fastest and deepest Healing Power available in this universe.

It is a bullet pathway to God if these energies are harnessed and merged in purity, love and integrity. It is a way to feel love, freedom and no mind *directly*, which is why it has been so derided, bought and sold, as well as misinformed about even in most modern neo-Tantric circles. Materialism and spiritual materialism are part of these negative forces, cleverly dressed up to appear spiritual.

'Keep me in the shadow of Your Love and Infinite Truth and Light every hour and moment of every day.'

When we pray this, we are asking for Divine Truth and Love to show us the way, for Love is our only real protection. Love is the only healer, so we ask for more Divine Love to flow through us so we can feel the places within us where it is not able to go at this moment. Then the Divine Light can illuminate us further, allied with our own willingness to recognize and see our own flaws.

The shadow of God's Love is a resting place, allowing us the spaciousness to become more vulnerable and to keep opening further into our souls and the places we fear to tread within. Many sincere practitioners in all sacred traditions have had to evoke guardians, protectors and even wrathful deities in order to allow them to go deeper into the purity of their practices. This is because of the powers of the negative spirits.

Divine Love is the only real protection. As we feel and become aware of the unfelt emotions in our souls and release them, we can allow this Love to ripple throughout our soul in all dimensions.

Gratitude to God for revealing to us our deepest fears and pains is our natural response in humility, and gratitude for actually receiving the Divine Love that comes through embracing these fears is one of the greatest feelings we can ever feel. God is always there, and never went away; we just closed our eyes and ears to God through our own choice, listening to the false wisdom of our wounds and the reflections in the world and in our relationships that our wounds attracted to us. *If we are not grateful for what we have, how can we receive more?*

'I give God all the glory, honor and love that my pure soul can give.'

Giving God the glory, honor and love allows us to become more humble and receive even more love. Giving glory, honor and love to God is immensely joyful and fills one with gratitude. This is the proof of the soul. More love arises from these simple actions. In giving, you receive.[74]

God deserves love from our pure soul, as does every living creature, including our own good selves!

We know we have been created, and are not the Creator. We do not claim anything to glorify our own self. We do not claim the fruits of our actions, but give it back to God, allowing the very (e)motion of creation to keep flowing through us unimpeded in the universal law of giving and receiving, the universal circuit that keeps on flowing through us, to God, and back again.

In comes Divine Love, and if we hold onto it, it stops its flow. How can one dam a limitless ocean? As the Love flows out through us, to others, to all life, and back to God, more can then flow into us and to all others. And so the circle keeps flowing. *This is a Divine Law – what we receive must also be given back.*

This is how your soul starts to connect with God consciously once you have healed many of your wounds – there is an infinity loop between you and God; a bridge occurs. There is no longer a big separation or a 'felt' divide; there is a growing sense of God always being there, and nothing else is as important, no other person, no other relationship, apart from this One.

You need this one; all others can come and go, and it matters not. It may look like you are alone, but you may prefer it like this, as it gives you time to Be with God and rest in this burgeoning and ever-growing connection.

This is a deep moment for the soul to cognize, in deep peace, light and knowing. A Divine Law manifests in your soul. We are finite until we merge with the infinity that God is. The infinity loop is the bridge to this, the reminder of our finiteness and the infinite

Love that can also flow into us, and back out again, forever circulating in moments of Grace, moments of the sheer power of Divine Love that our souls can bear.

Yeshua gave this line in the Divine Love Prayer so we can also overcome the flaws and errors of our ancestors, including those who walked away from love, truth and God. They have passed on their own errors to us in our DNA, and in this prayer we can wash clean many of these errors.

Giving God all the glory and honor means the death of your small self.

DIVINE HEALING PRAYER

Right from the beginning of Prayer, it is important to make a distinction. Who is God? For many people on Earth, God has become an impersonal force, a myth of legend, a wrathful god, a false god, a god of religion and punishment, a god that is not loving.

Maybe this god is a mischievous or negative spirit, a demi-god disguised as God, pretending to be the One God. Maybe you have been partially giving away your love and devotion to this spirit, or you have been giving it away to stay in a victim mode, to stay in a subservient place where you do not have to take responsibility for your life, instead giving away the responsibility to this 'god.'

All of this is not God, who is Divine Love and Truth.

Right from the beginning of your prayer, it is important to *differentiate* your true heart's yearnings and desires from your memories and conditioning about what God is, and what god is supposed to be like as told to you by religions, society, parents and friends.

Start afresh with pure loving desire from deep in your heart.

God is Our Father, a Loving and Beautiful Mother, and with Him, anything is possible. God desires you. She wants you, He wants you, She wants you so much. She has designed everything for you. Everything in your life is designed to bring you back to this Love. There is nothing that God does not Know or Love about you. He loves you totally. He is always smiling at you, even in your weaknesses.

He is always here, waiting for you, with a burning desire for you. His arms are wide open. There is nothing He wants more than to feel your soul fully. You are the greatest of His creations. You are what He has always wanted. There is nothing He would not do for you to bring you to the Love you have always secretly wanted but forgotten.

God is not what you have forgotten Him to be. Your soul was made in the image of His Great Soul. You are similar. So, address God in a way that leaves no doubt as to where your prayer is going: to That Great Soul of Divine Love, and not to any other destination.

The Healing Prayer to God is a foundation to begin to feel your wounds, and to establish a link through your loving desire to the Great Soul of God. Using the *Healing Prayer* is *a way to feel everything*. In this way it can be applied to anything and everything in your life.

Before starting, just feel into your heart-soul. Just start to feel all that is there. Feel the state of your soul, drop down into it, feel its true condition and feelings. Whatever is there is fine. Go deep into the core feelings and emotions there. Feel the heaviness, stress, love, feel your readiness, feel all the things that are bubbling in your heart, and in feeling all of this, you are ready to begin.

You start the prayer with a long, breathful inhale, and then the exhale of *AHHHHHHHH* ... letting go whatever emotion you are feeling: let everything out. Everything gets released. And you can do it a few times. Just let out your nervousness, your fears, your joy, your happiness, and your fatigue. Once these are released, do another AHHHH ... for your longing, your desire, and your love. And this then is the wave that your prayer rides on. *Then you are ready to begin.*

Deep soulful breath empowers all prayer. The ancient Hawaiians always started prayer with breath to both release the stress within them AND empower the prayer with manna, with vital force, with breath that connects to our soul, to spirit, to God. They were shocked when Europeans came to their islands and prayed without breath, without life force behind them.

AHHHH opens the space, connects and releases emotions, connects and empowers your prayer with life force, and then empowers your desire and expands it. You can do this breath into each of your seven main chakra centers to open and relax yourself, cleanse and quieten the mind, and empower your prayers.

Divine Healing Prayer

My Beloved Father, My Beloved Mother God,
Creator of my soul, Creator of Heaven and Earth, Creator of all Universes
God of all gods, God of Love

Please help me to feel all the *betrayals* of my soul I have done. Holy Father God, please help me to feel all the ways I have betrayed others. God, help me to feel all the ways I have betrayed Your Divine Laws.

Holy Mother, Holy Father God, I want to feel my *denials* of all my emotions now; I choose to feel *all* the deep feelings of my soul that I have chosen not to feel.

My Lord, please help me feel all the pain and harm I have ever received from anybody. Please help me to feel all the pain and harm I have ever done to anybody. Please help me to feel all the pain and harm I have done to myself.

Forgive me Father, forgive me Mother; have mercy on my soul, for all I have done. I am so sorry for everything harmful I have ever done to myself and others. I now choose to feel it ALL. Help me to be truly humble and feel all my hidden and unfelt emotions.

Father, Mother God, please help me to feel how I deny and stop Your Love and Your Divine Laws from entering my soul. God, please help me to accept and embrace every emotion of my soul, positive and negative. I choose to now feel them ALL.

Father, Mother God, please help me to feel what I *judge* myself about. God, I want to feel how others feel when I judge and hurt them. God, please help me to feel how I judge Your Divine Truth. Mother, please help me to feel the causes of all my judgments.

Holy Mother God, I want to feel all the ways I *abandon* my soul. I want to feel and know how I have compensated for this abandonment in my life. Father God, please help me to feel all the ways in which I abandon Your Divine Laws. Please help me feel and bring all parts of my soul back into Your Loving arms, so I can be One with You.

Holy Mother God, please help me to feel again. Please sensitize my soul to Your Divine Love and Truth. God, please, help me to receive Your Divine Love. I love You.

Holy Father, Holy Mother God, thank you for helping me feel ALL emotions in me that are still unfelt. Thank you for helping me feel ALL emotions in me that I still deny and avoid. Thank you for helping me feel ALL the emotions in me that I still do not trust. Thank you for helping me feel ALL emotions in me that are still unforgiven. Thank you for helping me feel ALL the ways I cut off from Love. Please help me to feel it all now.

May this Be how I Am in all my thoughts, feelings, words and deeds, with all people now, and forever more.
Amen.

NOTES ON THE DIVINE HEALING PRAYER

This Prayer works in many ways and reveals key Divine Laws that you can directly feel and put into action every day, practically and soulfully. *This Prayer works by asking to feel the obstacles we have created that stop Divine Love entering our soul*, revealing painful emotions that block the inflowing of Divine Love.

The key to Prayer is that it is truly, deeply, passionately heartfelt. A deep yearning and a soulfully felt, keen desire can be painful; painful because it is cleansing our hearts. Nothing else is more important than receiving and asking for this – and this is the desire through prayer that REALLY receives the full power of Divine Love's alchemy.

All desires have a sacred origin, no matter how odd they may seem. Fear, pain, and ignorance may distort them, but it is always possible to locate the Divine source from which they arose. In describing one of his addictive patients,[75] Jung said: 'His craving for alcohol was the equivalent on a low level of the spiritual thirst for wholeness, or the union with God.'

Hillman echoes the theme: 'Psychology regards all symptoms to be expressing the right thing in the wrong way.' A preoccupation with pornography or romance novels, for instance, may come to dominate a passionate person whose quest for love has degenerated into an obsession with images of love. 'Follow the lead of your symptoms.'

Where has your desire for the greatest Love gone awry?

God is My Love of loves ... the greatest of all Loves, the Love beyond all other loves, the only Love that is vital and necessary beyond all others, the Love that transcends all other loves. The love we try to find in more mundane things is a pale imitation of this Love, and all the time we forget the source of this Love; and it is this Source ONLY that will ever satisfy us. Human loves can remind us of Divine Love, but cannot even come close to Divine Love.

God, You are the substance of Love Itself that transforms and makes all things anew. You are my Creator, and it is You I desire to receive. You are the greatest love, the Love I have always wished for and looked for in the people and things of this world, but which I never found.

You are my Love of all loves. There is nothing I want more; everything else I can do without. I cannot do without You. All else can come and go, but You remain. And this, Your Love, is all I desire.

Only God can fulfill us: nothing and nobody else EVER can or will. So do not hold back, and give God every part of you, and allow Him into every part of you. Gather all the parts of you that are holding back, and bring them to Her.

Pick up the parts that are afraid, that hold back, that are ashamed and gently bring them to Her in this prayer. Do not just timidly press on God's doorbell: burst through with the power of your heart's desires in full flow.

We have all done harmful things (karma) and we need to feel the harm we have created in order to carve open our hearts, deepen our compassion and *enter true forgiveness*.

If we do not desire to feel the pain and harm we have created, we will repeat our mistakes again, creating more harm and karma. At this point in the prayer, you may also name and feel specific people in your life whom you *feel* you have harmed.

Part of breaking out of victim mode is to *stop beating yourself up* for the pain and harm you have caused yourself and all others, AND AT THE SAME TIME FEEL all the pain and harm you have caused yourself and all others. When we beat ourselves up, we contract inside and then we close down to FEELING and RECEIVING Divine Love.

As we become wide open, transparent, honest and real with ourselves and all others we will quickly bring to the surface all the ways we are not aligned in love with ourselves, others and God. And when we feel this truth, although it is painful, it leads to freedom and to more Love. It is actually joyful!

The harm we have done to ourselves and others *can be emotionally HUGE for us when we first feel it.* We can feel deep pain, grief, repentance, shame, fear and many other emotions as we confront and feel all these feelings *that have always been within us,* but which have been buried, minimized or rationalized.

Over time, as we excavate and feel the many layers of these emotions, past and present, the emotions and causes of this harm can be released from the soul forever.

Then, the notion of harm refines itself, and becomes subtler, and rather than being a big emotional release, it becomes a gradual deepening and a felt, soulful understanding of where we are creating harm by going against Divine Laws in subtle ways in our life. We can then correct it more smoothly. This soulful awareness comes to us in everyday activities, and we can deal with it instantly by recognizing it and putting it right in the next moment.

So, if we do something out of truth, the next moment we can rectify it, apologize to someone if it is affecting him or her, and pray to feel the underlying cause within our own self that created it. Humility, truly feeling all your soul's emotions, is a huge key to opening the heart.

God is our Father, our Mother, our first and true Mother and Father. How do YOU feel about your true Mother and Father?

Divine Love and Infinite Truth or Living Light is the deepest, most transforming alchemical substance available to anyone in any universe. To constantly ask for it, and to consistently receive it, will transform you *very fast*. However, there are energies that try to distract you from this focus, influences trying to battle for your soul, to take it somewhere else apart from back to God, back to Divine Love.

Gratitude for this Love is the most natural outpouring of our human heart. Gratitude just bubbles up! God loves us so much, and to feel this is the deepest gratitude a human can feel. When you feel it, you will know. Gratitude for what we have means more can come in.

Divine Will knows far more than you ever can. To trust this is to trust God with your life; that God knows what is good for you far more than you ever can if you can but see the opportunities presented to you for your own healing.

By fervently desiring and asking to feel the true causes of our souls' wounded and unfelt emotions, we accelerate our pathway to God. Emotions and awareness combine to ensure the same mistakes do not happen again because you understand what the initial mistake was all about.

Pray to know Divine Laws and Divine Truths, the laws of love that govern our universe, which are knowable through your own heart connecting to the heart of God.

You will know once you really tap into a CAUSAL emotion, like grief, because it is visceral and overwhelming. You may want it to stop, you may say 'this is enough, I can't handle this,' you may walk away from the emotion and distract yourself, you may feel totally overwhelmed and cry your eyes out and feel like crap, you may say you are not ready yet.

There are many excuses to not wishing to feel the pain of a causal emotion – but it is your passport to Love and Truth. And be gentle, be kind with yourself in this process – loving yourself is the process as well. All takes its good time. There is no time, but timing is everything.

Feel it, just like a child simply feels whatever is presented to him or her; and in so doing, the emotion releases. This is part of the *process of feeling and re-sensitizing your soul* to Love and Truth.

Once you feel these emotions, tender compassion naturally blooms within you for yourself and for the many, many others in the same situation, because you have suffered it yourself. This accomplishes a double greatness: we heal ourselves and we no longer judge others, instead we come to them with love and understanding.

We each have within us a great teacher; all our own experiences. It is these emotional experiences, once embraced, that will lead us closer to God.

'You' are your experience, and each experience or wound holds a key to your Union with your Pure Soul and God. It is each key of experience that, once embraced, becomes transcended and forgotten; a piece of yourself is deleted, then your soul expands.

So don't be in a hurry to transcend your experiences! For they hold your own unique keys that you have created for your own liberation, and once felt, they serve to open your soul further to the Great Soul of God.

This is the BIG undressing of yourself, of all your wounds, projections, denials, concepts and interpretation of your experiences. Rather than rationalizing them away, justifying or numbing them, feel the emotion behind them. Then, you can completely undress, and become less likely to pick up any new woundings or remain trapped in the cage of your experiences; you can remain naked through the feeling, open-heart soul.

These emotions clear FAST by the process of Divine Love as it acts on and transforms them. When it does, then grace, light, peace and gratitude arise in you, for a few hours or days; and then you go back into the next emotion ... and so on, and on. The process continues until you are free of all emotional-soul error. And are naked in love.

The more one loves God, the more this love will flow into your human life and relationships. This may also be painful, as this love will highlight areas where you do not love yourself, are in relationships where you are not loved as a result of your own lack of self love, have given your love away to a cheap imitation, or value another above your own soul and its relationship to God.

We own nothing. This is a Divine Law. All rules of ownership are man-made. To pretend we own something is not to trust deeply in life, in God. Of course, we all need to eat, travel, house ourselves. This is common sense. It is when these physical laws start to take precedence over Divine Laws that we start to lose our connection to life itself.

Life is a circuit, and it flows through this sacred hoop and cycle, continually circulating. Owning nothing is very liberating; your name may be on the bill you pay or deed you think you possess, but always remember these little things are of this world, not of Reality. Do not get caught in them, and keep humble. This is why most evolved souls own little or nothing.

As all our emotions and wounds are felt and embraced, the mind naturally quietens down, as there is less ammunition for it. However, during the healing process itself the mind may flare up into more chatter as its hold begins to loosen. Mental chatter arises from unfelt emotions.

God does not need our love, but to freely give it to God is an amazingly loving experience. Love loves love, so if it brings more love it is true. To walk this wherever we go, no matter what people say, think or do, is staying true to Divine Love and Truth.

RESOURCES

The Soul Centre is a unique Centre established in 2012 for the rapid growth of the soul into the embodiment of Truth and Divine Love.

The Soul Centre is situated in what is known as 'The Holy Grail' region of Provence, Southern France. Just outside Menerbes, widely regarded as one of the most beautiful small villages in France, it lies next to the Vaucluse Mountains, a short drive from many ancient sacred sites connected to the Divine Feminine, including the magical Cave of Magdalene in Sainte-Baume and Saintes-Maries-de-la-Mer, the place where Salome, Magdalene and Sarah, with several other Apostles, first arrived from Israel.

Artists such as Picasso lived in our village, and Van Gogh and Monet painted nearby because of the extraordinary quality of light and luminosity here. Art and the sacred merge in this peaceful oasis, the heart of France.

The Soul Centre features its own well and geo thermal waters, hot tub, swimming pool, infra red sauna, oxygen chamber, and many cutting edge healing technologies designed to unify soul and spirit with the Divine. There is a dedicated Spa Room, Healing Room and Teaching Space. It has been designed and initiated to create a high energy field for healing, soul sanctuary and deep soul growth.

The Soul Centre is a Loving Sanctuary for all Pilgrims of Divine Love, those of us that seek the sweet effulgence of our souls relationship to God. Our desire is for ourselves and all who enter to become closer to God, to taste the immortality of His-Her mystery and our relationship with our Divine Parents in a 21st century, non dogmatic and open Way.

Our passion, joy and souls purpose is working with the threefold flame of Love, Power and Wisdom, bringing this forth into embodiment in our daily lives. We specialise in tailormade healings and programs for individual souls to grow rapidly in a beautiful, safe and gentle environment that allows you simply to let go.

The Soul Centre works by donation only. Within the Soul Centre you will discover:

- Healing modalities that strip away the contractions of mind, wounded emotions and soul
- Powerful processes that cleanly awaken the raw and refined waves of Shakti
- Initiations and openings to ignite the soul's longing and desire for God, by purifying the soul from self-reliance

We sincerely welcome you here when you hear the Call.

For more about The Soul Centre, visit thesoulcentre.eu.

For a wealth of free audio interviews, spoken word meditations and more about Divine Love, visit www. christblueprint.com.

To sign up for newsletters sharing more about free healings and our regular offerings, go to the main page.

To go to an experiential and powerful workshop near you worldwide, go to EVENTS.

The companion books to *The Dimensions of Love* are:
The Christ Blueprint (NAB/Findhorn Books)
Sacred Wounds Original Innocence (available on www.christblue-print.com).

Further Reading

The Dark Night of The Soul: St John of the Cross
Interior Castle: St Teresa of Avila
Blessings of the Cosmos: Neil Douglas Klotz
The Forty Rules of Love: Elif Shafak
The Maqalat of Shams-i-Tabriz: various translations

The Padgett Messages: www.truths.com/TrueGospel1.pdf
See also www.new-birth.net

A.J. Miller for his teachings on emotional clearing: www.divine-truth.com.

ACKNOWLEDGEMENTS

Thank you to Aina for looking after me, creating the diagrams and typesetting, David Andor for the cover and initial graphic design, and Amanda for initial editing.

Thank you to John Hunt and O-Books for their rapid response and appreciation of this book, and for pioneering a new way in publishing that is much needed for the 21st century.

Thank you to Christ Yeshua for always being there for me.

Thank you Beloved Mother Father God for everything, and for bringing me back into your Divine Love.

Thank you to *all others* I may have left out who helped with this book.

Endnotes

1. Shams of Tabriz
2. Christ Yeshua
3. Pure desire becomes the main factor in soul growth the higher you rise in the Spheres. Pure desire and total humility before God are all that really matter to open your heart more to receive more Divine Love and Truth.
4. Rumi
5. A.J. Miller
6. *The Padgett Messages*
7. For more information on the Spheres see p 35 onwards.
8. Some of the most powerful times to pray to receive Divine Love are during and after making love with your partner.
9. Yeshua, *The Padgett Messages*
10. See the chapter on substitutes and Lucifer's Matrix for a full list in the book, *Sacred Wounds Original Innocence.*
11. *The Padgett Messages*
12. *The Padgett Messages*
13. Miranda Weisz, *Star Avatar – Emergence of a Messiah.*
14. Aïvanhov, *Cosmic Balance – The Secret of Polarity*
15. Henderson, *The Science of Soulmates: The Direct Path to the Ultimate*
16. Jeff Brown
17. Shams of Tabriz, *The Forty Rules of Love*
18. St Teresa of Avila
19. Until this time, the Merkabah of love, as taught by Drunvalo Melchizedek, is useful. At the Seventh Sphere, it will dissolve, yet it is advisable for this intention to be seeded into your merkaba now.
20. Apostle John
21. William Law
22. Eli Pariser, *The Filter Bubble*
23. Eli Pariser, *The Filter Bubble*

24. They also have very little negative spirit influence running them like puppets.

25. Not having self love means you can be easily run by your negative emotions and programs and in be turn exposed to negative spirits.

26. Synchronously enough, I wrote about the Five Deaths two months before I even knew about the Spheres and how they operated, and found the amazing correlations between the two.

27. St Teresa of Avila

28. This is why the cover of this book marks out 8 Spheres only.

29. *The Padgett Messages*

30. *The Padgett Messages*

31. John 14

32. St Paul

33. Luke 9, v 23

34. Henry Ward Beecher

35. Shams of Tabriz, *The Forty Rules of Love*

36. St Teresa talks about reptiles being the main blocks in the first sphere here; these are the same reptiles I talk about, who disconnected our DNA in the book *Sacred Wounds Original Innocence*. The best modern information on the reptiles and their agendas in controlling the world is available from David Icke.

37. Shams of Tabriz, *The Forty Rules of Love*

38. A.J. Miller

39. Shams of Tabriz, *The Forty Rules of Love*

40. A.J. Miller

41. Ben Okri, *Starbook*

42. Like homeopathy, first the soul must be infected with that which it will become impervious to; if it survives the attack, the foundation becomes impregnable. If it does not, a good person perishes and has to begin again from where they left off the struggle. Ben Okri, *Starbook*

43. Shams of Tabriz, *The Forty Rules of Love*
44. St Teresa of Avila
45. Prophet Muhammad
46. Christ Yeshua
47. Luke 9, v 24
48. Ben Okri, *Time for a New Dream*
49. St Johnof the Cross, *The Dark Night of the Soul*
50. Shams of Tabriz, *The Forty Rules of Love*
51. How trite it is to convey Divine Love using human similes!
52. Just as the Second Sphere holds touches and lessons that are of the Fourth Sphere, so does the Fifth Sphere open up into the Seventh.
53. *The Forty Rules of Love*
54. See *Sacred Wounds Original Innocence* for further information.
55. Part of the healing of this comes in the opening of the Male 4 Gates and the 7 Gates of a Woman. For more ways on how to open these Gates, see the books *Sacred Wounds Original Innocence* and *The Power of Shakti.*
56. All italics, Ben Okri, *A Time for New Dreams.*
57. Ben Okri, *Tales of Freedom*
58. St Teresa of Avila
59. *The Padgett Messages*
60. A.J. Miller
61. Hildegard of Bingen
62. *The Padgett Messages*
63. St John, *The Padgett Messages*
64. St John, *The Padgett Messages*
65. Listen to a beautiful Aramaic rendition of the Prayer sung by Colleen de Winton. See www.sacredchants.com.au
66. The Padgett Messages
67. A.J. Miller, www.divinetruth.com
68. *The Padgett Messages*
69. *The Padgett Messages*
70. *The Padgett Messages*

71. Shams of Tabriz, *The Forty Rules of Love*
72. Shams of Tabriz, *The Forty Rules of Love*
73. For more information see the chapter on Spirits in the book *Sacred Wounds Original Innocence.*
74. For a beautiful commentary on The Prayer, go to www.godswayoflove.org/Downloads/Publications/MillerAJ /AJ Miller-The Prayer for Divine Love.pdf
75. Rob Brezny, *Pronoia*

BOOKS

MySpiritRadio